CW01095648

BOOKS AND SOCIAL MEDIA

Social media and digital technologies are transforming what and how we read. *Books and Social Media* considers the way in which readers and writers come together in digital communities to discover and create new works of fiction.

This new way of engaging with fiction stretches the boundaries of what has been considered a book in the past by moving beyond the physical or even digitally bound object to the consideration of content, containers, and the ability to share. Using empirical data and up-to-date research methods, Miriam Johnson introduces the ways in which digitally social platforms give rise to a new type of citizen author who chooses to sidestep the industry's gatekeepers and share their works directly with interested readers on social platforms. Gender and genre, especially, play a key role in developing the communities in which these authors write. The use of surveys, interviews, and data mining brings to the fore issues of gender, genre, community, and power, which highlight the push and pull between these writers and the industry.

Questioning what we always thought we knew about what makes a book and traditional publishing channels, this book will be of interest to anyone studying or researching publishing, book history, print cultures, and digital and contemporary literatures.

Miriam J. Johnson is a Senior Lecturer in Publishing at Oxford Brookes University, UK. She also maintains the *Books are Social* website (https://www.booksaresocial.com/).

BOOKS AND SOCIAL MEDIA

How the Digital Age is Shaping the Printed Word

Miriam J. Johnson

LONDON AND NEW YORK

First published 2022
by Routledge
2 Park Square, Milton Park, Abingdon, Oxon OX14 4RN

and by Routledge
605 Third Avenue, New York, NY 10158

Routledge is an imprint of the Taylor & Francis Group, an informa business

© 2022 Miriam J. Johnson

The right of Miriam J. Johnson to be identified as author of this work has been asserted by her in accordance with sections 77 and 78 of the Copyright, Designs and Patents Act 1988.

All rights reserved. No part of this book may be reprinted or reproduced or utilised in any form or by any electronic, mechanical, or other means, now known or hereafter invented, including photocopying and recording, or in any information storage or retrieval system, without permission in writing from the publishers.

Trademark notice: Product or corporate names may be trademarks or registered trademarks, and are used only for identification and explanation without intent to infringe.

British Library Cataloguing-in-Publication Data
A catalogue record for this book is available from the British Library

Library of Congress Cataloging-in-Publication Data
Names: Johnson, Miriam J., author.
Title: Books and social media : how the digital age is shaping the printed word / Miriam J. Johnson.
Description: Milton Park, Abington, Oxon ; New York, NY : Routledge 2021. | Includes bibliographical references and index.
Identifiers: LCCN 2021004640 | Subjects: LCSH: Books and reading–Technological innovations. | Publishers and publishing–Technological innovations. | Social media–Authorship. |
Fiction–Publishing. | Electronic publishing. | Self-publishing.
Classification: LCC Z1003 .J65 2021 | DDC 028–dc23
LC record available at https://lccn.loc.gov/2021004640

ISBN: 978-1-032-03090-6 (hbk)
ISBN: 978-1-032-00135-7 (pbk)
ISBN: 978-1-003-18664-9 (ebk)

DOI: 10.4324/9781003186649

Typeset in Bembo
by Taylor & Francis Books

This book is dedicated to everyone who helped me through the project, from family to friends who've put up with me occasionally talking about it and reading it through. A special thank you to Dr Michele Paul, Dr Jane Potter, and Leander Reeves. Without y'all I'd never be where I am now. Thank you.

CONTENTS

ILLUSTRATIONS

Figures

Table

INTRODUCTION

New means of moving information will alter any power structure [and will allow] serious conflicts [to] occur within organisations.

—— *Marshall McLuhan*, Understanding Media

There's something about power that is evocative. People want to be a part of it, close to it, regardless of where they find it; they are drawn to it whether it's in public life, the world of business, or in the pages of books. The lure of power can manifest simply as wanting to be a part of the various institutions that create and share books. But is it a thirst for power that has the publishing industry overrun with applications for any job? Likely not. It is more likely that those who want to work with books have a desire to find new, amazing works of writing and to share them with the wider world.

Very few people would say that they are going into the publishing industry to become a gatekeeper, but the lure of becoming an arbiter of taste matched with a pure and admirable love of books can be seductive. There is a growing subset of authors who love books, love writing, and want to share their works with the wider world for whom the lure of the mainstream approach to publishing with its entrenched and conventional understanding of what a book can be has somehow lost its pull. For those writers, they choose to explore new outlets for their work.

Some simply don't care about monetary gain or the prestige of having a physical book published by a well-known publisher; they just want to share their work with readers and make a connection. It is these writers that I am interested in. These are the writers who have often been turned down by the gatekeepers of the mainstream industry and have gone instead to find where like-minded readers may be: online.

With low barriers of entry to online spaces, social media has become a key meeting point for writers and readers. Sites like Facebook, Twitter, Instagram, Wattpad, FanFiction.net, etc. have become places where some writers have chosen

DOI: 10.4324/9781003186649-1

to write and share works directly with an audience that is interested. They become citizen authors. While writing on social networking sites may have started out small, it has grown tremendously. Hashtags link stories or draw readers into a thread where they can find works of interest. Repositories like Wattpad and FanFiction.net allow for readers to find exactly the sort of stories they want to read and to comment directly on those works. The authors in these spaces have the ability to address comments, interact with readers, and develop relationships with them.

Some come to have large follower numbers and readers who adore their work. Those with substantial metrics gain the attention of publishers, who seek to cash in on the popularity of these authors and works by publishing them in the traditional fashion. The power these citizen authors have gained comes from themselves, their readers, and the relationships they have developed in these new social spaces. The mainstream industry is starting to understand the dynamic of these new creative spaces and seek ways to harness them.

This book examines the creative spaces for reading fiction and engaging with authors. It directly speaks to the changing ways of thinking about the book within the publishing industry and amongst authors, and how new technologies and social media platforms are perceived in this context. The framing of the book as printed, bound object, or a digital replica (such as a hyperlink text or an eBook), began to alter with the first online networking sites appearing in 1996.

Scholars such as DeNel Rehberg Sedo and Danielle Fuller have extensively studied the concept of social, or shared, reading as a way to build communities around works (Sedo, 2011; Sedo & Fuller, 2013), and while the role of book groups and mass reading is important in understanding the communicative roles of readers, here the focus remains on digitally social communities around works of fiction published directly onto social platforms, not traditionally published works read and discussed on these platforms.

Today, there are some 3.6 billion active social media accounts worldwide (Clement, 2020). And publishers have begun to tap into the works produced in this new space. They have published titles that pull content from social media, such as Penguin's *Twitterature* (2009), Hyperion's *White Girl Problems* (2012), Pan's *Shit My Dad Says* (2010), Prion's *The History of the World Through Twitter* (2009), and more recently Doubleday's *Hey, Harry Matilda* (2017), Andrew McMeel Publishing's *Milk and Honey* (2015), Gallery Books' *After* (2014), Hodder Children's *Arrowheart* (2018), Canongate Books' *The Beautiful Poetry of Donald Trump*, and Hamid Ismailov's *The Devils' Dance* (2018).

Even with so much readily available content and interactivity, there has been little research done into the ways that the publishing industry can use social-media generated content within and beyond the existing publishing models, apart from being a marketing tool.[1]boyd and Ellison noted in 2008 that "To date, the bulk of SNS research has focused on impression management and friendship performance, networks and network structure, online/offline connections, and privacy issues" (boyd & Ellison, 2008, p. 219). In 2020, this remains largely the case.

For my research for this book, I set out to see if people were writing on social media platforms, and, if so, who these authors were and what they were writing. In order to get the data I needed, I surveyed and interviewed authors and publishers. This was a key part in locating who was writing where, how the industry related to it, and what authors and readers considered to be a book in relation to the digital communities that have developed around written works that have not become part of the traditional industry's publishing model.

I do realise that the business models of publishing are not static. They alter between publishers, geography, and the advent and uptake of technologies. However, in this book, when speaking of the traditional publishing model I am referring to an author sending a manuscript to an agent, the agent sending it to publishers, the publishers editing it and publishing it in printed/digital/audio/serialised editions, and marketing it to an appropriate audience.

I use Foucault's archaeology to consider the wider discourse of the book, which allows for the creation of an archive where publishing and social media converge. I cover the time period from the early 2000s – and continuing until the present day.

Each participant that was surveyed or interviewed could only speak from their location in the industry, and the way they responded depended on their situation at the time, as any changing circumstances, such as having another book published or one publisher being taken over by another, would alter their position within the discourse and be filtered into their responses. While an effort was made to follow up on the status of a participant – i.e. an author having a second book published – this was not always possible. Having participants who were active in the publishing industry gave voice to a range of experiences of the industry that might be overlooked and so provided this research with varied points of view regarding the book, publishers, authors and their relationships to one another and to social media.

There were four distinct stages of this research: surveys, interviews, #Twitterfiction, and gathering comments across a specific work in Wattpad. The results of these stages were brought together to build an overview of the current publishing industry's relationship to social media as a content generator. The integration of the preliminary surveys and the sequential interviews allowed for an exploration of the relationships identified.

Participants in the surveys and interviews were over the age of 18 and were either associated with a publishing house or were themselves a published author. The inclusion criteria for publishers were to be publishing at least one book per year (eBooks, print books, audiobooks, etc.) and to have actively sought out new work (either via agents, in unsolicited submissions, or in other, unique ways). Authors who took part must have had at least one book-length work published and available within the United Kingdom or other English-speaking country. Limiting participants to those who have played a role in the industry ensured that the information gathered was relevant.

The number of respondents to the surveys and interviews was relatively small, but those responding were considered a representative sample, since it reached no less than 5–10 publishers across a range of business sizes (small, medium, and large) and

5–15 authors who have published works of fiction by traditional or non-traditional publishing routes. In future studies, reaching a wider pool of authors and publishers would solidify my findings.

The third and fourth stages of research were asynchronous stages that involved data-scraping and mining from the social media platform Twitter by pulling out the #Twitterfiction hashtag to generate a stream of fiction written within social media, and pulling and coding the in-line comments from Rebecca Sky's *Arrowheart* (part of *The Love Curse* series), chapter 1, off Wattpad.

Applying algorithms to digital texts that have been scraped, cleaned, and mined in order to locate potential fiction written within social media allowed for testing the concept of social media as a slush pile in a more practically oriented way. The data mining was particularly important in this research. It highlighted that writing on social, public, and digital platforms is possible and that authors are taking advantage of the easy access to these relatively new platforms and developing works of fiction that engage with the structures of the platforms (character limits, hashtags, and links) and the community of readers, authors, agents, and publishers that populate it.

Twitter Application Programming Interface (API)

The scraping of social media focused on testing whether or not a social media platform could be used as a place to locate works of fiction. This was a practical aspect to the research that showed how social media platforms are being used by citizen authors as places to generate new works of fiction. Scraping allows the industry to see how using social media as a content generator can be done without asking publishers to take the plunge and do it themselves.

In order to scrape a social platform smoothly, Twitter was chosen, as it has more unlocked accounts than Facebook and relies less on imagery than Instagram, though all three make use of the hashtag feature to create linked, searchable media streams. Facebook, in particular, focuses more on interacting with connections rather than the wider platform, and as such, many accounts are private.

The hashtag #Twitterfiction was chosen as a key datapoint as it separated out the works of fiction (fiction written on twitter) from the performative acts of writing with hashtags such as #iamwriting or #amwriting. Though other hashtags were considered around #twitterwriting, #twitterstories #fiction, the tag #Twitterfiction remained the most commonly linked to the topic of the research. I did not tag already written books (#fiction) or any term with 'writing,' as I was not interested so much in the act of writing on twitter but the output and connectivity with a digital readership.

"Due to the commercial value of the data, most of the major sources such as Facebook and Google are making it increasingly difficult for academics to obtain comprehensive access to their 'raw' data" (Batrinca & Treleaven, 2014, p. 90). With this in mind, an application programming interface (API) was created to capture all English language tweets with the hashtag #Twitterfiction. The API continued to run unaided, refreshing the collection every hour for twelve months; it ran from September 20, 2015 to September 20, 2016. This timeline was chosen due to the way "texts in social media contexts [...] happen in much faster timescales than traditional media ecologies" (Khosravinik & Unger, 2016, p. 217), which heeds that authors on social media can be expected to write and tweet from their mobile device and without setting aside a particular time and space dedicated to writing the work or chapter as a whole.

The first tweet was at 23:20 on September 20, 2015 and it ran until midnight on September 20, 2016. The final number of tweets reached 7,604 before sorting and mining.

Using open-source data manipulation software to process the scraped Twitter data

Though there is much software available to apply data-mining processes and varying algorithms to a cleaned database of #Twitterfiction data, Knime was chosen due to its ease of use and open-source ethos. In addition, the mapping format of the main workflow allowed for a visual understanding of the processes and their links, which corresponds to the mapping of the discourse of the book.

It is important to note that this sort of search and scraping was controlled by a rate limit that limited results to 180 queries in 15 minutes (Twitter, 2016) and gave access to less than 1% of the entire Twitter firehose, made up of the entirety of tweets from around the world, around 9,283 per second[2] (Twitter, 2020), in a chronological fashion (González-Bailón et al., 2014, p. 16). Narrowing the specification of a search API to the #Twitterfiction feed "on the basis of content or location might yield better estimations because it reduces the scope of interest and maximises the information retrieved" (González-Bailón et al., 2014, p. 17).

As part of the mining process, the #Twitterfiction tweets needed to be organised and cleaned. Once the initial stage of scraping the Twitter data was completed, the spreadsheet was uploaded into the Knime workflow. Once the numbers of tweets rose above two tweets per user, the amounts of users who were tweeting larger numbers dropped in proportion. For instance: while there were sixty-nine people that tweeted three times, there were only five people that tweeted eight times. As numbers of users who tweeted multiple times with the #Twitterfiction hashtag dropped, the numbers of tweets they produced rose steadily, reaching three people who tweeted twenty-seven times, two people who tweeted forty-six, and single users who tweeted higher numbers such as one who tweeted 770, and two who tweeted over 800 and 900, respectively. This highlights that many people branched out from the #Twitterfiction hashtag over extended numbers of tweets, which limited the numbers of potential works of fiction that could be found, as writers may have used other hashtags to mark their writing.

Locating usable tweets

From the original 7,879 tweets that came in over the twelve-month period, after pulling them together by username, there were 1,066 unique user IDs that tweeted

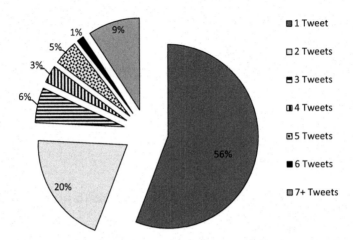

FIGURE 0.1 Numbers of tweets per user: September 20, 2015 to September 20, 2016

with the hashtag #Twitterfiction. 606 of the 1,066 user IDs were peripheral, low-frequency users who wrote only one #Twitterfiction tweet and made up the majority of 57%. All user IDs that tweeted less than five tweets with the #Twitterfiction hashtag were removed, leaving 137 unique users who have tweeted more than five times with the hashtag.

Of the remaining 137 unique users, each set of tweets were sorted manually to remove the users that only re-tweet other users, those that were nonsense texts, those that solely promote #Twitterfiction contents and writing, and those that did not tell any sort of story in the body of their tweets.

Once the unique user IDs that were not writing works of fiction were removed, there remained forty-four citizen authors who wrote fiction in the body of tweets.

The most interesting numbers lie beyond the single tweets, or even the double/triple tweets. Though there are several competitions to tell a Twitter-length story (Project Pen, Short Story, and Society of Authors), what matters here is locating fictions that could be pulled out of the 'slush pile' in the social platforms where they were written and re-formatted for a more traditional publication.

For this purpose, I considered 800 words as a minimum length for a short story. In order to compare this word count to the character count used in Twitter, an 800-word story translated into around 4,620 characters with spaces, which was thirty-three, 140-character tweets.[3] The data that was extracted for further transformation and analysis consisted of nine unique user IDs which had at least thirty-three tweets.

The nine users' tweets were pulled into a spreadsheet and cleaned by removing hashtags, replies and other non-fiction-based content. Some hashtags that were part of the storyline itself, such as when @ErikHandy writes "#InMyOldHoodWe ignored the whispers from the woods. They never went away" (@ErikHandy, 2016, 30 March), were left in, as they were deemed to be necessary to the tweet itself. The nine works ranged from just under 1,000 to over 13,000 words in length, which were then analysed for content.

Wattpad in-line comments

The fourth and perhaps most interesting stage of research for this book was based on the in-line comments from a Wattpad novel. Wattpad was chosen because it is a social platform where authors write and share works, hashtag them with genres and search-able phrases, and interact with their readers. The available in-line commentary on Wattpad stories makes it an ideal place to observe and understand how authors and readers are speaking to each other and developing a community in these social spaces. Though there are over 350,000 stories on Wattpad (Wattpad Books, 2019), I chose to pull the comments from Rebecca Sky's work *Arrowheart*, since this work was written on Wattpad and after gaining popularity online was published in paperback version by Hodder Children's Books in June 2018. Sky also fits the profile of a typical Wattpad author: young, female, and writing genre fiction (fantasy romance).

In using *Arrowheart*, I was less interested in the content of the story itself and focused instead on the in-line commentary around the first chapter. This consisted of 262 individual comments from both readers and Sky herself. I did not look at the overall comments on the chapter, of which there were 1,800. I wanted to work only with the in-line comments to discover if there were feedback loops between the author and the readers, and how the interactions on the text itself played out in the digital community and related to aspects which became important to this research, such as gender.

These 262 comments were coded for editorial feedback, interactions of note, negative/questioning, positive excitement, and positive feedback. The commenta-tors were also gendered. To do this, I used the available information on each commentator, which included username, avatar image, and on their profile any gendered information they provided, including checking any links to their social media they include for public viewing. The information available on most profiles gives an indication of gender that is sufficient for this study, but I recognise that this method has limitations where some profiles are completely gender neutral and the use of avatars can disguise demographics entirely.

Using this blend of established and emergent techniques allowed me to ground my exploration in a solid framework while leaving room for the innovative or unexpected to emerge and be observed. The complex interplay at the edges of this fascinating new frontier of publishing provided no shortage of material for analysis. My work merely summarises the potential for books as social objects to continue their growth well beyond the bounds of previously accepted definitions of what a book is or might become.

Notes

1 For more information on using social media as a means of marketing and its effect on sales, see Criswell and Canty (2014).
2 Up from 6,000 per second in 2017.
3 In November 2017, Twitter doubled the limit on its character count from 140 to 280. This research was carried out prior to this change and as such all tweets that were mined are based in the 140-character limit, and the research and numbers of tweets per story use the 140 character limit as a basis for determining lengths.

Bibliography

@ErikHandy, 2016. #InMyOldHoodWe ignored the whispers from the woods. They never went away. #Twitterfiction #horror. [Twitter]. Available at: http://twitter.com/ErikHandy/statuses/715200250953252864. [Accessed 26 December 2020].

Batrinca, B. & Treleaven, P., 2014. Social Media Analytics: A Survey of Techniques, Tools and Platforms. In *AI & Soc.* Vol. 30, pp. 89–116.

boyd, d. & Ellison, N.B., 2008. Social Network Sites: Definition, History, and Scholarship. In *Journal of Computer-Mediated Communication.* Vol. 13, pp. 210–230.

Clement, J., 2020. The Number of Social Networks Users Worldwide from 2017 to 2025. Statista. Available at: https://www.statista.com/statistics/278414/number-of-worldwide-social-network-users/. [Accessed 26 December 2020].

Criswell, J. & Canty, N., 2014. Deconstructing Social Media: An Analysis of Twitter and Facebook Use in the Publishing Industry. In *Publishing Research Quarterly.* Vol. 30, pp. 352–337. Available at: doi:10.1007/s12109–014–9376–1.

González-Bailón, S., Wang, N., Rivero, A., Borge-Holthoefer, J., & Moreno, Y., 2014. Assessing the Bias in Samples of Large Online Networks. In *Social Networks.* Vol. 38, pp. 16–27.

Khosravinik, M. & Unger, J., 2016. Critical Discourse Studies and Social Media: Power, Resistance and Critique in Changing Media Ecologies. In Wodak, R. & Meyer, M. (Eds), *Methods of Critical Discourse Studies* (pp. 205–233). London: Sage Publications.

McLuhan, M., 2013. *Understanding Media: The Extensions of Man.* Berkeley: Gingko Press. [eBook].

Sedo, D. (Ed.), 2011. *Reading Communities: From Salon to Cyberspace.* Hampshire: Palgrave Macmillan.

Sedo, D. & Fuller, D., 2013. *Reading Beyond the Book: The Social Practice of Contemporary Literary Culture.* Oxfordshire: Routledge.

Twitter, 2016. The Search API – Development Documentation. Available at: https://dev.twitter.com/rest/public/search. [Accessed 22 November 2016].

Twitter, 2020. Internet Live Stats – Usage Statistics. Available at: http://www.internetlivestats.com/twitter-statistics/. [Accessed 26 December 2020].

Wattpad Books, 2019. About. Available at: https://books.wattpad.com/about. [Accessed 12 September 2019].

1
WHAT IS A BOOK?

On first glance, 'What is a book?' is, perhaps, the most simple question with an obvious answer: a book is a bound object that has stories or images inside. That answer is correct. But it also falls dangerously short of truly tapping into what a book is and can be. In defining a book, we must first look at how the things around a book are changing, and how those changes seep into the outer edges of the traditional printed book and begin to alter it. These changes are often related to technological advances, but it is not enough to stop short and say, 'eBooks and audiobooks are great advances and are still books.' We have to take into account the changes that these technologies allow to happen. Specifically, digital technology and the widespread use of, and access to, the internet has given rise to social media, which in turn has changed how authors and readers relate to content and how they form communities around writing on social media platforms.

Historically, the book publishing industry has enjoyed long periods of stability followed by revolutionary upheavals that lead to radical changes in the way that books are written, published, and distributed. The most easily recognised shift was from the codex (AD 150) to the printing press (AD 1450), which gave rise to the traditionally bound books that we have today. Other technological advances such as magazine printing, mass-market paperbacks, eBooks, and audiobooks have also come of age in recent decades and have contributed to the evolving definition of a book by changing the format of a book in such a way that it retains tight connections, real or virtual, with the physical item itself.

From the time of inscribed clay tablets (2500 B.C.E.) until the digital revolution (1990s), a book had been a physical object that was usually portable, often collected, and prized as a "storehouse of human knowledge" (Kilgour, 1998, p. 3). The book itself has undergone physical changes over time, and book historians now use "the word 'book' in its widest sense, covering virtually any piece of written or printed text that has been multiplied, distributed, or in some way made public" (Eliot & Rose,

DOI: 10.4324/9781003186649-2

2007, p. 3). While this definition invites inclusivity for new forms of technologically produced writing, it is as vague as it is broad, and the question remains as to how this definition can evolve more specifically to encompass new and as of yet undiscovered forms of the book that develop around the traditional format.

Though the focus here is not book history, it is valuable to use book historians' definitions to give a baseline for what the wider industry considers a book. That being said, we must keep in mind that every understanding of how a book is defined is grounded in what that particular person is able to say from their place of knowledge within the industry. Those with different experiences will have different considerations.

The publishing industry slowly but continually shifts and changes. As new technologies and media converge and grow both vertically and horizontally, the definition of a book must capture the essence of content while remaining fluid enough to encompass existing and future packaging of that content. In order to facilitate a suitably adaptable and forward-thinking definition of the book, it is necessary to first understand how the book is currently defined in the different areas of the industry and how those definitions have gained traction.

Digital publishing and the convergence of new technologies have altered the available formats of the book, with the development of eBooks and audiobooks, and different ways of getting content to readers, and we must, in turn, alter the discourse surrounding the book to reflect this change. In discussing ways that the themes of continuity around the definition of a book can be hindered by preconceptions, a good starting place is Foucault, who in his *Archaeology of Knowledge* states that to best prepare ourselves for understanding a discourse "we must rid ourselves of a whole mass of notions," in this case, the set descriptors of a book. He goes on to explain that the specific notions "that must be suspended above all are those that emerge in the most immediate way: those of the book and the oeuvre" (1989, pp. 23–23).

Foucault alludes to the evolution of the book when he states that "The book is not simply the object that one holds in one's hands; and it cannot remain within the little parallelepiped that contains it" (1989, p. 23). By stripping out the "interpretation of the facts" (p. 29) about what a book is, we can better define a book by looking at the "rule of simultaneous or successive emergence of the various objects that are named, described, analysed, appreciated, or judged in that relation" (p. 32). In other words, we must look at all the instances of a 'book' in order to understand what it can, and cannot, be. In the current age of technological advances, that includes texts written and shared within digitally social environments.

At the Shenzhen-UNESCO International Conference on "Digital Books and Future Technology," Hitchens mentioned how "digital companies will most likely join the fold as publishing companies shift resources towards the burgeoning eBook industry" (2014, p. 13). However, he neglects to go further to examine how this shift will encompass media more broadly and only hints at the digitally social communities that can grow up around a published product, and he does not touch on the power dynamics such a shift contains. He does, however, suggest that "that the future of eBooks will be based on much more than text on a screen" (2014, p. 13). This can already be seen in the marketplace with publications such as Faber & Faber's interactive book app of T.S. Eliot's *The Waste Land* (2011) or read-aloud books for kids that add sound and effects to stories. Likewise, new forms of interactive literature such as UNRD provide a new format for experiencing real-time stories via a mobile device which showcases the convergence of ePublishing technologies and the way books, and the ways we interact with them, are changing.

The rise of new reading/writing-based technologies, algorithms, and formats does not herald the end of the printed book. In his talk for UNESCO, Hitchens concluded that "the demise of the physical book is still far from inevitable" (2014, p. 16). Thus far, the numbers agree, with recent Nielsen data showing that print book sales in 2019 rose 0.4% in the UK and 3.3% in Ireland, with 1.8 million ISBNs selling at least one physical copy in 2019 (Whelan, 2020).

Furthermore, Phillips, in his book *Turning the Page: The Evolution of the Book*, explores the current state of the book and its future potential. He discusses its forms, and he labels printed books "pbooks" as a way of acknowledging that although published products are often called books, "traditional routes of production are being left behind" (2014, p. xiii). The definition of a book is broadening to accommodate changes in technology and how we are all linked closely together via the internet in a global village. Along with this, we see movement in the power strategies, how digital communities grow, and the role of authorship in these new spaces.

Changes within the publishing industry regarding the definition of the book have not always been easily accepted. In 1998, Kilgour wrote that the eBook

> has met with an unenthusiastic reception, chiefly because it presents a radical physical change for the user: from the familiar bound book in the hand to the monitor screen of a desktop computer or the flat-panel display of a laptop machine.
>
> *(p. 151)*

By 2006, when Kelly wrote that "publishers have lost millions of dollars on the long-prophesied e-book revolution that never occurred" (p. 2), eBooks had become an accepted, if still unpopular, form of the book that echoed the physical book in the rear-view mirror but one that is held under glass.

Moving away from the traditional formats, if we took the content out of the container what is there to define a book? Let's take, for example, a trade bestseller. The publishers distribute it in hardback, paperback, eBook formats, all of which are comfortably considered to be books. But what happens when the publisher converges media and creates an audiobook that resembles the bestseller only in that the content, not the format, is (mostly) the same?

Is an audiobook still a book? Michael Bhaskar suggests as an answer that an audiobook isn't a real book, claiming that "Audiobooks are a halfway house – at one level they are sound, at another just another format of a text like a paperback or an eBook" (2013, p. 32). Is it, as Bhaskar argues, "sufficiently close to a book to easily absorb the associations of 'book publishing'" (p. 32) or does it fall out with commonly accepted definitions of the book? This links to the seeming contradiction that lies between the repetition of the framework of the book in the wider discourse as an understood and recognisable object – hardback, paperback, eBooks, or audio, etc. – and the un-repeatability of new forms and uses of technology that have yet to become established as recognisable books.

Going back to Eliot and Rose, they state that a book is a text that has been "multiplied, distributed, or in some way made public" (2007, p. 3), but this definition lacks clarity in two key ways. Firstly, the issue of multiplication, distribution, and making it public must be scrutinised, as each of these elements limit the definition of a book. When a book is defined by being "in some way made public," Eliot and Rose seem to discount those books that are printed and never made public at all, such as pulped books and private print runs that sit in a room, never shared. Bhaskar also disagrees with the usefulness of the phrase 'to make public' by claiming that the "weakness of such a view lies in the lack of clarity about making public" (2013, p. 168). When there is no clarification of what 'making public' means, then does the non-distributed item still retain the nomenclature of a book simply by virtue of being multiplied or in some way distributed? Likewise, would a single issue of a bespoke photography or picture book not be considered a book due to its lack of printed text, multiplication, public exposure, or distribution?

The single issue of a bespoke book that deteriorates the edges of Eliot and Rose's definition is not the norm and can, perhaps, be glossed over in favour of the inclusivity their definition provides, where it can include print-on-demand and single edition prints. However, the second, more pressing issue with their definition deals with their lack of engagement with terms that specifically relate to technological advances or the sociality that, in many ways, is driving the current market. In their omission, Eliot and Rose are remaining conservative by keeping their definition from aging. But the vagueness which keeps this definition of the book alive and modern is also what makes their understanding of the book an umbrella term that prevents it from becoming contextually relevant when engaging with future technologies.

Where Eliot and Rose stop, Cope and Phillips step in, going a bit further, claiming that "A book is no longer a physical thing. A book is what a book does" (2006, p. 7). The question that follows from this is: what does a book do? According to Cope and Phillips, a book does two things:

- It has a characteristic textual, and thus, communicative, structure.
- It has book-like functions because it is defined, registered and recognised as a book. This means that, when we need to 'do books', it can be found in bibliographical listings, it is acquired through bookstores and libraries; and it can be referenced as books.

(2006, pp. 7–8)

This dual definition of what a book does creates areas of friction within itself, the most obvious of which is where Cope and Phillips mention the "characteristic textual, and thus, communicative structure." Within this statement, there seems to be lacking a theoretical or practical link between a book's textuality and its communicative structure. What is there to presuppose that a book's text is communicative?

Cope and Phillips overstate the connection between these two elements by presuming that because the structure is textual is it also communicative; where, in fact, the communicative nature of a text is potential instead of actual. Again, we can use the example of the bespoke photography book used above, a book that was published but never read, or printed and then pulped without trying to sell a single copy. These examples show text in its potential to be communicative but also highlight that one does not necessarily lead to the other, meaning that an item can be a book in structure even if it is never communicated to any readers and, vice versa, it can also be a book if it is communicated to others but not structured as a book, as with audiobooks, podcast books, or serials.

In looking at their second point in what a book does, we must question the book-like functions they describe and whether they relate to a book's function or the physicality of the book. Importantly, this raises questions on whether this definition of a book allows for new formats such as Keitai Shōsetsu, collaborative fiction, and social media writing, which, noticeably, lack some of the features mentioned above.

Cope and Phillips mention earlier that a book is "a structured rendition of text and possibly also images" (2006, p. 7), which they quickly narrow down as "extended text (of, say, more than twenty thousand words and/or twenty images)" (2006, p. 7). To truncate the length of text considered to be a book overlooks a wide array of genres, presentation styles, and eProductions that all, rightfully, should fall under the mantle of the book. By narrowing down the understanding of a text as it relates to their interpretation of a book, Cope and Phillips do not allow for an open and forward-thinking definition of what a book is and can be.

The role of innovative formats in defining a book

A traditionally published book that has been moved online, where comments on the text are allowed without altering the original book, does not in and of itself, as Bob Stein seems to suggest, create a future where the definition of a book expands to become a place of communication (Stein, 2008). However, there is scope for the dialogue in digitally social places to give rise to a book. This is explored by Phillips, who discusses the social platforms of blogs as places that have "attracted a whole new set of writers" (2014, p. 16). Many printed books have been pulled together from blog feeds creating what is known as a blook. Some of these, such as Julie Powell's *Julie and Julia* – a blog based on the author's adventure of using a printed version of a famous cookbook for a year – later shifted media again to be made into a film. Printing blooks even gave rise to a Blooker prize that was run by Lulu.com in 2006 and 2007, further legitimising the content of blogs by rewarding the efforts of publishers to pull the content offline and issue it in a traditional format.

In 2008 and 2009, Bob Stein, co-founder of The Institute for the Future of the Book, hit on the community-driven definition of a book and began to describe the "future of the book as 'a place where readers (and sometimes authors) congregate'" (2008). By taking a book out of its static printed or locked digital form and opening it up to become a meeting place for authors and readers, Stein envisioned the book publishing industry to be less about the book as an object and more about the content and the dialogue created in and around communities of reading and writing. With this in mind, the Institute for the Future of the Book ran several projects around generating collaborative dialogues in the margins of a digital book, including "The Golden Notebook Project."

This was a collaborative project in which seven readers were asked to conduct a conversation in the digitally provided margins of an online version of Doris Lessing's *The Golden Notebook*. The website for the project seems to be stagnant, but by clicking through to the "read the book" section, where any reader can gain access to the same text that the original seven read and commented on, the user is faced with an onscreen design that mimics the pages of a printed book. In fact, along with clicks left and right to change pages, at the top of the interface there are changeable fields which tell readers how the online, UK print, and USA print versions correlate page by page. The rear-view mirror aspect of the interface reminds users, who may have been unfamiliar with onscreen reading of novels when the project was begun in 2008, that what they see onscreen directly corresponds to a printed page, lending the screen version a sense of legitimacy (McLuhan & Fiore, 2008 [1968]).

With that consideration, I open up the definition of a book to consider other formats. Both Phillips and Bhaskar briefly address the rise of new writing outlets in the Asian market, specifically looking at mobile storytelling forms of Keitai Shōsetsu in the Japanese market and what Bhaskar calls "original fiction" from China. Keitai Shōsetsu "are novels being written on cell phones, or keitai's, by individuals in Japan. These novels are tapped out on mobile phones in a form similar to long text messages" (Keckler, 2010, p. 2). The rise of mobile fiction in Japan has been heavily intertwined with the proliferation of cell phone usage, especially among young adults and young women, who are most often the readers and writers of the form (Keckler, 2010), much like the gender balance of the readers and writers discussed later in this book. Authors in Japan pen their stories on their phones when they have time and upload them to dedicated websites such as Maho no i-rando, which was followed by Magic i-land and Wild Strawberry, among others.

In China, the market shifts away from phone-written fiction and focuses instead on websites that act as portals for readers to find and read new original fiction. Reading Base, a mobile platform run by the country's largest mobile provider, China Mobile, is just one of the dedicated 'original fiction' outlets that are helping to fuel the "5 billion yuan industry" (Bhaskar, 2013 p. 52). The platforms in China work on a freemium model, where a user has free access to some content and has to pay for others. "Popular work is upgraded to pay-as-you-go VIP areas" (Bhaskar, 2013, p. 52).

Keitai Shōsetsu and China's 'original fiction' have generally been accepted as new genres of fiction within that market (Bhaskar, 2013, p. 51), but there is no clarity on at what point these cell phone novels are considered books. This leads to the question of whether the format of the printed book still retains privilege as the prized goal that only then allows a work to be called a book. It would seem as such, with journalist Normitsu Onishi pointing out in 2008 that "Of last year's 10 best-selling [printed] novels, five were originally cellphone novels" (2008, para 2). Similarly, in China, one step beyond the pay-as-you-go VIP area, there are publishers that are dedicated to bringing the most popular works to the printed page.

Much like Keitai Shōsetsu and 'original fiction,' these works, written within or uploaded to, community websites and repositories online "represent new ways of writing and a new end product" (Bhaskar, 2013, p. 52). Such works are often written and exist in an entirely digital setting, which could seem to undermine the validity of calling them books, but this would be a mistake. Writing repositories online are prime slush piles for publishers, with the added benefit that the slush has sometimes already been filtered (the VIP area in China, fan fiction with the highest views in the West) and the publishers can choose to bring books to print that already receive a high number of views and are likely to sell well in traditional containers.

Content and containers as a means of defining a book

There is less concern now that print is dead. Instead, there is a new debate arising about how digital and communicative technology can redefine the book, and it is reshaping the publishing industry as a whole. Early in his discussion of the book, Phillips declares "The whole debate over print vs. digital is over" (2014, xii).[1]

Foucault notes that "the unity of the book, even in the sense of a group of relations, cannot be regarded as identical in each case" (Foucault, 1989, p. 23). Lichtenberg also addresses the lack of unity in the format of the book, in saying that "With the book, since Gutenberg, the form factor itself defined both container and content." He goes on to say that "The internet and digital technologies have broken them apart" (2011, pp. 105–106).

Bhaskar mentions how:

> We still talk of 'the book' both as the physical codex on our shelf but also as 'the text' or 'the work' in a more abstract sense; moreover we use these distinct terms interchangeably [...] suggesting we do not, in day-to-day circumstances, recognise a disjuncture between content and media.
>
> *(2013, p. 80)*

Much of what Bhaskar discusses relating to the content and context of the publishing industry is influenced by O'Leary's 2011 work "Context First: A Unified Field Theory of Publishing," where he says that the containers (books) are used to "define content in two dimensions, necessarily ignoring that which cannot or does not fit" (p. 212). O'Leary goes on to say that the 'container first' model, which limits content, is already obsolete (2011, p. 212). While O'Leary doesn't heavily involve himself in the formats that the future book could take – beyond a few digital predictions regarding workflow and bundling – Bhaskar attempts to relate content to "frames." Frames are Bhaskar's term for content containers, which he considered to be "not just delivery systems or packages for content but content's experimental mode" (2013, p. 84).

Prior to Bhaskar or O'Leary's consideration of frames is McLuhan's use of the 'rear-view mirror' as a frame for understanding older media: "The objectives of new media have tended, fatally, to be set in terms of the parameters and frames of older media" (McLuhan, 2013). But, in the context of Bhaskar's use of frames, their experimental modes can be shuffled and twisted to hold an array of content, shifting again when the content expands, as in the form of collaborative story-writing communities like StoryMash, or shrinking to become packets of books delivered straight to your cell phone. If we follow Bhaskar further, we see that he breaks down digital frames to mechanisms that assist content delivery systems: screens, HTML, coding languages, fibre optic cables, electricity, and more (2013, p. 85). All of these frames play a role, however small, in defining a book within the digital environment and beyond. This relates directly to what #Twitterfiction author Simon Grant highlights about using digital structures to pull apart what a book might look like when he says of his own writing on social platforms:

> Many of the stories with more explicitly experimental structures have no set length or pre-existing form. Forcing them to be beholden to traditional notions of what a book can be would undermine the discovery process and the structural freedom that gives social-media composition such rich potential [...] the necessary linearity of a book would force structure to lose some of its unique interconnectedness.
>
> *(8 February, 2017)*

Grant is an author who embraces the mechanisms of social media that assist in the delivery of his work as a way to enhance it and help the audience to navigate it in a way that would be impossible with a traditionally printed book.

Phillips, too, hits on the breaking apart of content and container when he describes reading onscreen, saying that the "actual experience of reading a book is already coming close to reading web pages" (2014, p. 119), where pages can be scrolled continuously, and readers can find imbedded links to enrich and inform their experience.

Hitchens points out a modern incarnation of McLuhan's concept of the rear-view mirror affecting eBooks: "most eBooks are functionally the same as reading a print book" (2014, p. 13). To highlight lean back technology, akin to McLuhan's rear-view mirror, Phillips mentions the skeuomorphic design of the iPad, which relies on a wooden-styled bookshelf to hold a user's books (2014, p. 36). In fact, most eBook readers, platforms, and apps have embraced print book-centric functionality, such as white reading screens and page-turning visuals and sounds that serve no purpose other than to allow the reader to connect to their current media through attributes of an older one. The rear-view mirror also has an effect on how a book is defined, but we must be careful not to limit the definition of the book to include only those already existing technologies and instead open it up to future forms of framed content.

Today, the book has moved beyond the eBook to encompass a variety of ePublications facilitated by advances in media and technology. In his article "Evolution of the Book Publishing Industry," Keh is forward thinking when he describes how, "In the information age, the publisher no longer views himself as the purveyor of physical products, but of ideas and information. The publisher's asset lies in the contents, to which he adds value by providing them in different formats" (1998, p. 118). Keh's observations are relevant today, as the current publishing model continues to develop slowly and expand both vertically and horizontally, allowing for innovative ways of connecting and controlling new content delivery technologies. Grant echoes this when he says that social technologies provide "restrictions as a mechanism for heightening creativity, complexity, and novelty."

Bhaskar agrees with Keh in the idea that a publisher is a purveyor of content, but he goes further than Keh in saying that the "content is framed – packaged for distribution and presented to an audience – according to a model" (2013, p. 6). While I agree that the future of the book is content based, what Keh and Bhaskar both lack in their content-focused discussion is the integration of digitally social technology that goes beyond marketing to create a place where communities can be built and where new writing can emerge.

Redefining the book in the social age

Scholars such as Bhaskar (2013), Keh (1998), Phillips (2014), and O'Leary (2011) champion the idea of content as what makes a book and agree that a digital text is simply another format of that content, but they stop short of taking it forward to the next level. Specifically, they neglect to take into account instances of disruption brought on by the rise of social networking sites that have unlimited resources, an unfathomable amount of user data, and innovative authors who are willing to publish their intellectual property directly within these digital communities. The discourses that develop around these disruptions can be related to other areas such as the wider publishing industry, socio-economic considerations, and gender balances in the industry and online. To develop an understanding of how they work can lead to an understanding of the shifting power relations among the industry's key players.

While Phillips ends *Turning the Page* with a plea for "advocates of the [(inferred) printed] book to stand up and be counted" (2014, p. 127), Bhaskar ends his book by coming slightly closer to the point by declaring that "It [publishing] is a social machine. One problem: the Machine Age has ended" (2013, p. 195). The Machine Age *has* ended, but publishing is no less social than it has been in centuries past, perhaps even more so in the current digital age, where the world is, as McLuhan suggests, shrinking to the size of a village (2013).

Venturing further than Bhaskar, we can say that books are now social. Using that premise as a starting point, the definition of a book must be more inclusive and open to digital changes while being careful not to age itself at the moment of writing. It must reflect the content created around new technologies, genres, and digital communities; it cannot alienate certain forms or remain prejudiced around print, distribution, or multiplication. Defining what a book is in the face of a rapidly changing and developing publishing model, and digital technology is never clear-cut. Keeping that in mind, I define a book as any piece of framed content that has a basis in text or image that can potentially be reproduced and that has an element of sociality, insomuch that it has the possibility to be shared or made public at some stage in its development.

This description should not be considered the final word in how a book is defined, but should be used as a guideline, a starting place from which the understanding of a book can grow alongside the publishing industry and not be relegated to the objects of the past. It will help locate where new objects and technologies are giving rise to new understandings of the book within social communities and how they relate to the power structures that frame the wider industry and who has the say in declaring what can be a book.

Note

1 Certainly the debate has calmed down since the sudden upheaval of digital publishing spurred academics and industry experts to write books and articles such as: *The Book Is Dead (Long Live the Book)* (Young, 2007), 'Books Survive the Orgasm of Closure' (Matthews, 2008), and 'Flogging a Dead Book?' (James, 2011), amongst others.

Bibliography

Bhaskar, M., 2013. *The Content Machine: Towards a Theory of Publishing from the Printing Press to the Digital Network*. London: Anthem Press.

Cope. B. & Phillips, A., 2006. Introduction. In Cope, B. & Phillips, A. (Eds), *The Future of the Book in the Digital Age* (pp. 1–18). Oxford: Chandos.

Eliot, S. & Rose, J., 2007. Introduction. In Eliot, S. & Rose, J. (Eds), *A Companion to the History of the Book* (pp. 1–6). Oxford: Blackwell.

Foucault, M., 1989. *The Archaeology of Knowledge*. Translated from the French by A.M. Sheridan Smith. London: Routledge.

Grant, S., 2017. Interview with Simon Grant. Interviewed by Miriam Johnson [email].

Hitchens, A.D., 2014. *eBooks: The Revolution Will Be Digitized*. The Shenzhen-UNESCO International Conference on "Digital Books and Future Technology". Nov. 29–30, 2014. Shenzhen: UNESCO.

James, S., 2011. Flogging a Dead Book? In *Journal of Scholarly Publishing*. Vol. 42, pp. 182–204.

Keckler, S.L., 2010. Koizora: A Mirroring of Keitai Shōsetsu in a "Novel" Approach to Modern Literature. PhD dissertation. Washington and Lee University.

Keh, H.T., 1998. Evolution of the Book Publishing Industry: Structural Changes and Strategic Implications. In *Journal of Management History*. Vol. 4, No. 2, pp. 104–123.

Kelly, K., 2006. Scan This Book!. In *The New York Times Magazine* [online]. Available at: http://www.nytimes.com/2006/05/14/magazine/14publishing.html?pagewanted=2&_r=5. [Accessed January 2015].

Kilgour, F.G., 1998. *The Evolution of the Book*. Oxford: Oxford University Press.

Lichtenberg, J., 2011. In From the Edge: The Progressive Evolution of Publishing in the Age of Digital Abundance. In *Publishing Research Quarterly*. Vol. 27, pp. 101–112. Available at: https://doi.org/10.1007/s12109-011-9212-9.

Matthews, B., 2008. Books Survive the Orgasm of Closure. In *Eureka Street*. Vol. 18, pp. 37–38.

McLuhan, M., 2013. *Understanding Media: The Extensions of Man*. Berkeley: Gingko Press [eBook].

McLuhan, M. & Fiore, Q., 2008 [1968]. *The Medium is the Massage*. London: Penguin Books.

O'Leary, B.F., 2011. Context First: A Unified Theory of Publishing. In *Publishing Research Quarterly*. Vol. 27, pp. 211–219.

Onishi, N., 2008. Thumbs Race as Japan's Best Sellers Go Cellular. In *The New York Times Magazine* [online]. Available at: http://www.nytimes.com/2008/01/20/world/asia/20japan.html?pagewanted=all&_r=0. [Accessed January 2015].

Phillips, A., 2014. *Turning the Page: The Evolution of the Book*. New York: Routledge.

Stein, B., 2008. A Book Is a Place.... *If:book: A Project of the Institute of the Future of the Book* [blog]. 29 December. Available at: http://futureofthebook.org/blog/2008/12/29/a_book_is_a_place/. [Accessed January 2015].

Whelan, S., 2020. *The UK Book Market and All the Data Behind It* [lecture]. October 2020. Oxford Brookes University.

Young, S., 2007. *The Book is Dead (Long Live the Book)*. Sydney: NewSouth Publishing.

2

FOUCAULT'S ARCHAEOLOGY AND MCLUHAN'S GLOBAL VILLAGE AND REAR-VIEW MIRROR AS ANALYTIC STRATEGIES

Academics and students who are interested in using Foucault's theory of archaeology and method of genealogy often find that his texts are both dense and fluid, making a complete use of his theory and method rather difficult (Dean, 2003). But, in working within a Foucauldian framework, I find that the best way to approach Foucault's methods is via his own words: "I would like my books to be a kind of tool box which others can rummage through to find a tool which they can use however they wish in their own area" (translated in O'Farrell, 2005, p. 50).

Using these tools, we must take on the roles of archaeologist, genealogist, and media analyst. First, the archaeologist seeks to analyse, within a particular slice of history, what can be visualised, the relationship between statements or groups of statements, the position of the speaker, the way that some institutions are able to gain authority, and how all of these phenomena relate to one another. The archaeologist must then become a genealogist in order to use the archaeological structure to explore the knowledge and power relations between the discursive and non-discursive elements within the archive, and how these knowledge and power relations become manifest within the social structures and industries. In addition, these tools allow for media analysis by appropriating McLuhan's theories of the global village and the rear-view mirror within the wider archive.

Foucault's archaeology and a 'slice of history'

Using Foucault's concept of the book as more than an object you hold in your hands (1989, p. 23) allows us to explore the changing ideas of what is considered a book by taking into account the possibility of innovation. Specifically, this refers to the advent and adoption of social media as an authorial tool giving rise to the citizen author, who finds their place writing in an online community which is imbued with power structures. This new location for authors and readers develops

DOI: 10.4324/9781003186649-3

creative outputs within and beyond the current publishing models and encompasses the working definition of a book detailed at the end of the previous chapter.

Using Foucault's archaeological method narrows the wide scope of history that does not necessarily adhere to a chronological timeline. This 'slice of history' (Foucault, 1989) approach considers the items of interest within a specified period of time, allowing for the categorisation of the different ways various groups define a book and the understanding of whom these definitions of the book serve in the hierarchy of publishing.

As one of Foucault's earlier works, *The Archaeology of Knowledge* is regularly overlooked within the field of publishing studies and can be considered as "rather a book for specialists" (Downing, 2008, p. 51). However, utilising the archaeology to create a theoretical framework as a way to structure a cohesive study of the elements within a specified period allows for the linking of the discourses of the book, publishing models, social media, and the citizen author with the non-discursive aspects of the publishing industry itself and digitally social technologies.

Foucault's works can be used to critically comment on social structures, such as the disconnect between new publishing technology, citizen authors, and traditional publishing models, but though his archaeology can highlight the flaws of the institutions, his work does not propose anything to take their place (O'Farrell, 2005, p. 109). To bypass the limitations of Foucault's archaeology, the parameters of this book include the discourse of the book, which incorporates definitions of the book, publishing, social media, socio-economic factors, technology, and the citizen author, while acknowledging that other discourses do exist and will cross over with the topics at hand. A further limitation of the archaeology is considered by Blanchot, who draws out the "the illusion of autonomous discourse" (1990 [1987], p. 80), wherein one can trace a particular discourse within the wider archive, forgetting that there can be infinite discourses that run parallel, all equally valid and true.[1]

We move away from "a uniform model of temporalisation" (Foucault, 1998, p. 200), where the history of objects and events lead from one to another in a linear fashion. Through his work, Foucault shows that it is more advantageous to remove this uniform model of linear chronology in order to consider objects, statements/definitions, and events as places of dispersal – where new things are created. In doing this, this book focuses on the space around the objects of interest (such as books, readers, authors, etc.) to define connections, missed connections, and other links that do not follow linearly, such as why genre communities grow and experiment in online spaces, often bolstered by a supportive (and gendered) community of readers, but the same genres progress at different paces and often with less experimentation in format and content when they are traditionally published.

Dean describes this non-linear study as a form of critical history that "seeks series, divisions, differences of temporality and level, forms of continuity and mutation" (2003, p. 93), which allows for the understanding of what a book can be to alter based on these "series, divisions, and differences." Dean goes on to say that "A general history would be a non-reductive, non-totalising one, which specifies its own terrain, the series it constitutes, and the relations between them" (2003, p. 94) and allows for several histories to occur simultaneously.

That being said, this book focuses on a selected historical range from the early 2000s to the present to explore this slice of history as a way to "select a *problem* rather than a historical period for investigation" (Kendall & Wickham, 1999, p. 22) (original emphasis). The 'problem' under consideration is whether social media can be a slush pile for traditionally published products and what the role of social media means for the relationships within online communities and the power hierarchies they can challenge.

Historical research tends to be studied chronologically, where we can follow the rise of the book from the papyrus, to plates, to the printing press in c.1440, and into the modern world of digital publishing and beyond. The issue with looking at the history of the book from horizon to horizon is that it presupposes a linear evolution from point to point and expects the history of the book to alter in a continually regular fashion. Within the history of ideas, this evolution often coincides with the history of something other. For instance, the history of the book can be paired with the economic and industrial histories of a nation, but in fact, each of these discursive formations have their own unique historical trajectory that may cross, split, deviate, and come together again at different points. Likewise, every discursive formation has an order that is intrinsic to its structure and does not rely on a chronological grid that builds up as it moves forwards (Foucault, 1989, p. 187). Therefore, discourses must be considered in relation to the rules governing them. Instead of looking at the history of the book, publishing models, and social media in a wide arc, a 'slice of history' allows me to consider "history as a practice within a definite present" (Dean, 2003, p. 14).

McLuhan and the global village

Digital communities of authors and readers, who write and share work on social media platforms, allow for the creation of stories that are often formatted as 'chapters' and 'books' and that can be placed into online spaces separated into genres. McLuhan's concept of the rear-view mirror aids in explaining why this happens: "When faced with a totally new situation, [such as the rise of social-media generated content] we tend always to attach ourselves to the objects, to the flavour of the most recent past" (McLuhan & Fiore, 2008, p. 74), in this case, the traditional book format.

Building on McLuhan's work[2] in reducing the electronically connected globe to 'no more than a village' allows us to define this interconnectivity in terms of "dialogue on a global scale" (McLuhan & Fiore, 2008, p. 16) as it relates to social media as a decentralising mechanism for the publishing industry and its gatekeepers (Levinson, 1999) and its effects on the production of books and the power surrounding them.

The creation and adoption of social technology defines cultural development as it relates to the publishing industry in ways which depend on the position of the person who is able to say what a book can be, the group to which that person belongs, and the knowledge and power relationships within themselves, their group, and the wider industry. The archaeological structure provides a means of exploring the potential of McLuhan's concepts of the global village and the rear-view mirror within the wider discourses of the book, publishing, and social media. In his early work, *The Gutenberg Galaxy*, McLuhan begins to flesh out the idea of the global village when he states that "The new electronic interdependence recreates the world in the image of a global village" (1962, p. 31). Later, he writes that "Our speedup today is not a slow explosion outwards from center to margins but an instant implosion and an interfusion of space and functions" (2013, p. 75). This implosion does not take the average reader out into the world but instead brings the world, and the publishing industry, directly to them through the means of media and new technologies, such as mobile phones, laptops, tablets, and smart devices. Social media has created communities that connect publishers, readers, and writers within them, that directly influences the rise of citizen authors who choose to publish their work on these platforms.

In allowing publishers, readers, and writers to develop an accessible dialogue, social technologies have enhanced the global village, where the aforementioned groups use it as a place for creating (Wattpad, Facebook, Twitter, etc.), marketing (Twitter, blogs, Facebook, Tumblr, Snapchat, etc.), connecting (Facebook, Snapchat, Instagram, etc.), and as a 'local' marketplace (Amazon, AbeBooks, Facebook, Instagram, etc.). As Taylor and Saarinen state "There is no communication without amplification" (1994, p. 8). They go on to say that "[e]ffective publications [eBooks, social media] require electronic amplification on a network that knows no bounds" (p. 8). New media and digital publishing opportunities grow in direct relation to the shrinking digital distance between users.

Technology's ability to facilitate ongoing conversations between publishers, readers, and writers progressed from the potential suggested by McLuhan to the actual in the form of the Bulletin Board System (BBS) in 1978, which was quickly followed by AOL (1985), Livejournal (1999), Myspace (2003), Facebook (2004), Twitter (2006), Instagram (2010), Snapchat (2011), TikTok (2016), and Vero (2018), etc. McLuhan explored this when refining his view of the global village: "Electric circuitry has overthrown the regime of 'time' and 'space' and pours upon us instantly and continuously the concerns of all other men. It has reconstituted dialogue on a global scale" (McLuhan & Fiore, 2008, p. 16). With so much information coming directly to a user, the scope must be whittled down to focus on the statements and discourses that are directly relevant.

Since new, digitally social technologies have closed distances and times, in that users can receive content instantly, beyond borders and time zones, the range of general history is simply too wide to conduct an in-depth analysis of the connections and diversions between how the definition of a book relates to the rise of the citizen author within digital communities and furthermore, how these communities are gendered and genre-led spaces that create new power structures within them, and between them and the publishing industry.

The use of the rear-view mirror also allows us to "move into the future with our sight on the past" (Levinson, 2004, p. 58) and to feel more comfortable engaging with new media. As Paul Levinson notes in his book, *Digital McLuhan*, "the proximate effect of the rear-view mirror was to obscure some of the most important revolutionary functions of the new medium" (2004, p. 414). A more recent example includes the social networking site Pinterest, which takes the traditional format of the scrapbook and updates it for a digital environment while maintaining certain aspects of manual scrapbooking such as the use of boards, pinning, note making, and sharing.

As we move towards the future of publishing, we will see more of "McLuhan's notion of older media becoming the content for newer media, therein becoming more visible to the point of being mistaken for the newer media" (Levinson, 2004, p. 415). The rear-view mirror allows for the movement from one form of media to another, helping the user to understand the new via the codes of the old. We are already seeing this in the advent of book apps and websites that turn the content of other social sites, such as Twitter, into a series or chapbook of personalised poems, creating a loop effect where we are continually looking to the past through the lens of the new media.

As media extends the reach of man in the form of presenting new ways to generate and access works of fiction, drawing the world closer together into a global village, it increases the measure of control that the objects of media, and their producers, have over consumers. This, in turn, brings into play a key element of this book: the interplay of knowledge and power.

Defining a book as a means of understanding the relationships around it

It is through the lens of Foucault's archaeology that what constitutes a book can be explored as a way to understand the relationship of the book to reading audiences, the publishing industry, new social technologies, and the rise of the citizen author. In the *Archaeology of Knowledge*, Foucault defines archaeology as "an attempt to reveal discursive practices in their complexity and density" (1989, p. 209). This definition requires some unpacking. It is best approached by explaining the central discursive element and then working outwards to the related objects, concepts, strategies, discursive formations, and, ultimately, the archive of the book itself.

The function of the statements around what is considered a book

Statements are important in this research, as they relate to what has been allowed to exist within and around what is considered a book in relation to the industry, social media, and community. Here, we can focus on statements of the book that have come to exist in places of diversion from the traditional publishing model. These include the rise of the citizen author and digitally social communities as a means to circumvent the power structures of the publishing hierarchy, as well as the roles that gender and genre play.

A statement enables "groups of signs to exist, and enables these rules or forms to become manifest" (Foucault, 1989, p. 88). Statements of the book have a bearing on our understanding of the book as a cultural object, wherein it has direct relation to the groups of signs, stories, and genres each book contains. These signs, in turn, can affect other statements within the associated fields of the book such as: publishing, economics, authors, and social media.

A statement comes into being at the moment it diverges from another statement, or definition, creating a material existence, which itself is situated among a series of connected groups of statements. We are not concerned with understanding statements and definitions of the book at the "level of what things said mean, but how statements are able to come into existence and remain in circulation and disappear" (Topp, 2000, p. 366). This relates to the rules of materiality that govern the definition of the book, in so much that the definition must conform to the order of the institution, or non-discursive element, i.e. the publishing industry, a particular publishing house, or the digitally social platforms to which the statement is subjected. In this conformity, there is an inherent power relation between those who have the power to publish, readers, writers, and those who refuse to accept the curatorial position of cultural gatekeepers.

The "laws of possibility, rules of existence for the objects that are named, designated or described within it" (Foucault, 1989, p. 91) make up the referential of a statement. This referential sets the conditions for a place where the statement of a book comes into being and differentiates between the objects and subjects it brings into play in its emergence. In doing so, it gives meaning to the sentence (1989, p. 91) and validates it as a new statement within the discourse. Within this research, an example of the referential of the statement of the book can be the potential advances in technology (5G and mobile devices) and the rules that govern those advances (costs of devices, access to networks, etc.), which give validity to the formation of new outputs that exist within the discourse of the book but outwith the publishing industry such as eBooks, Twitter novels, and blogs, just to name a few.

Differentiating speakers via their location in the discourse

A particularly useful aspect of Foucault's archaeology is the ability to question where the speaker of a definition of the book is positioned within the discourse and what their position provides in the way of knowledge-power.[3] This creates a dispersive instead of unifying effect and presents a way to both decentre and organise the way we consider what a book can be.

By focusing on the "the place from which they come" (1989, p. 50), we can identify three elements put forth by Foucault to describe the speaking subject not as a person but as a unique position within the framework of a selected period of historical research. This allows the subject to "speak within the body of knowledge" (Topp, 2000, p. 369). These elements can be best understood by framing them as questions, as Topp suggests. In relating the following three questions to the discourse of the book and its myriad relations, we are able to better understand the multiplicity of a subject's potential positions.

First we must ask: Who is speaking? Statements regarding the book "cannot come from anybody; their value [and] efficacy [...] cannot be dissociated from the statutorily defined person who has the right to make them" (Foucault, 1989, p. 51). In evaluating the knowledge and power of the speaker, we need to know what qualifications they have in making those particular statements. For instance, writing a blog post blaming the fall of erotica on the pay-by-page scheme implemented by Amazon has less impact when written by an angry fan whose favourite author has given up writing because they are self-published than it would if a similar blog about Amazon stifling new erotica voices had been written by the head of Harlequin Enterprises.

The second seeks to question the "institutional sites" (Foucault, 1989, p. 51) from which the statements come. The site where knowledge is based can be outside of the publishing industry and still have a bearing on the statements created within the discourse of the book. The institutional sites of a statement of a book can be a publishing house, digital platforms, governmental organisations, and what Foucault calls the "'library' or documentary field" (1989, p. 51), which can include books, articles, blogs, social posts, and other objects that provide rules for regulating the possible statements of a book.

Finally, we must consider what positions within the discourse the speaker can occupy in order to understand their "perceptual field" (Foucault, 1989, p. 53), relating to what they can and cannot know or express in relation to the book. Within each institution a speaker can hold several positions. The statements provided by these different positions are "defined by the situation that is possible for him to occupy in relation to the various domains or groups of objects" (Foucault, 1989, p. 52). Though the discourse of the book is created by statements made within a publishing model, or house, the position of the speaking subject will alter depending on where he or she is placed within that organisation. A speaking subject can also be positioned in several different locations within the body of knowledge, which will create different relations depending on which 'hat' the subject is wearing when a particular statement is made. For instance, in a small company the president may take the subject position of the editor, designer, and finance manager, all of which create a different relation to the statement of the book, especially when the roles are combined.

The blanks and gaps

The things that do not become definitions of the book are as important as those that do. It is the space between these statements that allows us to see the relationship between what does and does not come to exist. For every new statement that arises, such as a piece of fiction written in a social community, there are other statements that do not. This can be manifest in what a character did or did not do in a work of fiction, or it can be seen in more tangible objects within the discourse such as why certain eBook readers (Kobo and Kindle) were a success while others (Pocketbook Pro or Samsung Papyrus) were not.

The blanks and gaps seek to understand why those 'other' definitions were unsuccessful. When we look more closely at the gaps, we can see the importance of the holes and negative spaces. For instance, at the point of the digital revolution and access to new technologies, eBooks became an accepted output or object of the discourse, which some publishers embraced and others ignored. In order to understand the conditions that allowed the eBook's specific appearance, we look at things such as the speaker, their location in the discourse, and their knowledge and power in their field. This leaves the question of why an unlimited number of other objects did not emerge at that particular moment. Part of the means of answering why some statements come into existence and others do not employs McLuhan's media concept of the rear-view mirror, which claims that we "attach ourselves to the objects, to the flavour of the most recent past" (2003, p. 74).

Using this concept as a basis, we can see why the format of the eBook was created to resemble the physical book as closely as possible as a means of segueing later adopters of new technology from one medium to another. This makes it easier to classify the gaps surrounding the creation of the eBook, where what was not developed is directly related to the relationships between McLuhan's concept of the rear-view mirror, economic considerations, and concerns regarding the potential decentralisation of the industry which the eBook could herald.

The interaction of statements and definitions of the book

We should consider the idea of the book to be tied to the whole of the "material individualization of the book, which occupies a determined space, has an economic value, and which itself indicates, by a number of signs, the limits of its beginning and end" (Foucault, 1989, p. 23). In this sense, the book is the representative of the cultural output of the publishing industry.

The relations between the definitions of the book draw attention to other, differing definitions with every division or agreement. Within the wider discourse, understandings around the book, the publishing model(s), authors, media, etc. interact with and diverge from each other. In his work on Foucault, Deleuze claims that "statements can be opposed to one another, and placed in hierarchical order" (1998, p. 3) depending on the rules that guide their ability to come into being, and when they branch off from one definition of the book, they create new definitions and statements which may become accepted in the wider discourse, or not – and fade away.

For example, when an author creates a new definition of the book based around their use of social media as a platform for creating and distributing work and interacting with their reading audience, it re-energises the definitions and statements of the publishing model and those of the reader and social media. The "intricate web of practices" (Henriques et al., 2005, p. 102) involved allows us to locate the places where these ripples and divergences happen. These statements then create new objects, concepts, and strategies that surface in the discourse of the book.

The objects, concepts, and strategies that make up the discourse around the book

Once we know what definitions and statements are said by whom, we can begin to look for the objects they produce. The object is brought into being by the statement or definition, and in turn is directly relative to the unique position of the speaker. Therefore, we must look again to the places and institutions from which the speaker begins in order to see which objects emerge from their statements.

It can be helpful to list the objects that have surfaced within the wider discourse of a book, bearing in mind that for them to be a useful way of documenting the divisions within the discourse "[t]hese need not be objects that have survived" (Topp, 2000, p. 368). In fact, sometimes the objects that did not survive tell as much as those that do. For instance, why the UNRD has flourished when oolipo did not can tell us much about the play of socio-economic power within the book/story app market.

In the discourse of the book and its relations, we can consider the example of the book app. Here, we must identify where book apps emerge as objects and who has the authority to bring them to life. In this example, we must ask if the concept of book apps came from a group of editors, writers, app developers, or marketers, and we must decide what gives the identified group the power to come up with this idea. We do this by asking who is speaking, from what institution, and from what position they are speaking from in relation to other domains.

A statement or definition also has its own set of concepts that are "found at the intersection of different systems and are cut across by the statement" (Deleuze, 1998, p. 8). These families of concepts are ideas within a larger discourse; in this case, that of the book. In order to place these concepts within the discursive framework, we must find how to best organise them in relation to the statements from which they develop. To do this, we must first look at the forms of succession and decide how we place the concepts in relation to one another and provide a set of rules that govern the general arrangement of the statements. Once we have identified their forms of succession we must determine which locations allow for the co-existence of multiple statements.

Finally, in order to locate and define the family of concepts related to the discourse of the book, we must define the procedures that enable actions that permit those concepts to develop. If I stay with the aforementioned example of book apps, we can see that the procedures of intervention are the means by which the book app is developed. For instance, the book app may have written rules that adhere to computer languages (css, html, sml, python, etc.), likewise it may have editors who divide submitted works into those that can be adapted to a book app and those that cannot based on formatting and story design. These 'procedures of intervention' help to guide what is created in the expression of the book app.

Discourses give rise to "certain organizations of concepts, certain regroupings of objects, certain types of enunciation, which form, according to their degree of coherence, rigour, and stability, themes or theories," which Foucault labels "strategies" (1989, p. 64). In simpler terms, the strategy of a discourse is a way to navigate the possibilities of a book and to understand who has the ability to make those decisions and how they are influenced by their own desires.

There can be several groups of statements within a discourse, and these can alter depending on the ever-changing relations within it. Kendal and Wickham stress that "discourses are not closed systems – the possibility of innovation in discourse is always present within any discourse itself and within tangential or succeeding discourses" (2003, p. 41).

Genealogy and the role of the rear-view mirror

Perhaps pre-empting his own course of research, in an interview with Bellour in 1967, Foucault says that "there is nothing to be gained from describing this autonomous layer of discourses [archaeology] unless one can relate it to other layers, practices, institutions, social relations, political relations, and so on" (1998, p. 284). Almost ten years later (and two years after writing *Discipline and Punish*, where he first began sketching out the genealogy), Foucault clarifies the connection between the archaeology and the genealogy saying:

> If we were to characterise it in two terms, the 'archaeology' would be the appropriate methodology of this analysis of local discursivities, and 'genealogy' would be tactics whereby, on the basis of the descriptions of these local discursivities, the subjected knowledges which were thus released would be brought into play.
>
> *(1980, p. 85)*

Where the archaeology creates a theoretical structure for identifying the statements and relations within an archive, Foucault's genealogy puts the archaeology to work as a means of understanding the inherent power relations between the discursive and non-discursive elements.

In exploring the strategic power relation brought to the fore by the genealogy, it is important to note that this relation is not a form but a force and is not situated between two elements as knowledge is. Instead, "power is a strategy, a strategy that maintains a relation between the sayable [discourse] and the visible [the non-discursive]" (Kendall & Wickham, 1999, p. 49). Whereas knowledge is structured and organised in the archive, the relationships of forces of power are transient, moving, and can almost seem invisible, depending on the position of the speaker. Which individual has the right to speak can alter depending on the other relationships in the discourse, and these alterations shift the power dynamics around the book.

In publishing, the viewpoint that directs selecting and publishing works of fiction often comes from the larger, centralised publishing companies, who have an eye on profits and cultural curation. *Publishers Weekly* identified fifty-seven companies, in 2015, which control the majority of the industry worldwide. This allows the creative output of the larger corporations to be dictated by, and to dictate to, the marketplace for works of fiction.

This form of centralised curation with an eye on economic gain created a circular model of publishing within the industry that does not often publish fiction that will not guarantee a certain degree of financial return for the investment.[4] However, digitally social technologies are being continually upgraded and content has become "malleable, updatable, [and] transferable" (Bhaskar, 2013, p. 49). Bhaskar states that "In a world of convergent new media, it may no longer make sense to simply print books" (2013, p. 48). With the rise of desktop publishing, typesetting programmes, and website and app building technologies available to the public, the tide is beginning to shift towards a more digital publishing environment; and the power structures in place within the publishing industry are altering. Editing, printing, and publishing books, a job that was once the major role of publishers, has become open to the public, closing the distances between readers, writers, and publishers in the creation of the global village, whereby the power of choice and curation is brought back to a local level. The global village itself amplifies this local level by removing borders and traversing distances instantly. This, in turn, gives rise to a citizen author, who chooses to embrace these new digital technologies to produce their own works, which has a tendency to boost publishing subgenres by creating new villages where people can digitally socialise around objects and topics of interest.

Social aspects of the global village will draw powerful social networking sites into the foray of publishing models, creating a different power dynamic between new publishers (social platforms), traditional publishers, and authors. This is already being seen with Twitter novels and Instapoetry, and with the choice of large news and magazine publishers (*National Geographic, The New York Times,* etc.) utilising Facebook as a way to publish new content directly into a user's social space. The wide availability of social networking sites is allowing for small steps towards social platforms becoming a decentralising mechanism within the publishing industry itself by allowing authors to publish their works directly in their newsfeeds. While this is reminiscent of Japan's Keitai Shōsetsu and China's 'original fiction,' social media publishing is taking on a different approach by using existing and up and coming social networking platforms as delivery vehicles for written content.

In exploring the relationship between power and knowledge, it is helpful to turn to Deleuze's work on power, where he suggests that you do not ask "What is power and where does it come from?" but instead "How is it practised?" (1998, p. 71). In order to better visualise the genealogy, we can understand it as a 'diagram' that is a "display of relations between forces which constitute power" (Deleuze, 1998, p. 36). We can ask how power relationships work here, allowing for an in-depth analysis of how certain forms of social technology and ePublishing devices have embraced the rear-view mirror to create new publishing models that, in turn, will affect the non-discursive publishing industry and the citizen author who utilises the new technology.

Notes

1 I focus more on utilising Foucault than criticising his works, although it should be noted that Foucault's work is still frequently criticised and misused almost as much as it is practised (O'Farrell, 2005; Apperley, 1997; Hook, 2001; Bové, 1998).

2 After the publication of *Understanding Media* and *The Medium is the Massage*, McLuhan became hugely popular in the 1950s and 60s, spawning terms such as France's McLuhanisme (Theall, 1971, p. 1). His theories of the global village (2013), hot and cold media (2013), and the rear-view mirror (2008) became metaphors for the way media extends the senses of man. In using these metaphors to 'probe' into different issues of media and its relationships to man, McLuhan gained many followers, who found his aphoristic style enlightening in the way it opened up the world of media to a form of study that is not unlike poetry. But, he also generated a circle of critics (See Miller, 1971; Mumford, 1970; Schramm, 1973; and perhaps most interestingly "medium *slants* the message" in Scheuer, 1999), such as Theall, who, in his book *The Medium is the Rear View Mirror*, points out numerous 'failings' in the works of McLuhan. Theall considers one such "great failure" of McLuhan's to be his "treatment of the history of media as a history of the way technology determined man's development" (Theall, 1971, p. 151). I disagree with Theall, and argue instead that the history of media is, in fact, a history of the way technology continues to determine and shape the growth of civilisation and culture.

3 Here, the enunciative modalities seek to ask where the speaker of a statement is located – is it a publisher/editor/marketer/reader/published author, etc. – and how does their particular location add to or detract from their knowledge and power to say a particular statement. For instance, an editor with a multinational publishing house has a different place within the discourse of the book to say what is or isn't a book – working within the publishing house could also give them knowledge and power (authority) to be the accepted voice on how a book is defined.

4 This relates to the "bandwagon effect" (Gaffeo et al. 2006, p. 5), where those who create demand (the big publishers) also create the effect where smaller publishers try to emulate this success by publishing similar titles.

Bibliography

Apperley, A., 1997. Foucault and the Problem of Method. In Lloyd, M. & Thacker, A. (Eds), *The Impact of Michel Foucault On the Social Sciences and Humanities* (pp. 10–28). Houndsmills: Macmillan Press.

Bhaskar, M., 2013. *The Content Machine: Towards a Theory of Publishing from the Printing Press to the Digital Network.* London: Anthem Press.

Blanchot, M. & Foucault, M., 1990 [1987]. Michel Foucault as I Imagine Him. In *Foucault | Blanchot* (pp. 61–109). New York: Urzone Books.

Bové, P., 1998. Foreword. In Hand, S. (Ed.), *Foucault* (pp. vii–xl). Translated from the French by Seán Hand. Minneapolis: University of Minnesota Press.

Dean, M., 2003. *Critical and Effective Histories: Foucault's Methods and Historical Sociology.* New York: Taylor & Francis e-Library.

Deleuze, G., 1998. *Foucault.* Translated from the French by Seán Hand (Ed.). Minneapolis: University of Minnesota Press.

Downing, L., 2008. *The Cambridge Introduction to Michel Foucault.* Cambridge: Cambridge University Press.

Foucault, M., 1980. Two Lectures. In Gordon, C. (Ed.), *Power/Knowledge: Selected Interviews and Other Writings 1972–1977 (pp. 78–108).* Translated from the French by Colin Gordon, Leo Marshall, John Mepham, & Kate Soper. New York: Pantheon Books.

Foucault, M., 1989. *The Archaeology of Knowledge*. Translated from the French by A.M. Sheridan Smith. London: Routledge.

Foucault, M., 1998. On the Ways of Writing History. In Faubion, J.D. (Ed.), *Aesthetics, Methods, and Epistemology* (pp. 279–295). Translated from the French by Robert Hurley and others. New York: The New Press.

Gaffeo, E., Scorcu, A., & Vici, L., 2006. *Demand Distribution Dynamics in the Book Publishing Industry*. Paper prepared for the WEHIA 2006 Conference Bologna, 15–17 June 2006.

Henriques, J., Hollway, W., Urwin, C., Venn, C., & Walkerdine, V., 2005. *Changing the Subject: Psychology, Social Regulation and Subjectivity*. New York: Taylor & Francis e-Library.

Hook, D., 2001. Discourse, Knowledge, Materiality, History: Foucault and Discourse Analysis. In *Theory and Psychology*. Vol. 11, No. 4, pp. 521–547.

Kendall, G. & Wickham, G., 1999. *Using Foucault's Methods*. London: SAGE Publications.

Levinson, P., 2004. *Digital McLuhan*. New York: Taylor & Francis e-Library.

McLuhan, M., 1962. *The Gutenberg Galaxy: The Making of Typographic Man*. Toronto: University of Toronto Press.

McLuhan, M., 2013. *Understanding Media: The Extensions of Man*. Berkeley: Gingko Press [eBook].

McLuhan, M. & Fiore, Q., 2008. *The Medium is the Massage*. London: Penguin Books.

Miller, J., 1971. *Marshall McLuhan*. New York: Viking Press.

Mumford, L., 1970. *The Myth of the Machine. Vol. II, The Pentagon of Power*. New York: Harcourt Brace Jovanovich.

O'Farrell, C., 2005. *Michel Foucault*. London: SAGE Publications.

Scheuer, J., 1999. *The Sound Bite Society: Television and the American Mind*. New York: Four Walls Eight Windows.

Schramm, W., 1973. *Men, Messages, and Media: A Look at Human Communication*. Taiwan: Harper & Row.

Taylor, M. & Saarinen, E., 1994. *Imagologies: Media, Philosophy*. London: Routledge.

Theall, D. 1971. *Understanding McLuhan: The Medium is the Rear View Mirror*. McGill-Queen's University Press: Montreal and London.

Topp, W., 2000. Knowledge System Diagnostics: Applying Foucault's Archaeological Framework to Organizations. In *Systems Research and Behavioral Science*. Vol. 17, pp. 365–374.

3

THE CREATIVE POSSIBILITIES OF THE BOOK

When we take books into the realm of social media and open up the opportunities for what a book can be in relation to new digital technology, we come to see that there are many ways that a book can be created outside of the traditional industry format and how such technology can influence the publishing industry in turn. In their work on data and books, Brouillette and Doody (2015) found that companies like Amazon are already mining the data of their readers and discovering what their digital reading habits are, how they read, and when and where they stop in a work. This is important information that publishers could take more advantage of, like Barnes & Noble, in the US, who are sharing this data with publishers who sell on their platform (Flood, 2012; Neary, 2013; Alter, 2012).

Though publishers are comfortable with using data mined from eBook platforms to help their writers create work that has a ready market, there are issues with data mining to locate works that are being read in the digitally social communities, which Batrinca and Treleaven (2015) discuss in their work on the commercial value of data sets from platforms such as Facebook, Twitter, or Google. This impeded access to raw data from platforms is a key issue for publishers who are looking to test the waters of data mining. Though, as Batrinca and Treleaven note, access to the raw data is costly and unwieldly, and in the case of sourcing content from a social platform, access to the raw data is not necessary anyway. In fact, data mining can be done on a small scale, in-house, using programmes that are low-cost or free to pull valuable content from the data sets (Norton, 1999). This could potentially open the door for publishers to begin branching out into this modern, rich area of new content.

If a publisher is unwilling to data mine for content, there are other ways they can access content from digital spaces. One of these is by locating social media influencers. Hall (2010) and Freberg et al., (2010) both discuss the role of an influencer, a social media personality that has a reach beyond their direct friends

DOI: 10.4324/9781003186649-4

and followers. These are personalities that can help to shape audience opinions on a brand, a book, author, or even a publisher.

It is in the grey area of writing on social media that we see the rise of self-publishing and the citizen author. Because of this, the publishing industry has had to rely more heavily on what Martin and Tian (2010) call the 'intangibles,' which consist of the aspects of the publishing industry that allow the publisher to leverage their understanding of the process, connections, and curatorial experience to locate and produce a product that will bring financial returns. However, much of the publishing industry that has weathered the rise of the digital aspects of publishing feel they've overcome the challenge of digital publishing, and some believe that though eBooks and e-technology have their place, for the most part "the digital side is always only advertisement" and that "a book is perfectly good" (McPherson, 2016).

Some business models of the publishing industry tend to lag behind those of the music and film industries. Where the music industry saw the rise of Napster for downloads give way to the free and paid services like Spotify and Apple Music, the film and television industries went a different route, breaking down the hierarchy of the cinema release and moving to subscription services that are more diverse and unique in their offerings, such as Netflix, Disney+, Hulu, Amazon Prime, Mubi, and many more. The publishing industry, for the most part, has kept itself at a level of taking part, not innovation. However, this is not true for all publishers; in fact, publishers such as Faber & Faber, Unbound and a slew of digital-only publishers dedicate much time and resources to re-thinking the relationship between digital texts, content, and delivery. Others have ventured into pay-per-views or advertising, and others still have begun to mimic the models, and even small publishers are setting up accounts on platforms such as Patreon.

If we now consider the book to be social, it would be at the publisher's peril to ignore the potential opportunities to develop ways of better integrating digitally social technology and the business of publishing. This is especially true of the big five publishers, who maintain a dominance in the industry that could potentially be disrupted by new business models and distribution channels that echo those in other media industries mentioned above.

This is why it is important to explore how socially created content can be collected, collated, and pulled offline into a traditionally published product. Keeping in mind that there is always a possibility of further innovation, writers and publishers can utilise social media as a place to generate and share content. Examining the connections between the different types of personalised, computer-generated fictions and what we call a book highlights the places of cohesion and rupture within the wider discourse where such fictions challenge the taxonomies of the book. The social platforms must be considered in relation to the forms of creativity and writing they foster and should not exclude cross-platform writing and engagement. Instead, it is important to engage with the sociality of the platforms as a means of making reading and writing a more social endeavour within an online community.

Publisher's potential use of data scraping and mining

If publishers were more willing to look beyond the existing industry structures and seek innovative content from non-traditional locations such as social media, it could potentially lead to wider use of data scraping and mining to locate creative works within those digital communities.

In addition to using data scraping and mining, there is also an abundance of data that can be gathered from digital reading which tells publishers about readers and their reading habits, even down to which parts of an eBook they sped through, or where they stopped reading altogether. In the current publishing climate, this means that those booksellers, not publishers, who use data mining are using it to enhance the selling of books. According to Brouillette and Doody (2015) big booksellers such as Amazon and Barnes & Noble are already sharing reading data with publishers to better curate books based on real reader behaviour. This sort of data mining "arises from the realisation that improvements can be made to the way a business is run" (Ahlemeyer-Stubbe & Coleman, 2014, p. 19).

As early as 2012, Barnes & Noble were sharing the data knowledge of their eBooks with publishers to "help them create books that better hold people's attention" (Hilt, qtd. in Alter, 2012). Publishers, in essence, are becoming more comfortable with collecting and analysing big data to direct the content of their books to enhance sales. This is using data mining for marketing purposes. It plays a role in the way that publishing will progress, with more direction from the publishers to their authors as to what should be written and what sells (though we are yet to see this in practice). However, publishers could go even further and consider how they can use similar data mining techniques to generate fiction from social media platforms.

Many publishers now have social media feeds across all the major channels that are run in-house and will have access to the data they need to test the waters of data mining.[1] Once a publisher has decided that they want to use data mining (for marketing or as a content generator), they must first decide from where they want to scrape the data. The most obvious examples are Twitter, Facebook, Instagram, and blogs. Though each platform has different APIs (application programme interface) for scraping data.

In order to get access to the raw data, a publisher has three main options[2]: contact the social media head office and get quotes for price and scope of access[3]; use an intermediary social analytic platform, the more powerful of which have price packages tailored to an organisation's needs and can even provide the publisher with the option to have the social analytic intermediary perform the mining functions for them. Examples include: GNIP, NUVI, NetBase, etc. Or, they can collate the data themselves.

Restricted access to this data brings to the fore the power dynamics between the publisher and the social media platforms that house the data, where the publisher relies on the platform or an intermediary to have access to large quantities of data in one go. This reflects the limited access that authors have to the publishing industry itself, in that it may only be accessed using an intermediary (like an agent or a company to scrape data) or paying for the privilege.

With respect to the hesitance of publishers to invest money into digital slush pile strategies that are, as yet, mostly untested for return on investment, the focus here is on the third, self-reliant method of data scraping, which allows publishers the freedom to trial data scraping and mining in-house using either paid or open-source mining programmes.

Two of the ways that a publisher can scrape the social data themselves are by batch scraping of large amounts of data in one go, or by generating an API for each platform that allows them to scrape targeted feeds such as those with a particular hashtag marker, location, time, or username. There are many programmes that function for scraping off batch data from a particular platform. Using programmes such as NVivo, or browser extensions such as Chrome's Webscraper (both have free and paid versions), a publisher can pull up tens of thousands of entries from the chosen platforms in a single go, adding them to a spreadsheet to create their own database. The publisher can choose to do this as many times as they want, increasing the size and depth of the database that they can then mine to pull out content of interest.

A second method of creating a database is more targeted and requires a publisher to create APIs for the individual platforms and scrape specifically tagged feeds such as #Twitterfiction, #facebookfiction, #iamwriting, #Fictionwriting, #Instragramnovel, #Instafiction, etc. A targeted API scraper requires little knowhow to set up as long as the publisher has an account with the chosen platform. The scraping can be set to continue automatically on a prescribed basis and will pull the selected content into a spreadsheet for later cleaning and mining. The benefit of using targeted scraping is that a publisher will have a much clearer view of the content and significance of the data they are databasing and the clean-up is more straightforward. However, it should be noted that some platforms, like Instagram, are notoriously harder to pull data from. There are now tools that enable such pulling out of data. That being said, publishers should also note that some platforms (Instagram and Facebook) have explicit listings in their Terms of Use that prevent data scraping, and these Terms alter regularly. Though this is a grey area if publishers are using data to then locate an author who they contact directly for content and do not publish the data that has been scraped.[4]

Batch scraping highlights the width of information a publisher can database. Not only can batch scraping pull out all the hashtags mentioned above but it will put out thousands of posts that are not immediately relevant. This form of scraping is the equivalent of sticking a very small pot under a waterfall and pulling it back out – you will certainly catch some content, but not nearly all. While this may seem counterproductive to generating coherent content from a social media feed, in the cleaning and mining process that comes next it can also give insight into stories and fictions that were not immediately apparent by the standard tagging. For those publishers who are more interested in local publishing, they can tap into areas to mine for interesting content based on location, which they can then take forward in the publishing process.

Once the data has been cleaned the publisher can mine it for useful information using mining programmes to implement complicated algorithms that separate out certain data and store it in the database alongside the original data. Publishers can pull out feeds based on selected criterion to develop a new, collated feed. For instance, if there are 30,000 tweets over the course of two months and all 30,000 of those use the #Twitterfiction hashtag, a publisher can pull out each stream by username and collate it, remove the non-essential tweets and see the story that the Twitter user is writing. Likewise, the publisher can add in a few more steps to arrange those tweets by username, date, time, and location, to narrow down the feeds more. The publisher can then remove the Twitter handles and hashtags from the stream they have isolated and apply an algorithm that restructures the text itself into a more reader friendly format, allowing for the fiction to be read on par with other submitted fictions.

Much in the same way that data scraping and mining can be used to develop streams of fiction in Twitter, Facebook, and Instagram, APIs can be quickly developed with little technological expertise that will scrape existing blogs to create a database that can be cleaned and mined, pulling out links, phrases, timelines, and more.[5] Though blogs will rarely be so simply coded as those from other social platforms – in relation to hashtags – they still often have 'category' and 'tags' that the blogger uses to make it easier for their readers to find related content on their site. Once the blogs have been cleaned and separated out by writer, publishers can use these 'categories' and 'tags' to pull together streams much in the same way they would with other forms of data, allowing a publisher to read through the content and make an educated decision on the viability of the content as a published item.[6]

Follower-led content

At present, many publishers do not have the time or resources available to put into practice data mining techniques, but some are open to approaching social media-based content generation in a way that would be more likely to ensure a return on investment by approaching and working with a social media influencer. One of the ways this can be done by the publisher is for them to collate the social influencer's most popular social communication into a book. A second way publishers can harness the power of the influencer is to contact them and directly commission a work, based on their social content, to be written and produced offline, such as Kate Siegel's *Mother Can You Not?* Both processes provide the publisher with an author that has a large digital following and the potential to generate sales, while the latter, commissioning, approach has the added benefit of creating a marketing buzz around the writing process, which can raise the profile of the book even before it goes into production. These approaches take into account that "Influence is the foundation on which all economically viable relationships are built" (Remorin, qtd. by Booth & Matic, 2011, p. 186) and factor in the potential symbiosis between social media as marketing and as a place to create publishable, fictional content.

Social media influencers

Social media influencers are individuals who have a significant[7] following within and across social media networks. They can have a real-world presence, such as an actor, author, politician, or as someone who is simply influential in a particular field[8]; they can be social media-based representations of characters, such as Superman or Harry Potter, and have their own Facebook page or Twitter account from which they interact with followers; or they can be entirely fictional personas with no manifestation outwith social media.

This is a developing field, however, where the metrics that were once thought of as significant are now viewed as less so, and there is the potential for backlash against what influencers do or do not say. That being said, they still play a role in the ecosphere of social media, and according to Hall, influencers "generally do not have many direct 'friends' and 'followers', but what makes them truly valuable is the number and relevance of their extended or indirect connections" (2010). In this way, they function as "independent third party endorser[s]" helping to shape audience perceptions and attitudes towards a brand, product, idea, book, and author (Freberg et al., 2010, p. 90).

Technologies have been developed that allow for ranking social media influencers in the field of literature; many of these are based on blog hits, follower numbers, interactions, shares, and likes across four main platforms: Twitter, Facebook, Instagram, and blogs. Booth and Matic (2011, p. 188) suggest ranking social media influencers into tiers based roughly on followers, outputs, status, and knowledge, in order to better understand their reach and how it connects with the publishers' target market. They rank bloggers on three tiers which can be adapted across platforms for use by the publishing industry: A – those with many followers, who deal with newsy items such as new books coming out, announce opportunities for readers and writers, retweet interesting information, and do not often engage in direct conversations; B – has fewer followers than A, but they are more engaged and passionate about books and writing, with a point of view that is unique within their area of interest and who are willing to use their reach to gain and monetise more recognition; and C – those who have fewer followers than A or B but whose followers are more dedicated to the influencer and their outputs. One key factor that Booth and Matic note about tier C is their obvious passion, which translates into more social interaction with their followers, a devout following within their sector, and a frank delivery of facts as they see them, which may be distinct from the majority's perception (2011, p. 188).

By taking into account these three main influencer groups, publishers will have a better overview of the potential markets that an influencer could reach, providing them with a firmer understanding of the value of approaching and working with a social media influencer. However, it should be noted that not all influencers will have followers that can be converted into sales of published items. In fact, though influencers on social media often imply an advertising model in which they use their platforms to share paid[9] content or posts on behalf of an item or brand, this isn't always the case. There are social media influencers who work towards social media engagement instead of paid endorsements. This engagement can be wielded by the influencer to share work more widely, or to provoke the interest of a publisher, or to attain a book deal in the traditional industry.

The publisher should look closely at the numbers and types of followers and decide how they fit in with the publisher's mission statement and brand identity, and they should not discount micro-influencers: those who have 10,000–100,000 followers. In addition, they should take into account the potential distortions caused by non-human accounts when looking to follower numbers and interactions, as well as look out for professionally managed accounts that do not directly reflect the voice of the influencer (Ruths & Pfeffer, 2014, p. 1064).

Collating a social media influencer's feed

Once a publisher has identified the social media influencer that they believe will be the best fit with their brand and who has the potential for creating publishable content, they can approach the influencer and work out how to draw together their content into a usable format. Across the social media platforms, blogs, with their long-form written style, are the most straightforward social media platform for repurposing content into a traditional book. October 2014 boasts the highest number of blogs posts made on Wordpress or Wordpress-affiliated sites, with over 64 million blogs posted in that month alone (Wordpress, 2016), making the blogosphere a treasure trove of content if publishers developed a business model that included exploring their potential more fully.

Blog posts have been a gainful way to source new writing since they started popping up on the web around 2006. Blogs give new and established writers an outlet where they can test their work on readers, grow their following, and potentially leverage influence in the digitally social sphere. Popular blogs such as *Julie and Julia, Belle de Jour: Diary of a London Call Girl, TuckerMax*, and *Save Karyn: One Shopoholic's Journey to Debt and Back* were able to gather enough of a following that they were picked up by publishers and printed as books, with all four of them also being made into movies or prime-time television programmes.

The relationship between blogs and books is one that is unique in the publishing world and highlights the privilege still given to traditionally published books over self-publishing in the online, social format. An interesting aspect of this dynamic is not that the blogs shut down once the writers got their foot into the door of the traditional publishing world, it is instead that the writers turned their attention to expanding their influence on other social media platforms such as Twitter, Facebook, and Instagram as a way to promote the book further. It is also worth noting that many non-fiction books that began as blogs continue on as blogs even after the book is published as a way for the author to continue to build their brand and influence within a recognised field.

The result of some blogs being published as books was brought up by Unbound Associate Editor Scott Pack, who said that when it comes to new ways to locate content that could turn a profit, "Publishing tends to get very excited about new things, and then ruin it very quickly [...]" (8 April, 2016). This can be seen when blogs become books and the blogs themselves (*Julie and Julia, Belle de Jour,* and *Save Karyn*) are shelved or taken offline entirely once the book deals have been made.

Pack goes on to say that:

> Initially there were three or four blogs that were turned into books that were really successful, and then publishers started paying sixty grand to bloggers, and one hundred grand to bloggers [...] they were paying big money to bloggers and as soon as you start doing that there will be failures. There will be books that don't make their money back and then publishers think, 'I won't do it now.'
>
> *(8 April, 2016)*

This is indicative of the wider industry and their wariness to engage with new technologies and social platforms that could cost them money and not bring any tangible returns.

Some social media accounts have been created in the likeness of the characters in blogs, such as @Belle_Baxter (*Diary of a London Call Girl*) on Twitter. This is not an unusual occurrence on social media networks, with the rise of 'social fiction' where characters from books are given their own lives on social media. This often extends beyond the original storyline of the book from which they came and introduces ways that the characters can interact with the global community (Ramachandran, 2013). They can also be used to give their point of view to the story, such as @the_Joker from *Batman*, @FrodoBaggins from *Lord of the Rings*, @DeathtoMuggles (Voldermort) from *Harry Potter*, and @SparkleCullen (Edward Cullen) from *Twilight* on Twitter, and Jack Lancaster from *Twenty Something* on Facebook, just to name a few.

Looking beyond blogs by social media influencers as a slush pile for content, Twitter and Instagram feeds have influencers that have huge numbers of followers and interactions with their audiences which are based on and around their artistic outputs. While it can be argued that social media platforms, beyond blogs and fiction repositories, are best suited to sharing works of poetry, many well-known authors, who are social media influencers in their own right, have taken to Twitter to write works of fiction that have been later published elsewhere. After a successful marketing campaign where David Mitchell wrote a 6,000-word story on Twitter entitled "The Right Sort," which was based loosely on the universe that his novel *The Bone Clocks* (2014) was set in, he took the story and turned it into his most recent novel *Slade House*. To keep the momentum going, Mitchell has created a Twitter handle for his narrator, @I_Bombadil, which develops the story in a different angle – creating a new, parallel fiction as well as creating allusions to the text in his upcoming novel.

The relationship that Mitchell's publisher, Sceptre Books, has with the release of the original story on Twitter is significant. "The Right Sort" itself was released in segments across a week by David from his @david_mitchell account, but before he began releasing the story on July 14, 2014 he tweeted: "@SceptreBooks are delighted to present a story written by David for Twitter, serialised twice a day this week. We give you **#THERIGHTSORT**…" (@david_mitchell, 2014, 14 July, bold in original), indicating that the publishers themselves were presenting a work by Mitchell. However, the publisher did not release any of the tweets themselves, nor did the tweets from the story have the publisher-created hashtag #THERIGHTSORT pulling them into a coherent stream. Sceptre Books acted instead in a marketing role, drawing attention to the stream by presenting themselves as an outside observer by sending tweets that suggested they too were reading along, as when they posted, "Can twitter just be quiet for 20 minutes please while we read the last instalment in @David_Mitchell's #THERIGHTSORT" (@SceptreBooks, 2014, 20 July).

Mitchell's work led to the creation of two social media based stories that eventually were pulled offline and evolved into works of fiction, but an earlier author who wrote collaborative fiction on Twitter is Neil Gaiman. In 2009, he worked with BBC Audiobooks America and sent the first sentence of a modern fairy tale from his account. It read, "Sam was brushing her hair when the girl in the mirror put down the hairbrush, smiled & said, 'We don't love you anymore.' @BBCAA #bbcawdio" (@neilhimself, 2009,13 October). From here, Twitter users were encouraged to write in the next line of the story and mark it with the hashtag #bbcawdio. Over the next eight days, the tweets were reviewed by BBC Audiobooks America and added to the story. At the end, 874 of over 10,000 tweets were chosen to create the 14,000-word story called *Hearts, Keys, and Puppetry*, which was then published as an audiobook and is available from all major retailers.

In 2012, Pulitzer Prize winning author Jennifer Egan shared a science fiction story called "The Black Box" over the course of 600 tweets, which was later published in print by *The New Yorker*. Though Egan is a social media influencer, which helped her secure a place in a well-established print publication for her Twitter fiction, on a smaller scale, authors such as Sovern (*Tweetheart*) are continually working directly on Twitter in real time, mimicking the popular cell phone fictions of Asia where the conception of a book as content isn't as bound to the physical ideal. While others, such as Matt Stewart, first wrote their novel and then shared it on Twitter in a steady, well-marked stream. The momentum Stewart created on Twitter with his work titled *The French Revolution* drew the interest of Soft Skull Press, which published a print version of the novel in 2010.

"It was a straight-up gimmick to get attention," Stewart says of his decision to tweet his novel, which worked, as his novel was published. But he goes on to clarify the type of attention his book received on Twitter and off:

> Readers are not reading it like candy, they're not. They want reviews. They're snooty. I mean that's one thing I learned when I went to the world before the book actually came out, as the people who are going to buy this book don't care about twitter, and the people who care about twitter would go 'it's so cool', but they wouldn't actually buy it. The people buy a book because it's

> like a good use of time over money. Honestly. Spending like 10 hours with a book it better be pretty entertaining.
>
> *(1 June, 2016)*

Even Stewart's book was an interesting experiment for the publisher at a time when books were beginning to be written on social platforms and shared via hashtags and other linked means (such as within groups).

Other platforms have fared better at having works written on them. Platforms such as Instagram lend themselves to creating writing which is based around a visual prompt. Instagram works particularly well for graphic artists and poets, and in recent years has seen the meteoric rise of Instapoets such as Rupi Kaur, who writes poetry, draws images, and publishes them on her 3.2 million follower-strong Instagram account. It also is the chosen medium of authors that have a fan fiction or science fiction slant, such as Anna Todd, author of the One Direction fan fiction book *After*.

While straightforward fiction that is written on Instagram is, as of yet, harder to find than Twitter fiction, that is changing. Authors such as Rachel Hulin use the platform in an engaging way that draws in readers and leaves them wanting more. Her novel *Hey Harry, Hey Matilda* uses Instagram and a dedicated website to tell the story of two twins who are struggling with a dark secret. Immediately after she began posting the novel online she gained a huge following and was approached by several large publishers seeking to sign a print deal.

One thing each of the aforementioned examples showcase is the interest that publishers have in authors who are social media influencers and the potential audiences that their original posts can bring. When publishers pull a work of fiction directly from a social feed, it is in their interest to ensure that the influencer has enough support and interaction to indicate that those followers would be likely to follow the influencer into a traditionally printed medium.

Commissioning work from a social media influencer

Though pulling an author's feed offline and publishing it in a traditional format may currently lead more to the genres of novelty and poetry books than works of fiction, connecting to a social media influencer and commissioning work directly is a means of harnessing their influencer status in a way that could translate into sales of traditionally published items. Publishers such as Pan, Crown Archetype, Penguin Random House, and most recently Unbound, have begun to capitalise on this phenomenon by seeking out social media influencers and offering them contracts to turn their popular feeds into a printed work.

Unbound is a London-based publisher that works on a crowd-funding publishing model that pulls in the social influence of the writer to gain a certain level of fiscal backing before Unbound will publish the book. Scott Pack explained in an interview that the key to this publishing model is to capitalise on an author's following and minimise the risk to the publisher (8 April, 2016).

He cites examples such as Mr Bingo's *Hate Mail: The Definitive Collection* Kick-starter campaign (not published by Unbound), which allowed the illustrator to raise over £135,000 to print a collection of his pay-by-card, personally illustrated hate mail to send to friends and family – an amount that would have been impossible to raise if Mr Bingo had tried to go down the traditional author-agent-publisher route to market. Unbound has had several similar, though lesser funded, success stories with their publishing model and for several years had a deal with Penguin Random House that meant copies of a trade edition of each crowd-funded book that Unbound published were placed in bricks and mortar shops. In 2018, Unbound moved their sales and distribution back in-house.

Pack has turned his attention to Twitter for sourcing new writing talent. Through his personal Twitter network of around 10,000 followers, he keeps an eye on well-loved, if not well-known, authors and approaches select ones to crowdfund a book with Unbound. Brian Bilston is one such author. He was approached directly by Pack to work with Unbound to publish *You Took the Last Bus Home: The Poems of Brian Bilston*, which is an edited collection of his poetry that he posted on Twitter. The book was fully funded by the middle of the third day. Pack suggests that this model works for Unbound as a way to tap into a writer's immediate followers, as each of the authors he approaches are middle-hitters in Twitter follower numbers (10–50,000) but have readers who are loyal and are happy to give money "as a way to thank the guy" for publishing their work for free on the social network (8 April, 2016).

Other publishers have preferred to connect with an author directly and ask them to create new works based on, and not directly pulled from, their social feeds. Two examples of this type of social influencer commissioning can be seen in Crown Archetype's *Mother Can You Not?* by Kate Siegel, and Penguin Random House's *Harlow & Sage (and Indiana)* by Brittni Vega. *Mother Can You Not?* began in November 2014 as the Instagram feed of @crazyjewishmom, run by Siegel, to showcase the 'helicopter mother' effect of being a Jewish girl in her mid-twenties living in Brooklyn and not yet married. The account documents the interaction between mother and daughter with the ever-present adage of "no ring on the finger, you must not linger." People reacted on Instagram and Siegel gained over 300,000 followers in as little as four months.

In April 2016, at the height of her popularity, the Instagram account of @crazyjewishmom had over 811,000[10] followers. With such numbers, Siegel was able to wield a large amount of influence among her followers. If we go back to January of 2015, we can see that @crazyjewishmom began to market products on her Instagram feed, touting t-shirts with a pink "no ring on the finger" logo. Later that year, images of products and television shows appeared in both Instagram and Twitter feeds. Soon after she began doing interviews and making television appearances with her mother, Siegel announced that she was writing a book, which was published by Crown Archetype in April 2016.

Unlike the commissioning that Pack is doing with Unbound, which pulls content directly from Twitter and re-packages it, *Mother Could You Not?* is not a direct drawdown of the social media feeds that made the author and her mother famous. Instead, it is a series of related short stories about the relationship with her mother that form the undercurrent of the social media accounts. The obvious benefit to the publisher is a collection of new content, and the forceful advertising from Siegel and her mother, who banter back and forth about the book and Siegel's lack of job security as an author. They did promotional interviews and spent days in Times Square to encourage large numbers of people to pre-order and later to buy the book. Especially with books by influencers who have a niche market, pre-orders are important to secure sales before the book is printed to help cement the marketing strategy and return on investment by the publishers. It can also propel the book into the bestseller list upon release and give the most die-hard fans the first chance to positively review the book (Coker, 2015).

While *Mother Could You Not?* develops a backdrop to the popular social media feeds, *Harlow & Sage (and Indiana)* is a book developed from social media to tell a fictionalised story using the characters in the feed: Brittni Vega's dogs, Harlow, Sage, Indiana, and Reese. In the book, she tells of the dogs' lives and exploits through the fictional voice of her Weimaraner, Harlow. The book was briefly on the *New York Times* Best Seller List in November 2014, the month it was released. The @HarlowandSage Instagram account began in 2013, and as of November 2020 it has 1.7 million followers.[11] She regularly posts photos, videos, and items supporting charities, businesses, and their own branded merchandise. Penguin Random House released a second book, based on the growing Instagram account, *Harlow & Indiana (and Reese)* in October 2015, which uses the voice of Indiana to teach Reese the ropes of her new family.

Publishers are beginning to take note of the power of social media influencers to drive sales of books and associated merchandise. Publishers such as Unbound choose to commission middle-range authors in whom they spot potential and who happen to be social media influencers that have a passionate follower group to help them get more books in hands than traditional publishing would, while larger publishers such as Crown Archetype and Penguin Random House are more cautious in their approach. They choose social media influencers with a wide reach, commissioning them to create a new work based on their social media feeds that will use the feed to add value to the book. But many publishers are beginning to look for works of fiction that are ready-made in that they are already written, have a huge following, and lots of potential print sales.

Ready-made fiction

Though many fiction repositories exist online, there are distinctions in the way they market themselves to their particular audiences. Sites such as FanFiction.net (1998) began as a bare-bones repository for fan fiction, while others such as Wattpad and Medium, who came on the scene in the 2006 and 2012 respectively, have set themselves up as social networks based around reading and writing. All three sites allow readers and writers to interact in the comments section of their stories by leaving reviews, and all three also have forum functionalities to allow users to communicate, facilitated by the users setting up profiles within the site. The main differences can be seen in the user-friendly set up of Wattpad and Medium vs FanFiction.net, which may have something to do with the amount of venture capital behind Wattpad and the founders of Medium also having co-founded Twitter.

Though FanFiction.net has the functionality to allow for comments and has a forum, the community aspects of the site do not measure up to the participatory communication fostered by Wattpad and Medium. This, however, has not hindered writers from posting their works on the site, nor has it scared off potential publishers. One of the most well-known works posted in an online fiction repository is the *Fifty Shades of Grey* trilogy, which originated on FanFiction.net as a series of *Twilight*-based fan fiction known as "Masters of the Universe." James then went on to self-publish the first book (now called *Fifty Shades of Grey*) through a small writers' community. Within the year, it sold over 300,000 eBooks. James' work was soon after picked up by Random House's Vintage Books.

Medium tends to focus more on non-fiction and community-styled reporting, along with paid journalism articles. It denounced its position as a 'publishing' platform when co-founder Evan Williams published a story on the site in May of 2015 entitled, "Medium is Not a Publishing Tool." In the article, he speaks of Medium being a writing tool that is "creating network value […] a network of ideas that build off each other" (Williams, 2015). Evans focuses on the highlighting tool and responses function to written works and segments of a work that create a sense of interaction and community in Medium. Much like Twitter and Instagram have social media influencers, Medium also has well-read and interactive authors, who, though they mostly write essays and non-fiction, are able to influence their audience, extend their own brand, and are potentially the right people to approach to collate and print their online work.

In April of 2016, Medium altered part of their focus as a platform to offer specific platforms for publishers within their site, via Medium for Publishers. Through this new format, publishers can carve out their own, customised domain within Medium where they post their content. *Electric Lit, The Awl,* and *Pacific Standard* are three online magazines with a mix of fiction and non-fiction that have migrated to Medium as a way to create an interactive dialogue between their readers and writers.

Where Medium is for non-fiction, Wattpad is the hub of online fiction. With over 40 million monthly users and stories in over fifty languages, "Wattpad takes everything you love about storytelling, and turns it into a social, on-the-go experience" (Wattpad, 2016), creating a feeling throughout the platform that books are social. It does this by placing the ease of mobile navigation and connectivity at its fore and by having users create profiles as a starting point. From there users can curate book lists and interact with other readers and writers through clubs, contests, hashtags, discussions, and the ability to comment at the end, and in-line, on stories within the site. The chapter-end and in-line comments are visible for the author and others to see, facilitating a dialogue between the readers and writers.

Wattpad deals in information of its users, and stories are hidden behind registration walls that require readers to register their info in order to gain full access to a work. In August of 2016, Wattpad USA implemented Wattpad Futures, a programme that includes ads between chapters of popular stories. This means of using the demographics of readers, specifically targeting younger audiences, is already paying some pre-chosen, popular Wattpad authors 1–2,000 USD per month in sharing the advertisement profit with the author. In addition to this, Wattpad has implemented annual awards called The Wattys. In 2016, there were nine categories, including: Trailblazer, Voracious Reads, Collectors Edition, and HP Love. For the winners and shortlists in 2016, aside from Wattpad acclaim and a rise in reader hits, they will also have their story put forth to Sourcebooks editors to be considered for traditional publication. In 2020, the categories have evolved with the readers and now include: New Adult, Fan Fiction, Fantasy, Historical Fiction, Horror, Literary Fiction, Mystery and Thriller, Paranormal, Romance, Science Fiction, and Young Adult. In 2020, one winner, Loridee De Villa, was chosen by the judges to have her work traditionally published by Wattpad's publishing arm, Wattpad Books.

Wattpad also implements a 'ranking' system across the site that is the reader-facing results of a complicated, malleable algorithm that determines the amount of support in the Wattpad community – meaning the more views and stars/votes a story has, the higher it appears in the Wattpad rankings. While the rankings may be of use to readers who want to find the best fiction without having to trawl through the 200 million-plus stories, it is also a valuable resource for publishers for the same reasons.

In 2016, Wattpad provided a Q&A section on their website that enabled their writers to navigate the potential for being contacted by a publisher. On this page, they provided a list of "trusted publishers who have worked with Wattpad and Wattpad writers" (Wattpad, 2016), including the big names in publishing such as: Penguin Random House, HarperCollins, Simon & Schuster, Macmillan, and more. Wattpad also provides a forum with peer-to-peer resources on your Wattpad publishing journey.

Wattpad created the publishing arm of the company in 2019. Their mission statement is worth quoting in full:

> [Wattpad Books] takes the stories people have obsessed over, and gives them a platform so their creators can be heard. Through an innovative, data-driven approach not yet seen in the industry, Wattpad Books is poised to disrupt traditional publishing by harnessing data to unleash the most ground-breaking stories from Wattpad directly onto bookshelves.
>
> *(Wattpad Books, 2019)*

By using "story DNA Machine Learning technology" (Wattpad Books, 2019), Wattpad Books represents a new form of business within the publishing industry that takes technology and data and combines it in a way that should produce viable results in the form of books that sell well for their intended audiences. With the launch of six books in late 2019, and several more in 2020, their overall sales in the UK remain low, with volume sales reaching just over £3,000 (Nielsen, 2020).

Some markets are more open to purchasing and reading different formats of fiction. The Asian market has always been more open to mobile fiction, with Maho no i-rando (Japan) and Reading Base (China) being hugely popular,[12] and Wattpad's hold in places like the Philippines should come as no surprise, but the Western publishing world has traditionally been more wary of social, online fiction. However, this is rapidly changing. Publishers and agents in the English-speaking world are sitting up and taking notice of writers on Wattpad who draw big numbers of readers and are approaching them to publish the work offline. These include Beth Reekles (Random House); Abigail Gibbs (Harper Collins); Lillian Carmine (Harper Collins); Taran Matharu (Macmillan); and Jordan Lynde (one book with Random House and one with Sourcebooks) (Herman, 2014).

Anna Todd is perhaps the most well-known success of Wattpad. Todd began writing *After*, her One Direction-based, erotic fan fiction on Wattpad at the end of 2013 after moving the novel over from being written in long Instagram comments. On Wattpad, *After* has been viewed over one billion times, but even with all the internal fame on Wattpad, publishing houses didn't jump. Instead, Wattpad approached Todd after seeing the views she was receiving and helped broker a deal with Simon & Schuster imprint Gallery for a four-book deal, which allowed *After* to remain on Wattpad and eventually scored Todd a rights sale to Paramount in 2014, who sold them on later.[13] It should be noted that once the fan fiction is taken out of its context, the names and some identifying markers from the original fan fiction have to be altered for copyright reasons.

Though romance, fan fiction, and teen fiction are the three big genres noted by Wattpad's communication manager Khan, science fiction is making steady gains (Herman, 2014). If we trace the rise of Taran Matharu's work *Summoner: The Novice*, we can see how citizen authors who choose to forgo the traditional publishing route and put their works on fiction repositories have the potential to gain huge numbers of followers and readers, which, in turn, brings agents and publishers to them. When Matharu published his work on Wattpad, he was writing the novel for NaNoWriMo, a competition to write a 50,000-word novel in a month, and he uploaded his work to Wattpad as he went. By the end of the month he had over 100,000 views. Soon after agents started approaching him, publishers wanted to print his work, and he signed a three-book deal with Feiwel & Friends, an imprint of Macmillan, of which the second book is not published on Wattpad.

Computer-generated fiction

Where ready-made fiction has an audience and comes already as a whole work, computer- generated fictions are those that are written based on algorithms or AI, and not usually reposited in online spaces. Computer-generated fictions are of interest because they relate to the changing definition of the book and its relationship to social media as a digital slush pile. They are considered to be those works of fiction which are based on human-written code as well as those which are written by machines and learn from themselves as artificial intelligence (AI).

Though most publishers across the UK have taken some steps towards integrating digital workflows (O'Leary, 2011), if not digital outputs, into their business strategies, those that take into account the potential for automated writing itself are few and far between but are becoming more popular. Publishers holding onto the formatting of a traditionally published book even as technological advances uncouple the content from the container, making it harder for the industry of publishing to understand and embrace what the book could potentially become.

Most artificially intelligent writing and computer-generated works are used across the web to fill in edits in Wikipedia, such as updating out of date information to aid editors (Moore-Colyer, 2020). Other forms of "algorithmic news" (Clerwall, 2014, p. 519) write and flag up journalistic news articles that are based on previously searched or read content. According to Clerwall, the systems of algorithmic news are perceived to have "no significant differences in how the two [computer-generated and journalist-written articles] are perceived" (2014, p. 526) by the reader and are more prolific than readers may think. For instance, by 2010, companies such as Statsheet and StatMonkey were already publishing 150+ word summaries of sporting events that were hard to distinguish from human-written equivalents.

Where computer-generated work is able to overcome quality-based, human gatekeeping mechanisms, it pushes for new definitions of what a book can be.

Writing about sports scores and games is several steps away from writing fiction, due to the nuances of character development that are involved in fiction which are not necessary in the formulaic writing of sports scores and game roundups. The intangible elements that make a storyline saleable are harder to code in a way that machines can interpret and create something new. However, in recent years, there have been inroads into the progress of computer-generated fiction, creating opportunities for writers and coders to develop programmes that can write convincing works of fiction with minimal human input. This can cause tensions where the author no longer has a fixed relationship to the book and the authorial process.

Writing with code

The changes that coding brings to the industry challenge the understanding of a book at the place where authors, readers, and publishers interact with new forms of technology and the coders that develop them. The interaction between writers, the industry, and new technology has become evident with the rise of programmes such as the National Novel Generation Month (NaNoGenMo), modelled on the popular National Novel Writing Month (NaNoWriMo), which encourages writers to complete a 50,000-word work in a single month. Much like the fiction written for NaNoWriMo, their computer-generated counterparts fluctuate in quality and readability, where the value of a work is judged based on human perception of a work's cultural merit.

While some of the fictions written in NaNoGenMo are technically readable in that they are comprised of words instead of nonsense text, they often do not create any sense of coherence. Strings of words such as, "Redwood. Medium carmine. Burnt umber. Burnt umber. Russet. Coffee. Field drab. Field drab. Dark brown. Field drab" (Regan, 2015, Chapter 587) will never sell enough copies to convince publishers that computer-generated fiction has any fiscal value. The precept of power involved in human value judgements of a work prevents innovative, but nonsensical, computer-generated fiction from reaching a wider market as a work of quality fiction.

Other entries such as Nick Montfort's 2013 *World Clock* show more potential for meeting gatekeepers' standards of quality that remain vital to the publishing industry and the power dynamic it embodies. Written as a 165 line of code in Python language, Montfort, a professor of digital media at MIT, developed a code that created a new character, location, and situation for every minute of a single day. The book was published free online as a pdf and in a print edition by Bad Quarto. It is engaging but choppy, with a lack of full character development that makes it a book more for dipping into and out of than reading straight through. However, Dzieza calls it the "breakout hit of last year" (2014). Its overarching themes of connectivity in the mundaneness of everyday activities across spatial-temporal boundaries can be seen as a commentary on the way technology highlights connectivity and similarity in the wider global village.

World Clock's non-traditional format, where the whole work is to be taken as small vignettes that work together in their relative positioning to one another to create an overall impression and tenuous links, would not meet the standards of most publishers who work with traditional, fictive storylines and who must pay attention to the economic viability of a work. Though *World Clock* is available for free online and in printed book format, there have been no critical evaluations to discuss the cultural value of the original text.

In 2014, *World Clock* was published in Polish by re-writing the original code in the Polish language to re-generate the novel entirely. Unlike the English version, *Zegar światowy* has been reviewed in Polish eight times (Montfort, 2014), picking out similar themes to those that can be discerned in the original English language version (Kushz, 2014; Szymański, 2015).

Other works of computer-generated fiction, such as Matsubara's team's entry into the 2016 Hoshi Shinichi Literary Award competition, have worked to overcome the low standard of quality that bars most computer-generated fiction from being considered 'good' literature. Matsubara's work shows that technology has advanced enough to allow an AI story to meet standards set by gatekeepers and progress onto the longlist of a literary award system in a blind reading. The story is based on a computer that becomes aware of itself as it writes a novel and is appropriately called "The Day a Computer Writes a Novel." However, much of the basis of the story was composed by the programmers and re-worked, or co-written, by the AI. Regardless, a translation of the final sentence from the Japanese shows the potential for AI writing and computer-generated fiction: "I writhed with joy, which I experienced for the first time, and kept writing with excitement. The day a computer wrote a novel. The computer, placing priority on the pursuit of its own joy, stopped working for humans" (Schaub, 2016).

Sarah Thorne notes the growing use of AI in video games and in film but reminds us that "narrative applications of AI have lagged behind, and efforts to develop AI agents that can generate stories are far more experimental and less likely to be implemented in commercial products" (2020). However, it is worth noting that there are programmes like OpenAI which have developed Talk to Transform systems that seek to write a few paragraphs based on a user prompt. And other companies have developed bots to write stories, such as Botnik Studios, which have written fairy tales (Thorne, 2020).

World Clock, "The Day a Computer Writes a Novel," and the cases highlighted by Thorne showcase new formats of writing fiction using code that are expanding the definitions of the book by pushing the boundaries of what we consider a book to be and how that relates to the connectivity of coding and the human-centred gatekeeping mechanisms of the industry. Coding is further changing the publishing industry by challenging the perceptions of who or what an author is and how we understand the place of technology as moving towards a more central role in the industry.

The constraints of code

Exploring the concept of the definition of the book in relation to computer-generated fictions through a lens of archaeology highlights the constraints of writing fiction with code and brings to light the importance of knowing what is missing. While the above-mentioned works are generated by computers, they are based on coding developed by humans, as noted by the chairman of Japan's Society of Artificial Intelligence, Matsubara, who states that in "AI-generated fiction, 80 percent of the creative process is actually handled by humans" (qtd. in Otake, 2016). Computers and artificial intelligence, at present, tend to work from a base code that tells the computer how to draw together and organise content to create works of fiction (Barrie, 2014). This can be the rendered names of pixel colours, images pulled from Flickr or other sources, or out of copyright works from public repositories like Project Gutenberg, among a myriad of other sources. A programmer must decide first what sources they want the computer to use. Once a source of content has been chosen, the source must be put under constraints in order to tease a new text out of it.

Composing a completely new work of fiction is much harder for artificial intelligence than is using existing works as a start for re-structuring (Matsubara, qtd. in Otake, 2016). Part of why creating a new computer-generated fiction from scratch is difficult links back to McLuhan's rear-view mirror, where new works of computer-generated fiction disrupt the industry's conception of what a book and author should look like. Some works, like Borenstein's *Generated Detective*, crawl through particular genre-coded texts searching for sentences of a specified length that contain certain key terms. Others, such as Jeff Lee's book of *Computer*

Generated Short Stories, search through online blogs and use code to write stories that plot new ways through the existing texts.

Another issue facing the creation of computer-generated fiction is the presence of human gatekeepers that are the arbiters of 'quality' of a work of fiction. A work of fiction written by AI that has X number of words coded in by the programmer may be comprised of recognisable words marked by their part of speech, but they would not necessarily be combined in a way that creates coherent sentences or storylines. Though technically these written works that carry little cohesion may be considered works of fiction, the power dynamic within the publishing industry ensures that they do not reach the traditional publication stage where a book has a particular meaning rooted in the traditional printed object and its digitally produced counterparts. They may, however, be published in the wider digital sphere in non-traditional formats. Works of fully dynamic, computer-generated fiction that would meet gatekeepers' standards have only just begun to be written and published. It is in the absence of many of these computer-written works that we can better understand the relationship between the current industry standards and expectations of quality that are governed by a human-led gatekeeping system and the computer-generated fictions that do and will come to exist.

It is the Oulipian constraints written into the coding that allow a work of fiction to be written. The constraints in coding computer-generated fiction do not restrain the output of the code, which can be as guided or general as the programmer wishes. Code tells the programme what can be taken, re-shaped, and formatted together to form a new work, by indicating to the programme which markers and structures may be used. As seen in the popularity of the three years NaNoGenMo ran, constraint within the code is by no means restrictive. Instead, it gives the programmer freedom to develop unique codes that write sometimes surprising, sometimes unusual, works of fiction. However without the code instructing the computer, there would be no output or work of fiction, but with the growing abilities of AI and computer learning, this is set to change.

Learning machines and AI

Exploring the use of artificial intelligence alongside the book expands the definition of the book further by enlarging the field of possibilities and in paying attention to the spaces where AI has not yet developed into a replacement for the author. When a computer programme reads fiction, it can replicate the structure and track different literary storylines and endings. AI learning machines can copy sentence lengths, complex structures and grammar, while sentiment analysis can note the feelings or emotions that are imbued in different parts of a story by coding words to their associated emotions, as programmed through a glossary or larger dictionary. Though the technology exists to technically create a new novel using AI, it is likely that what would be produced would lack the nuances of language and character development of a work written by a human author, as in most AI programmes "the responses are very factual" (Dai, qtd. in Kantrowitz, 2016). To enhance the voice of AI, since

2016, Google has fed 2,865 romance novels to its AI engine to teach it to speak more conversationally. This is because "Romance novels make great training material for AI because they all essentially use the same plot to tell similar stories with different words" (Dai, qtd. in Kantrowitz, 2016).

In order for computer-generated fictions to have the nuance of a human-written work of fiction, the AI programming behind it must learn as a human does. Google breaks this down into two types of learning: memorisation and generalising, which they call Wide & Deep Learning (Cheng, 2016). As it relates to the current study, this sort of technology can work to memorise things such as plot structures (boy meets girl, has crisis, ends in triumph), locations (streets of Seattle), and even feelings (being hurt makes characters cry). By memorising specific episodes where many similar plot structures, locations, and feelings take place, the AI can generalise further that similar plots may be able to contain two men as central love interests or generalise the loneliness of big city streets to specific places such as Paris and Tokyo.

Wide & Deep Learning in TensorFlow from Google is one of the ways that programmers and writers are pulling together connective and general memorisation and learning in AI to create products and services that learn what consumers will like based on the inputs, mistakes, and generalised connections (Cheng, 2016). Though Google is currently using this sort of Wide & Deep Learning in connection with feeding AI romance novels to teach it to mimic the subtleties of human speech and language, there is no reason that it could not provide a feedback loop that generates guidelines for creating its own unique work of fiction. To say that the next big novelist will be Google's AI programme is not a completely accurate depiction of things to come. However, the use of AI programming to create works of fiction that are generalised from the works that have been fed into them increases the potential of the book in the digital sphere, and the publishing industry needs to account for this growth.

When the computer becomes the author, it disentangles the human author from a work and broadens the definition of the book as a work that does not, necessarily, need to be created by a human. As it relates to the industry, AI-generated fiction expands the understanding of the book in that AI can use the six major arcs in storytelling and can be programmed to write works that closely match the arcs of those stories that have stood the test of time and have been remunerative (LaFrance, 2016). Using already published genre fiction to create an AI programme that can build rich characters and plotlines by mining the fictions it is fed links back to McLuhan's rear-view mirror, where, in relation to AI, new works are developed based on existing, previously published fiction. This allows the reader to be comfortable with the tropes and plotlines the AI programme presents in its output. This recognition prepares them to accept the AI writing on the same level as the works of fiction written by human authors. By basing AI fiction on works that have already passed through the publishing industry's gatekeeping tools, the developers of AI technology are more likely to create new works of fiction that could be of publishable quality. In doing so, creating works of AI fiction based on repositories of previously published writing within a particular genre changes the power dynamic surrounding the book by challenging the industry, meeting gatekeepers' standards, and decentralising the author of a work.

However, it is important to note that though this book focuses on how publishers may be able to source fiction from digital locations and formats, the introduction of AI to the publishing workflow is most likely to first manifest itself in developing ways of testing the readability or marketability of a work prior to signing a contract for publication.

From AI to personalised fiction

As AI and computer-generated fiction continues to improve in quality, publishers are beginning to take more advantage of advances in printing technology and are finding that printing works as needed instead of basing print runs on sale numbers of similar, previously published items allows them to take on board technology-based ideas of putting the end user first.

One of the ways that the publishing industry is slowly working to put the individual end-reader closer to the heart of the industry is by using print-on-demand technologies that involve small, medium, or even large print runs in a variety of styles, papers, covers, and inks (Mason, 2016). In the process of decentring the author of a work, publishers are now replacing that author with the reader, making the publication process revolve around the end user and thus allowing some publishers to cash in on "Generation Me" and the importance it gives to the reader in the discourse of the book. One of the ways publishers are doing this is to provide customers with personalised books and reading experiences that, in this study, fall within computer-generated fictions.

Personalised fiction

Personalised fiction is a form of writing that takes a reader's personal information and incorporates it into the content of a book. The growth of personalised fiction can be linked to the wider cultural shifts that come with the enlarging global village, where those who have the privilege of access to the connectivity provided by it are also those who have come to expect to be the centre of their digital spaces, and indicates what McLuhan discussed as media becoming an extension of man (2013). Some publishers, therefore, are embracing the user experience mentality of technological advances to give the reader (the end user) what they have come to expect from their lives within media: a user-centric work that allows them to become a part of the media, which itself, in the incorporation of their personal information, becomes an extension of their physical and digital personas.

While there has been large growth in the market for personalised fiction, there has been little in the way of academic studies on the topic, and exact sales numbers are, generally, not currently available. There are, however, several publishers who specialise in creating personalised fictions for different markets. There are personalised cookbooks by This Is Your Cookbook (a subsidiary of Quarto), personalised photo books, and personalised travel pamphlets (Telescope Cards) in addition to children's and adult fiction markets.

The most visible market for personalised fiction is that of children's illustrated books with the success of Lost My Name[14] on Dragon's Den and its subsequent growth as a publisher. Parents who are active in online communities often use their connectivity to create media extensions to and of those around them, including their children. With 81% of the children of the world having an internet presence before they are two, it should come as no surprise that parents often consider their children as part of their digitally connected, global village (Bessant, 2017). As such, they are looking to extend new forms of media into their physical lives by making their children the stars of their own stories. Publishers such as I See Me (a subsidiary of the McEvoy Group), Egmont (who use the Mr Men stories for personalisation), Lost My Name, and Pen Wizard are getting involved and grappling for part of the market share. These companies specialise in creating illustrated books that take into account a child's name, city, ethnicity, and other details to generate a distinct product that is scalable; and it is.

In 2014, Lost My Name reported sales of over 132,000 copies of their personalised children's books in the UK, and in 2015, after winning financial support on Dragon's Den, a popular investment television programme, their book *The Little Girl (or boy) Who Lost Her (or his) Name* sold over 500,000 copies (Flood, 2015). In 2017, they raised over 8.5 million in Series B funding and in 2019 were poised to move into the Chinese market. Other publishers who target the illustrated children's market, such as Sourcebook's *Put Me in the Story*, focus on personalising branded items such as Frozen, Sesame Street, and Disney stories to redevelop a previously established brand with a personal touch.

Issues that surround the scalability of personalised children's books, such as printing and how to vary the storylines, are handled much more easily in the digital realm due to the digital workflows that make implementing changes simple and efficient. However, many of the attributes of personalised digital stories that allow interaction between the content and young readers does not carry over into the realm of personalised adult fiction.

The growth of personalised fiction for adults

With readers expecting to be at the centre of their media experiences and extending that to their children, they are beginning to embrace the growth of personalised adult fiction. Straddling the line between the industry, technological advances, and altering the definition of a book, personalised fiction allows the reader to become a central part of a new work of fiction or a past favourite.

The market for personalised adult fiction is growing as companies take advantage of the rise of genre fiction sales in the eBook market (Author Earnings, 2016). Publishers are taking the genres that work as digital sales, customising content and selling them as bespoke-printed items. Those such as Personal Novel, U Star Novels, and Prezzy Box focus heavily on romance and erotica, allowing a reader to become the star of their own love story/erotic fiction. Personal Novel also offers personalised genre fiction such as fantasy, sci-fi, and historical fiction. They allow the reader to name several characters and personalise certain traits (hair colour, etc.), essentially creating their own cast within a set story frame. By allowing users to change particular elements of the work which are not essential to plot development, the power relationship is altered within the discourse of the book, with published works that both fit into and bypass the gatekeeping mechanisms.

While Personal Novel, U Star Novels, and Prezzy Box work towards genre fictions, others such as *In The Book*, published by Signature, create personalised versions of classic works of fiction. The foray into personalised fiction encompasses a variety of genres, allowing a reader to choose from classics, Mills and Boon, Ladybird books for adults, and more. Buyers fill in a questionnaire for names of characters. The completed book is then printed on demand and shipped to the buyer, allowing them to be the star of their own novel.

Though there is a potential for linking social media with personalisation of books, as of yet, the publishers who focus on personalised fiction shy away from social media. In fact, these personalising publishers tend to have a much less involved social media presence than more 'traditional' publishers and often go for weeks or months without interacting. However, it should be noted that, currently, further interactivity with the content of the books does not advance much beyond the naming of characters and of simple biographical details being fed into a formulaic structure, and to explore the place where interactive works of fiction cross more fully into the realm of gaming is beyond the scope of such a book but is entirely possible.[15]

In creating personalised novels, media can become an extension of man/woman. This along with new printing technology and the centrality that many readers have learned to expect in their digital and digitally social lives gives the end user/reader a work of fiction that places them at the centre of the process. Personalised fiction develops new connections and themes between the industry, the book, publishers, authors, and social media. The strategies that these connections develop uncover ways that they can work together within and across discourses while keeping in mind that power is also a strategy, one that is played out in copyright of computer-generated and personalised fictions.

Copyright and computer-generated and personalised fiction

Personalised work and computer-generated fiction must consider who owns the content. "Under the CDPA all copyright works need an author (even if unknown)" (Stokes, 2019, p. 35); however, there is a distinction between computer-generated works and those works where the computer or programme is merely the writer's assistant. The simple way to consider this distinction is in the use of software that aids writers in the production of a work. For example, the copyright of a work that was originally written using a Word processing pro-gramme belongs entirely to the writer using the programme, not the creator of the programme itself.

In the same way, the copyright of works of personalised fiction do not move to the reader who has opted to insert their name, gender, or location, etc. The copyright will remain with the writer of the original text. It is likely that those out of copyright works that are being offered as personalisable fiction will be con-sidered to have two authors: the original author and the new publisher/editor/author. This can be seen where authors have used out of copyright works as a basis for new fictions, such as Grahame-Smith's and Austen's *Pride and Prejudice and Zombies* and Winter's and Austen's *Sense and Sensibility and Sea Monsters*.

However, if the process of personalisation moves further to include more per-sonalised biographical information input by the reader, the lines of copyright ownership and dual authorship begin to blur as their crossover lengthens. As technological capabilities increase and as personalised books become a more main-stream publishing venture, the publishing industry will need to reconsider how the laws of copyright apply and, importantly, look closely at what contracts are needed. This raises the question of whether a work of detailed, highly personalised fiction could have an audience outside of the individual reader's order, and if the publisher opts to do a larger print run, or digital edition, and sell the book on, at what point does the included reader's biographical information make the reader a co-author, or can the reader stop a publisher from reprinting a book containing their bio-graphical details?

If it becomes the case that a more general audience would purchase a particular work of personalised fiction that resonates beyond the original reader, the publisher should proactively consider how to handle the situation. They could replace the personalised identifiers, such as names, and argue that any remaining personal details are coincidental and generic. But with the prevalence of social media acting as a judge and jury of business activities, this is a risky move that could isolate potential readers and reflect poorly on the publisher's brand. However, if publishers manage this in a sensitive way that makes the reader unidentifiable as an individual, by decentring the reader from the work of personalised fiction, this could also help to circumvent issues of privacy.

At present, copyright of personalised fiction is, for the most part, relatively straightforward. Stokes states that when dealing with a work of computer-generated fiction (or other copyrightable works), "the author is the person by whom the arrangements necessary for the creation of the work are undertaken" (2019, p. 35). He goes on to clarify that "this will typically be the programmer but not necessarily so" (2019, p. 35). In the case of the computer-generated fictions of the NaNoGenMo competition, the Hoshi Shinichi Literary Award, and others, the code is the under-lying basis for the story itself. Here the authors are the programmers who write the commands that direct the computers to the archives of text, giving them parameters for choosing, restructuring, and presenting the output to create a new work of fiction. In these cases, it is the code that is the main directive of digital copyright, and any outputs by that code are also directed to the author of the code itself. The instance where this is not the case is in moral rights, which apply to works created on the internet and digital works but not to computer-generated works (Stokes, 2019, p. 101).

As artificial intelligence advances and computers begin to create things based on learned abilities, we must consider at what point, if any, the computer itself becomes the author and how that will create disruptions at the sites of inquiry based on the human author and develop new statements, concepts, and strategies in the discourse. According to the current digital copyright laws in the UK, the point where the computer becomes the author does not exist and the rights of any outputs belong to the human writer/ programmer who made the "arrangements necessary" for the completion of the work (Stokes, 2019, p. 35). As the technology for AI to write works of fiction is in its infancy, it is too soon to tell if the copyright paternity of computer-generated works will need to change, should AI learn to code and recode itself to produce new and better works of fiction than even those who are opting to remove themselves from the traditional publishing model and write directly onto new, innovative, social platforms.

Notes

1 The big five often have more than one account, plus accounts across platforms for each imprint.
2 There are more than three options, but these are the most likely to be engaged with by publishers of all sizes. Those with large turnovers, for example, can afford to hire individuals and companies to do this work on a commercial scale.
3 Some companies, such as Twitter, are already working with large educational institutions to provide access to social data.
4 This is an area of change, and researchers are continually considering the balance of ethics and legality around scraping and mining publicly available social media content.
5 A Google search for the phrase 'develop an API' (24 November, 2020) returned over 469 million hits, from services to step by step guides to building one in a huge array of programming languages.
6 The consideration of commercial viability must be touched on but it is often closely linked to 'quality' judgements, from which I'm striving to remain neutral.
7 'Significant' in this research would depend on the publisher's goals. The aim might not be to have an influencer with over 1 million followers, when a smaller, local influencer with 20,000 followers is more in line with what the publisher publishes and the markets in which they work.
8 Such as beauty influencers, travel influencers, foodie influencers, bookstagrammers, etc.
9 This can be in money or in items from a brand.
10 Down to 784,000 as of July 2018, 745,000 thousand in September 2019, and 679,000 thousand in Nov. 2020. This drop could be due to the fact that she is now married and with child, and the premise of the social feed was her mother pushing her to get married in comical abundance.
11 Up from 1.6 million followers in July 2018.
12 For more details on the role of mobile fiction in these markets, see Keckler, *Koizora: A Mirroring of Keitai Shōsetsu in a "Novel" Approach to Modern Literature*, 2010; and Bhaskar, *The Content Machine*, 2013.
13 This movie has since been produced and streams on Netflix (2019).
14 Now known as Wonderbly.
15 Based on conversations with Chelsea Apps.

Bibliography

@david_mitchell, 2014. @ScepreBooks are delighted to present a story written by David for Twitter, serialised twice a day this week. We give you #THERIGHTSORT... Twitter. Available at: https://twitter.com/david_mitchell/status/488563292898467841.

@neilhimself, 2009. Sam was brushing her hair when the girl in the mirror put down the hairbrush, smiled & said, "We don't love you anymore." @BBCAA #bbcawdio. Twitter. Available at: https://twitter.com/neilhimself/status/4837873679.

@SceptreBooks, 2014. Can twitter just be quiet for 20 minutes please while we read the last instalment in @David_Mitchell's #THERIGHTSORT. Twitter. Available at: https://twitter.com/SceptreBooks/status/490888426711822336.

Ahlemeyer-Stubbe, A. & Coleman, S., 2014. *A Practical Guide to Data Mining for Business and Industry*. Chichester: John Wiley & Sons.

Alter, A., 2012. Your E-Book is Reading You. In *The Wall Street Journal* [online]. Available at: https://www.wsj.com/articles/SB10001424052702304870304577490950051438304. [Accessed 1 June 2020].

Author Earnings, 2016. May 2016 Author Earnings Report: The Definitive Million-Title Study of US Author Earnings. *Author Earnings* [online]. Available at: http://authorearnings.com/report/may-2016-report/. [Accessed July 2016].

Barrie, J., 2014. Computers Are Writing Novels: Read a Few Examples Here. In *Business Insider* [online]. Available here: http://uk.businessinsider.com/novels-written-by-computers-2014-11. [Accessed 28 August 2015].

Batrinca, B. & Treleaven, P., 2015. Social Media Analytics: A Survey of Techniques, Tools and Platforms. In *AI & Soc*. Vol. 30, pp. 89–116.

Bessant, C., 2017. More Than 80% of Children Have an Online Presence by the Age of Two. In *PSYS.Org* [online]. Available at: https://phys.org/news/2017-09-children-online-presence-age.html. [Accessed 13 January 2021].

Bhaskar, M., 2013. *The Content Machine: Towards a Theory of Publishing from the Printing Press to the Digital Network*. London: Anthem Press.

Booth, N. & Matic, J.A., 2011. Mapping and Leveraging Influencers in Social Media to Shape Corporate Brand Perception. In *Corporate Communications*. Vol. 16, No. 3, pp. 184–191.

Brouillette, S. & Doody, C., 2015. Literary Markets and Literary Property. In *Anglistik: International Journal of English Studies*. Vol. 26, No. 2, pp. 139–148.

Cheng, H., 2016. Wide & Deep Learning: Better Together with Tensorflow. In Google Blogs [online]. Available at: https://ai.googleblog.com/2016/06/wide-deep-learning-better-together-with.html. [Accessed 20 July 2020].

Clerwall, C., 2014. Enter the Robot Journalist: Users' Perception of Automated Content. In *Journalism Practice*. Vol. 8, No. 5, pp. 519–531.

Coker, M., 2015. How Indie Authors Can Use Preorders to Crack the Bestseller List. In *Publishers Weekly*, 20 November. Available at: https://www.publishersweekly.com/pw/by-topic/authors/pw-select/article/68748-how-indie-authors-can-use-preorders-to-crack-the-bestseller-lists.html. [Accessed July 2016].

Dzieza, J., 2014. The Strange World of Computer-Generated Novels. In *The Verge* [online], 25 November. Available at: https://www.theverge.com/2014/11/25/7276157/nanogenmo-robot-author-novel. [Accessed 23 August 2015].

Flood, A., 2012. Big E-Reader is Watching You. In *The Guardian* [online]. Available at: https://www.theguardian.com/books/2012/jul/04/big-ereader-is-watching-you. [Accessed 1 June 2020].

Flood, A., 2015. Personalised Picture Book Becomes Runaway Bestseller. In *The Guardian* [online]. Available at: https://www.theguardian.com/books/2015/apr/20/personalised-picture-book-dragons-den-little-girl-who-lost-her-name. [Accessed 6 August 2016].

Freberg, K., Graham, K, McGaughey, K., & Freberg, L.A., 2010. Who Are the Social Media Influencers? A Study of Public Perceptions of Personality. In *Public Relations Review*. Vol. 37, pp. 90–92.

Hall, T., 2010. 10 Essential Rules for Brands in Social Media. In *Ad Age* [online], 22 March. Available at: https://adage.com/article/digitalnext/10-essential-rules-brands-social-media/142907. [Accessed 1 June 2020].

Herman, B., 2014. What is Wattpad? The 'YouTube for Stories' is Transforming Book Publishing. In *International Business Times* [online]. Available at: http://www.ibtimes.com/what-wattpad-youtube-stories-transforming-book-publishing-1710151. [Accessed 9 September 2016].

Kantrowitz, A., 2016. Google is Feeding Romance Novels to Its Artificial Intelligence Engine to Make Its Products More Conversational. In *Buzzfeed News* [online]. Available at: https://www.buzzfeednews.com/article/alexkantrowitz/googles-artificial-intelligence-engine-reads-romance-novels. [Accessed 2016].

Keckler, S., 2010. Koizora: A Mirroring of Keitai Shōsetsu in a "Novel" Approach to Modern Literature. Thesis. Washington and Lee University.

Kushz, A., 2014. *World Clock – Nick Montfort.* SZORTAL [online]. Available at: https://translate.google.co.uk/translate?hl=en&sl=pl&tl=en&u=http%3A%2F%2Fszortal.com%2Fnode%2F6310. [Accessed 24 August 2015].

LaFrance, A., 2016. The Six Main Arcs in Storytelling, As Identified By an AI. In *The Atlantic* [online], 12 July. Available at: https://www.theatlantic.com/technology/archive/2016/07/the-six-main-arcs-in-storytelling-identified-by-a-computer/490733/. [Accessed 27 April 2017].

Martin, B. & Tian, X., 2010. *Books, Bytes and Business: The Promise of Digital Publishing.* Surrey: Ashgate Publishing Limited.

Mason, C., 2016. The Print-On-Demand Revolution Opens New Doors for Authors & Publishers. In *Book Business* [online], 12 April. Available at: https://www.bookbusinessmag.com/post/print-demand-revolution-opens-new-doors-authors-publishers/. [Accessed 25 July 2017].

McLuhan, M., 2013. *Understanding Media: The Extensions of Man.* Berkeley: Gingko Press [eBook].

McLuhan, M., 2019. Home Page [online]. Available at: https://books.wattpad.com/. [Accessed 12 September 2019].

McPherson, J., 2016. *Upcoming Publishing Models* [Panel Session]. 2020: A Publishing Odyssey. Society of Young Publishers, Scotland. 18 March.

Montfort, N., 2014. Translating World Clock. In *Open Transcripts* [online], 8 November. Available at: http://opentranscripts.org/transcript/translating-world-clock/. [Accessed 23 August 2015].

Moore-Colyer, R., 2020. MIT Develops AI Tech to Edit Outdated Wikipedia Articles. In *ITPro* [online]. Available at: https://www.itpro.co.uk/technology/artificial-intelligence-ai/354766/mit-develops-ai-tech-to-edit-outdated-wikipedia. [Accessed 20 December 2020].

Neary, L., 2013. E-Readers Track How We Read, But is the Data Useful to Authors?. In *NPR* [online]. Available at: https://www.npr.org/sections/alltechconsidered/2013/01/28/170296373/e-readers-track-how-we-read-but-is-the-data-useful-to-authors [Accessed 1 June 2020].

Nielsen, 2020. Wattpad by Full Year 2020 to 7th Nov. Accessed via Nielsen Bookscan. [Accessed 20 November 2020].

Norton, M., 1999. Knowledge Discovery in Databases. In *Library Trends*. Vol. 48, No. 1, Summer, pp. 9–21.

O'Leary, B.F., 2011. Context First: A Unified Theory of Publishing. In *Publishing Research Quarterly*. Vol. 27, pp. 211–219.

Otake, T., 2016. Japanese Researchers Take Artificial Intelligence Toward the Final Frontier: Creativity. In *The Japan Times*. Available at: https://www.japantimes.co.jp/news/2016/06/19/national/science-health/japanese-researchers-take-artificial-intelligence-toward-the-final-frontier-creativity/. [Accessed 2016].

Pack, S., 2016. Unbound. Interview with Miriam Johnson [phone].

Ramachandran, V., 2013. 'Social Fiction' Brings Characters to Life Via Facebook and Twitter. In *Mashable*, 28 August. Available at: https://mashable.com/2013/08/27/hawk-funn-social-fiction-kickstarter/?europe=true#nlMdI8DdsPqL. [Accessed November 2020].

Regan, D., 2015. *The Cover of the Sun Also Rises* [online]. Available at: http://alsorises.org/book/. [Accessed 23 July 2016].

Ruths, D. & Pfeffer, J., 2014. Social Media for Large Studies of Behavior. In *Science*. Vol. 346, No. 6213, pp. 1063–1064.

Schaub, M., 2016. Is the Future Award-Winning Novelist a Writing Robot? In *Los Angeles Times*. Available at: https://www.latimes.com/books/jacketcopy/la-et-jc-novel-computer-writing-japan-20160322-story.html. [Accessed 23 July 2016].

Stewart, M., 2016. Interview on Publishing and Social Media. Interviewed by Miriam Johnson [phone].

Stokes, S., 2019. *Digital Copyright: Law and Practice*. 5th ed. Oxford and Portland: Hart Publishing.

Szymański, M., 2015. Illiterate Time: The World Clock of Nick Montfort as a Diagnosis of the Avant-Garde Literature Market. In *The Province* [online]. Available at: https://translate.google.co.uk/translate?hl=en&sl=auto&tl=en&u=http%3A%2F%2Fprowincja.art.pl%2Fczas-analfabetow-zegar-swiatowy-nicka-montforta-jako-diagnoza-rynku-literatury-awangardowej-michal-szymanski%2F. [Accessed 26 August 2015].

Thorne, S., 2020. Hey Siri, Tell Me a Story: Digital Storytelling and AI Authorship. In *Convergence*. Vol. 26, No. 4, pp. 808–823. Available at: DOI: doi:10.1177/1354856520913866.

Wattpad, 2016. About [online]. Available at: https://www.wattpad.com/about/. [Accessed 12 April 2016].

Wattpad, 2016. FAQ [online]. Available at: https://www.wattpad.com/writers/faq/m. [Accessed 23 April 2016].

Wattpad Books, 2019. About [online]. Available at: https://books.wattpad.com/about. [Accessed 12 September 2019].

Wordpress, 2016. Wordpress Activity, October 2014. Available at: https://wordpress.com/activity/. [Accessed July 2016].

Williams, E., 2015. Medium is Not a Publishing Tool. In *Medium*, 20 May. Available at: https://medium.com/the-story/medium-is-not-a-publishing-tool- 4c3c63fa41d2#.z99gr7rel. [Accessed July 2016].

4

THE RISE OF THE CITIZEN AUTHOR

What is a citizen author?

While it may be intuitive to think that what is called a 'citizen author' is indistinguishable from a self-published author, this is too simplistic of a notion. They have some similar traits, but the point where the citizen author differs from the self-published author is where they are writing. Citizen authors write on digitally social platforms that are available as apps, websites, forums, etc. The timeline of their rise coincides with the advent of digital technology and social platforms (early 2000s to present).

It is important that the publishing industry moves away from the term 'self-published author' and embraces 'citizen author' to highlight the differences between these two groups.

Though the citizen author may take on many duties ascribed to the earlier self-published author, in that they often edit, print, and absorb any fees related to selling and promoting the work (Felton, 2014), the key distinction is the place the citizen author occupies within the global village, which makes "creative dialogue inevitable" (McLuhan, 1969) and allows them to develop direct relationships with others who have access to their digital communities. While a self-published author may still subvert the traditional publishing system by publishing and selling their own work – in this case, print books and eBooks – a citizen author is someone who embraces the new digital technologies to produce their own works, create new networks, communities, and followers, bypassing the gate-keeping mechanisms of the publishing industry. In choosing to forgo the traditional business model of the publishing industry, the citizen author actively challenges the industry's conception of what a book can be.

Here, the focus on the rise of the citizen author is based within the wider discourse of the book and encompasses the use of new digitally social technologies

DOI: 10.4324/9781003186649-5

available to them, allowing them to create, publish, and disseminate their works on the open market, going beyond the step-by-step platforms for uploading their text to an eBook creator or self-publishing platform.

From self-publisher to citizen author

In order to understand how the self-published author developed into and continues alongside the citizen author, we must identify who the modern self-publishers are, where they exist, and what platforms they use. Carolan and Evain suggest that current self-publishers fall into three categories: "big fish in the big pond[,] big fish in the small pond[, and] small fish in the big pond" (2013, pp. 286–288). Essentially, authors who are usually read online by large numbers, often leading to traditional book deals and commercial success, are those big fish in the big pond. Secondly, the big fish in the small pond are those who are great at making a name for themselves within a niche community. The third, and largest group identified, is the small fish in the big pond. These are the authors who write and self-publish but never sell more than a handful of books (2013, pp. 286–288). While these general groupings are beneficial as a means of distinguishing the categories of self-published authors, having more in-depth demographic statistics is useful in knowing more about who the self-publishers are and how they disrupt the coherence of the discourse.

It must be noted that the term 'global village' is not unproblematic as it relates to the 'digital divide' between those writers and readers who do or do not use new digital technologies to connect (Grădinaru, 2016, p. 185). Scholars such as Vrasidas and Veletsianos state that the overarching term of 'global village' "may not always work when applied to experiences of marginalized people in online communications [...] and thus can be 'exclusionary'" (2010, p. 5). While access to the global village is dependent on the socio-economic status of the user, this imbalance echoes what is seen in an offline community. However, it is more difficult to trace the lack of users in an online space without knowing who they could be and where the digital communities are that they might join if all access was equitable.

It is this specific set of digital contingencies that allows for the development of the self-published author. In 2013, Baverstock and Steinitz conducted an in-depth survey of self-publishers and discovered that "There are no demographic barriers to self-publishing" (2013a, p. 213). While this may be the case within the relatively small (120 participants) group of self-published authors that responded to their survey, this cannot be generalised to a wider set of authors, due to the fact that not everyone has the same advantage of access to the computers, software, and connectivity that today's self-publishing, generally, requires. That being said, those that did respond can create an image of who these self-publishers are and provide a good baseline for distinguishing the self-publishers from the modern citizen authors.

In their 2013 study, Baverstock and Steinitz found that 65% of respondents were female, and the vast majority (88%) were over the age of forty (p. 214). Additionally, they found that most participants were educated to undergraduate degree level and above (76%) (2013a, p. 214), a number that highlights the potential for unequal access to the global village.

A second study, also in 2013, by Baverstock and Steinitz, found that "selling material was by no means the only goal of self-publishing authors – or even the most important one" (p. 274). The most valuable result of self-publishing among the 120 authors surveyed was the "completion" of the process of writing, editing, and publishing the book that provided the most satisfaction (p. 273). However, the satisfaction of completion does not preclude a self-published author from doing well monetarily. According to the May 2016 data from the Author Earnings Report, half of the 1,340 authors who earn more than $100,000 a year are independent, self-published authors and Amazon-imprint authors. For the 'hidden' authors who do not, for some reason or another, show up in the Amazon bestseller list, thirty of the forty-three listed, including the top earner of over $250,000, are self-published authors (2016, p. 3). By 2018, the ACLS Authors' Earning Report found that some 18% of authors who make a living by writing have self-published and of those authors the mean earnings were £30,627 (Kretschmer et al., 2019). This disparity creates tensions in the relationships between the publishing industry, the socio-economic climate, the book, and the author, and provides an opening for a new type of author: the citizen author.

Demographics of a citizen author

In defining the citizen author, the use of technology, social media, education, and socio-economic levels all play a role in giving the citizen author access to the global village where they develop relationships with each other and readers. They actively bypass the traditional gatekeepers of the industry by writing, sharing, and promoting their work directly within the global village.

The use of social media platforms, self-publishing, and early adoption of new technology can also be broken down into age of use to give a better overview of who the citizen author is and where they situate themselves within the global village. Baverstock and Steinitz found that most self-publishers are over the age of forty, whereas the readers and writers of FanFiction.net are mostly between the ages of 13–17 (Fan Fiction Statistics – FFN Research, 2011); and with the users of social media, the majority are aged 18–34 (Kemp, 2020). Though there is a decent uptake of social medial platforms among all ages, this slows as the user's age rises and digital natives give way to digital migrants, defined as those who were not born into the digital age but have adapted to it by taking part in social media platforms and embracing new technologies (Prensky, 2001, p. 2).

When it comes to who is writing in the global village and how easily they adopt new technologies, education also plays a role. Access to the technology in monetary terms and the ability to have leisure time to spend on the platforms are two considerations that relate directly back to the socio-economic status from which the citizen author arises. Over 70% of Baverstock and Steinitz's self-published authors were university graduates (2013a, p. 214). This is comparable to the use of social media platforms where 72% of Facebook users, 32% of Instagram, and 23% of Twitter users have at least some college or university education (Duggan, 2015, pp. 10–14). Unsurprisingly, there is strong correlation between an individual's education and income levels (Graham & Paul, 2011), and those users that have a higher annual income are more likely to be early adopters of technology such as social platforms and new hand-held devices that give access to the internet.[1] However, there will be outliers who have gained access to, and made a success in, the global village who have created a network based on cultural capital and their status within a subculture in the global village.

The rise of the citizen author is advanced by an awareness among readers and writers of the innovative use of technology that has created places to write and share works of fiction. They embrace new digitally social technologies not only as places to build networks but as communities where they can write and market their work using cross-platform techniques. By actively engaging with their real and potential audiences on social networks, adopting the rules of followers and following, and by replying to comments on works, the citizen author fosters their own social presence and the relationships they create with the reader. In doing so, the citizen author, much like the self-published author, decentres themselves from their work so that as a speaker they are in a unique place to engage with the global village in a way that can feed back into their book at a further point.

To better define who the citizen author is and their relationship to the industry and technology, we begin with their age, sex, income, adoption and use of digitally social platforms and social writing repositories. These traits, combined with Feldman's findings that early adopters are more likely to be younger, and male (2019), and Baverstock and Steinitz's demographic findings of self-publishers, show that the majority of citizen authors who are using innovative technology and social platforms to write and disseminate their works are likely to be female, but not overwhelmingly so, between the ages of 18–49, have at least some college or university education, and be of a socio-economic status that allows for access to, and adoption of, new technologies and digitally social platforms.

Where are citizen authors writing?

Popular social media platforms, blogs, fiction repositories, reviews, audio platforms, websites, etc., all are locations that appeal to the citizen author who lives in the global village. The different places where a citizen author chooses to write challenges the industry's understanding of where an author can produce work and how they bypass industry gatekeeping systems. The demographics of the new citizen author differ from that of self-publishers around the concept of digital natives. Though not all citizen authors are born into the digitally connected, global village, many are. This is due to many factors that have an impact on writing in online spaces, including a citizen author's age, education levels, and socio-economic status – which relates to access and their physical location within the world. Deuze et al. state that "there is no external to the media in our lives" (2012, p. 1), and the citizen author takes this continual flow between internal and external media into the process of where and how they write.

Though the citizen author can choose to forgo the traditional author-agent-publisher route to the market, even if the market deals in cultural currency instead of money, they are usually aware of, and keen to embrace, a traditional publishing deal should it be offered, as can be seen in recent publishing deals with citizen authors such as Anna Todd and Abigail Gibbs, who first found significant numbers of readers on Wattpad (Published Samples, Wattpad, 2017). In fact, many publishers now visit repositories such as Wattpad and Medium to seek out authors who are doing well digitally, and to offer them a traditional publishing deal. This creates a bit of tension, where on the one hand there is a balance between Wattpad and other such repositories using traditional publishers to draw interest in their platform as a place of quality literature, and on the other as an infinite slush pile where undesirable writing must also be read to find the gems worth removing from the sediment of poorly written and edited works. The result is the development of social repositories, which creates a new understanding of what a book can be in relation to the citizen author and the industry, and which takes advantage of the socio-economic state where publishers can seek out works that have proven themselves prior to the investment of traditional publication.

Sites like Wattpad and Medium have low barriers of entry, which makes them an ideal place for a citizen author to hone and test their writing, interact with readers, and get feedback, all of which increases the quantity and quality of their relationships in the global village. To gain access and expand the relationships around their writing, all the citizen author needs is a device that has connectivity to the internet and an email address with which to register with the social platform. The same goes for access to other social media platforms such as Facebook, Instagram, Twitter, and more, with several new ones cropping up and falling out of favour all the time, all of which are of interest as we explore how to define the book as it relates to the citizen author.

The citizen author discriminates between social platforms based on their own interests, needs, and what is available to them. By taking on board the roles traditionally enjoyed by "professional media workers – their ability to effectively find, create and gather, select, edit, disseminate and redistribute information" (Deuze et al., 2012, p. 5), the citizen author alters the available digitally social spaces to accommodate their needs as writers and producers of works of fiction, effectively creating new definitions of the book. In fact, we find again and again that those citizen authors who do not find a suitable place in the digitally connected global village to write their fiction often create one themselves. This can be seen most evidently in the proliferation of writers creating blogs and building websites to house their works. This not only gives the citizen author more control over the formatting, delivery, and dissemination of their work, but it also allows them to return to it again and again to edit the work, often based on a feedback loop between authors and readers, which can be facilitated by comments and author contact forms.

Other citizen authors choose to experiment with their writing by using the technology in innovative ways, but that often does not lead to publication deals or monetary gain. The use of podcasting apps and programmes to share an audio version of an author's work is likely not to get as much coverage as a work written and well-tagged in other digitally social formats, and indeed, it may even cost the author money to produce. Geo-locational apps such as Podwalk and Voicemap differ in how they allow the author to share the work, in that Podwalk charges the author to produce and share the work – which is then available for free – and Voicemap hosts the work while charging the user to listen to the recording, sharing the fee with the author. However, if an author's work is tied to a location, this social technology is a way forward that citizen authors are beginning to embrace as a means of engaging with the non-discursive elements of a physical space, tying together the real and global villages.

One segment of citizen authors chooses to write in-depth reviews that are works of fiction. Though these may not stand out in the traditional sense as 'stories,' some products have garnered more interest for their humour . One such example is the reviews for Haribo Sugar Free Gummy Bears, for which users Christine E. Torok (2012, October 3) and @StuPurdue (2012, 21 November) each wrote a several hundred word story based on their literal gut-reactions to the sweets. There is much hyperbole in the reviews, rendering them almost certainly fictional, but they still remain as influential (judged by their number of review stars) product reviews years after being posted. While this is an unusual outlet for a short story, it does stand as a testament to the citizen author's ingenuity in using technology to write and share their work.

What are citizen authors writing?

The focus of this book is on fiction that is written on social media. This is not to say that the only things being written are works of fiction. As citizen authors expand where and how they write, they are also expanding what they write. Poetry is the most obvious fit for several of the current, major social media platforms.[2] It provides snapshots of writing that can be quickly consumed while scrolling past and 'liked' or shared quickly. In 2015, three of the top ten bestselling poetry books were written by poets who are best known as Instapoets (Qureshi, 2015). Twitter, with its current 280-character limit, is a perfect example of a constrained format that appeals to a poet, who often focuses on the nuances of the language within the tight confines of pre-determined structures. For those who have a Twitter account but are not poets, there is even a website[3] that will comb your tweets and create poetry for you, each line linked to a different tweet. The citizen author, perhaps, does not even need to have poetical leanings to create interesting new poetry using digitally social technology, as the digital developments have created sets of contingencies that allow for these new expansions in the global community.

Poetry is not the only genre to have a resurgence on social platforms; non-fiction, travel guides, self-help, narrative non-fiction, and cookery/lifestyle genres have all flourished at the hand of the citizen author. There are works which cross platforms to create interactive fiction that differs slightly depending on the access route. A new form of historical text is being written in the digital age, one that consists of grassroots digital activism, local eye-witness reporting, the swift tagging of stories, and the organisation and interaction of movements. While the individual posts that are part of this new archive of digital history may not be, on their own, worthy of recording, it is when the connections within the discourse are made that a more complete understanding of a historical or social event becomes clear.

Authors such as Matt Stewart and Anna Todd chose different routes to publication. Stewart stepped directly past the traditional gatekeepers by choosing to release his novel, *The French Revolution*, on Twitter from his own account. Stewart wrote his novel first and used an algorithm to tweet each 130-character segment in a timely manner, sharing the entirety of the manuscript on Twitter in 2009. It took 3,700 tweets to share the 480,000-character novel. It was shared at pre-determined intervals in order to facilitate an easy way to time and deliver the work in an automated fashion. This created a relationship between Stewart, as a citizen author, and his readers in the global village as they waited for the next instalment and could reply directly to the author's Twitter account.

Stewart was not a well-known author when he used social media to write and publish his book. In fact, Stewart readily admits that as a marketer he wanted to raise the profile of his literary fiction manuscript that publishers were wary of taking a chance to publish traditionally. The media attention Stewart gained in tweeting the novel brought his work to the attention of Soft Skull Press, who opted to publish the work in a traditionally printed format in 2010. Stewart did not simply bypass the gatekeepers of the industry; he pushed the industry to bring his work back into the traditional publishing model.

Todd, unlike Stewart, chose to write her fiction directly onto a social platform. For her One Direction-based erotic fan fiction, *After*, she moved from Instagram images to longer-form works on Wattpad. By the time she published the first chapter on Wattpad in 2013, she was already boasting a huge network of readers. Soon after, Wattpad stepped in and brokered a traditional publishing contract with Simon & Schuster and hired a talent agency to option the film rights. Todd said that she "had no intention of [formally] publishing" her stories, and that she "wrote what [… she] wanted to be reading" (qtd. in Kircher, 2015). This process of simply writing what you want to read and having the tools and platforms on which to do it often encapsulates the citizen author, who engages with social platforms as a means to bypass the industry entirely in order share their works with like-minded neighbours in the global village.

A citizen author chooses where and what they write, and that allows for a series of recurring micro-instances to challenge the mechanisms of the traditional publishing industry, which relies on gatekeepers and monetisation of a work. By paying attention to these micro-instances and how they recur, we can begin to see larger patterns emerging (Mittell, 2001). One such pattern is that of the role of gender in the digital communities and how it plays a role in what is shared, where, and who feels capable of interacting.

Notes

1 Here we are talking about early adoption. It should, however, be noted that among UK social grades, the AB demographic has a slightly lower uptake of social media, year on year (Tankovska, 2021).
2 For more info on Instagram poets, see Gill qtd. in Bennett (2020); Atkinson (2018); Carlin (2017); and Kovalik and Curwood (2019).
3 Poet Tweet. Poetweet.com.br.

Bibliography

@StuPurdue, 2012. Amazon Review: "My Dinner with Andrea". Amazon. Available at: https://www.amazon.com/review/R30I8VJFBDG6TD. [Accessed 22 November 2020].

Atkinson, J., 2018. What is an #Instapoet?. National Poetry Library [online], 7 June. Available at: https://www.nationalpoetrylibrary.org.uk/news-stories/what-instapoet. [Accessed 22 November 2020].

Author Earnings, 2016. *May 2016 Author Earnings Report: The Definitive Million-Title Study of US Author Earnings.* Author Earnings [online]. Available at: http://authorearnings.com/report/may-2016-report/. [Accessed July 2016].

Baverstock, A. & Steinitz, J., 2013a. Who Are the Self-Publishers? In *Learned Publishing.* Vol. 26, No. 3, pp. 211–223.

Baverstock, A. & Steinitz, J., 2013b. What Satisfaction Do Self-Publishing Authors Gain from the Process? In *Learned Publishing.* Vol. 26, No. 4, pp. 272–282.

Bennett, S., 2020. #aroomofonesown: How Social Media Made Space for Young Women's Poetry and Why Publishers 'Liked' It. MA dissertation, Oxford Brookes University. Available at: https://radar.brookes.ac.uk/radar/items/9e046c8e-3cb2-43ef-a028-ff08fe653787/1/. [Accessed 21 November 2020].

Carlin, S., 2017. Meet Rupi Kaur, Queen of the "Instapoets". In *Rolling Stone* [online], 21 December. Available at: https://www.rollingstone.com/culture/culturefeatures/meet-rupi-kaur-queen-of-the-instapoets-129262/. [Accessed 22 November 2020].

Carolan, S. & Evain, C., 2013. Self-Publishing: Opportunities and Threats in a New Age of Mass Culture. In *Publishing Research Quarterly.* Vol. 29, No. 4, pp. 285–300.

Deuze, M., Blank, P., & Speers, L., 2012. A Life Lived in Media. In *Digital Humanities Quarterly.* Vol. 5, No. 1 [online]. Available at: http://digitalhumanities.org/dhq/vol/6/1/000110/000110.html.

Duggan, M., 2015. The Demographics of Social Media Users. Pew Research Center [online]. Available at: http://www.pewinternet.org/2015/08/19/the-demographics-of-social-media-users/. [Accessed 1 October 2016].

Fan Fiction Statistics – FFN Research, 2011. Fan Fiction Demographics in 2010: Age, Sex, Country. In *FFN Research* [online]. Available at: http://ffnresearch.blogspot.co.uk/. [Accessed 3 October 2016].

Feldman, R., 2019. Who Buys the Latest and Greatest Gadgets? YouGov [online]. Available at: https://yougov.co.uk/topics/technology/articles-reports/2019/07/03/who-buys-latest-and-greatest-gadgets. [Accessed 20 November 2020].

Felton, M-C., 2014. Self-Publishing in the 18th Century Paris and London. Bodleian Library Bodcast series, 5 June 2014 [online]. Available at: https://podcasts.ox.ac.uk/self-publishing-18th-century-paris-and-london. [Accessed 24 September 2016].

Grădinaru, C., 2016. The Technological Expansion of Sociability: Virtual Communities and Imagined Communities. In *Academicus: International Scientific Journal*, 1 July, No. 14, pp. 181–190. Available at: doi:10.7336/academicus.2016.14.13.

Graham, B. & Paul, C., 2011. Does Higher Education Really Lead to Higher Employability and Wages in the RMI?. Pacific Web [online]. Available at: http://www.pacificweb.org/DOCS/rmi/pdf/Education%20and%20wages.pdf. [Accessed 20 September 2016].

Kemp, S., 2020. Digital In 2020. In *We Are Social* [slideshare]. Available at: https://wearesocial.com/digital-2020. [Accessed 30 September 2020].

Kircher, M.M., 2015. This Woman Wrote One Direction Fanfic on Her Phone and Ended Up with a Major Book Deal. In *Business Insider UK* [online], 28 July. Available at: http://uk.businessinsider.com/anna-todd-earns-book-and-movie-deals-for-one-direction-fan-fiction-2015-7?r=US&IR=T. [Accessed 20 September 2016].

Kovalik, K. & Curwood, J.S. 2019. #poetryisnotdead: understanding Instagram poetry within a transliteracies framework. In *Literacy*. Vol. 53, No. 4, pp. 185–195.

Kretschmer, M., Gavaldon, A.A., Miettinen, J., & Singh, S., 2019. UK Authors' Earnings and Contracts: A Survey of 50,000 Writers. ACLS. Available at: doi:10.5281/zenodo.2649059.

McLuhan, M. 1969. Playboy Interview: A Candid Conversation with the High Priest of Popocult and Metaphysician of Media. In McLuhan, E. & Zingrone, F. (Eds), *Essential McLuhan* (pp. 222–260). London: Taylor & Francis e-Library.

Mittell, J., 2001. A Cultural Approach to Television Genre Theory. In *Cinema Journal*. Vol. 40, No. 3, Spring.

Prensky, M., 2001. Digital Natives, Digital Immigrants Part 1. In *On the Horizon*. Vol. 9, No. 5, pp. 1–6.

Qureshi, H., 2015. How Do I Love Thee? Let Me Instagram It. In *The Guardian* [online], 23 November. Available at: https://www.theguardian.com/books/2015/nov/23/instapoets-instagram-twitter-poetry-lang-leav-rupi-kaur-tyler-knott-gregson. [Accessed 4 October 2016].

Tankovska, H., 2021. Share of Respondents Who Had Set Up Their Own Social Network Profile in the United Kingdom (UK) from 2010–2019, By Socio-economic Group. Statista [online], 25 January. Available at: https://www.statista.com/statistics/271901/social-network-profile-creation-in-the-uk-by-socio-economic-group/. [Accessed 23 March 2021].

Torok, C., 2012. Amazon Review: "Just don't. Unless it's a gift for someone you hate". Amazon. Available at: https://www.amazon.com/review/R3FTHSH0UNRHOH. [Accessed 16 January 2017].

Vrasidas, C. & Veletsianos, G., 2010. Theoretical Foundations of Social Computing and Virtual Communities. In Zaphiris, P. & Ang, C.S. (Eds), *Social Computing and Virtual Communities* (pp. 1–20). Boca Raton: CRC Press.

Wattpad, 2017. Published Samples. Wattpad [online]. Available at: https://www.wattpad.com/44013622-wattpad-stories-published-as-books-pop-fiction. [Accessed 16 January 2017].

5

THE ROLE OF GENDER IN THE DIGITALLY SOCIAL COMMUNITIES

Gender in online communities

Gender plays a key role in how communities in online settings interact. In order to better understand how gender in online communities relates to the role of the citizen author we must look at the spaces the authors inhabit. These include, but are not limited to, social media platforms, fiction repositories, and other digitally social spaces where authors can write, share work, and potentially gain feedback from a digital audience. When we are looking for writing on social platforms, the size of the audience does not affect the roles of citizen authors or readers, and a private blog with one reader is equally as valid as an account on a social media platform with hundreds of thousands of followers. What matters is that people are writing, sharing, and talking about written works in these spaces.

The way people interact in these online spaces relates directly to the ratio of male to female users. And these ratios subtly alter depending on where the evidence is gathered and when. However, there are gendered trends that remain relatively consistent across sources. In 2020, a Statista report into the social media use of the UK by gender found that 84% of women use Facebook vs 73% of men. For Instagram, the gender split was 48% of women and 35% of men (Johnson, 2020).

Data mining into the registered users (authors/readers) of FanFiction.net in 2011 found that 78% of registered accounts were owned by female-identifying users (Fan Fiction Statistics – FFN Research, 2011). Likewise, "the Wattpad demographic [...is] 70% female and very much Millennials and Generation Z" (Williams, 2017).

A citizen author is more likely to be female in reports by other companies like Statisa too. One of the major social media platforms that bucks this female-driven trend is Twitter. In 2016, the UK Gov Poll for taking part found that Twitter is used by 53.3% male and 46.7% female users (DCMS, 2016). However, according to Statista, in the years 2017–2020, Twitter was used by 20–32% of the population

DOI: 10.4324/9781003186649-6

of UK internet users, with 48% identifying as men and 47% identifying as women (Johnson, 2020). Garcia et al. found that "Twitter contains a male bias not only in amount of users, but also in a lower degree of female independence," which may hinder female users from engaging "in the community in the same way as males do" (2014, p. 23).

In the digital community, male and female users behave differently in how they use the space and interact with other users, in that they often imitate the gender norms of the offline world (Miller et al., 2016) with the "dominant ideals of femininity and masculinity" (Miller et al., 2016, p. 116). The gender makeup of the community is one of the main characteristics that "affects the communication norms and community dynamics" (Shen et al., 2017, p. 191), which in turn alters the way the citizen authors and readers interact in these spaces.

In social spaces dominated by people identifying as male, such as Twitter, the mood of the content tends to be more brazen, more about candour and debate with other members in a collective monologue (Shen et al., 2017, p. 185), while on sites that tend to have more female-identifying users, such as FanFiction.net, Wattpad, and Facebook, there is more self-disclosure and direct address of other readers and authors, and an overall sense of encouragement and support (Shen et al., 2017, p. 183) among members. This is due to the fact that, as Shen et al. (2017) suggest, groups with a dominant gender makeup are more likely to adopt the gender norms associated with the dominant gender group (p. 185).[1]

In Wattpad writer Rebecca Sky's *Arrowheart* (Book One of *The Love Curse*), the link between the gender of the commenters and the tone of their comments is apparent from chapter one (the old chapter one, which has remained on Wattpad after Sky got a publishing deal with Hodder Children's Books). The chapter consists of 1,800 overall comments or 'marginalia' (comments written in the margins), with 262 of those in-line on the text itself, which can facilitate conversation between readers (Ramdarshan Bold & Wagstaff, 2017, p. 16). While much of the commentary is about the text and character/plot developments, there were eleven comments about the overarching chapter that are identifiably positive and supportive, as seen in Table 5.1.

These eleven comments are from female-identifying readers.[2] At different points in the chapter, they lift up the author, with four calling the work "amazing." Most of the time, Sky replies directly to the commenters with a heart emoji (<3 or ♥) and/or smiley face emojis where appropriate.

A further example of the gendered tone of interaction within this chapter of *Arrowheart* is seen when reader Dash (identified as a dash mark "–")[3] comments on Sky's grammar and other readers get involved in what could have turned into an ugly example of commenting culture. When occlumence (formerly TopherdeTopher, female identifying) says: "it's rude to point out mistakes" (3 August, 2015).[4] Dash retorts "Seriously? [...] If she has a problem with it, then she can tell me" (4 August, 2015). Once Sky intervened, the commenters apologised to each other with "I'm sorry for fighting with you about something so silly. No hard feelings?" (occlumence, 6 August, 2015). To which Dash replied,

TABLE 5.1 Selection of positive and supportive in-line comments from chapter 1 of Rebecca Sky's *Arrowheart*

Name	Comment
digitalchicktv Mar 09	Amazing opening.
AmethystAmber87 Jan 29	Instant hook.
amandasumrall Mar 08, 2018	I love the British quotes instead of the regular one ms when a character speaks.
nikithanagraj Mar 01, 2018	??? relatable
Sista92359 Feb 17, 2017	YOU SLAY TOO WITH UR WRITING BOO
AJ_Marie_Writes Jun 23, 2016	Er-mer-gerd, Cherlie! Lurve yer prerferl perc! ^__^
DoNotFuryUS12 Jan 07, 2017	@RebeccaSky Lol I know your going to say that, I will by the way its a great book… probably that nist unique book I read so far in wattpad
Icee_Lemon May 13, 2017	Short and sweet message, love it already
Milagrosqkd May 07, 2017	Is amazing
MaddieHorses2003 Jan 25, 2017	So far this is amazing
Renesmie12345 Mar 22, 2017	@RebeccaSky yes it is very amazing so far

No hard feelings. And I apologize if I came across as harsh in my reply. It's just that I remember correcting one author's grammar (they never replied, and I wasn't bagging on their writing), and these girls ganged up and started harassing me. I guess that I can get a little defensive.

(6 August, 2015)

What these examples highlight is that the gendering of these digitally social spaces echoes the gendered nature of the publishing industry, where "although 80 percent of the fiction readers are female, 'the tastemakers, our critics, remain chiefly male'" (Messud, 2014). Tastemakers, in this sense, refers to those within the publishing industry – an industry that has made strides in pushing for gender equality and where most employees are female but where the "representation of females gradually declines as seniority increases" (Publishers Association, 2019). Likewise, the Vida Count in 2019 shows that, for example, *The London Review of Books* reviewed only 32.64% women authors (The Vida Count, 2019). Other major literary publications have similar numbers of male to female content and reviewers.

This disparity in gender in the industry is especially obvious in the genre of science fiction, which is dominated by male writers, who make up 75% of the authors (Lovell, 2016). This is slowly beginning to change, with female authors and female authors of colour winning more awards;[5] however, lists of 'best science fiction books' from Forbidden Planet to MIT's *Technology Review* are heavily dominated by male authors.

Though science fiction skews the demographic of author gender, not all genres are dominated by male writers. In recent years, the genre of crime fiction has seen a growth of female authors, so much so that male writers have begun to adopt female-identifying or gender-neutral pseudonyms in order to tap into the market of majority-female readers (Gamerman, 2017). And these female readers, according to a 2014 Goodreads survey, are 30% more likely to read books by women than they are to read books written by men (Elizabeth, 2014). Furthermore, in almost all genres, readers prefer to read books written by their own gender (Thelwall, 2017).

It is due to the disproportionate ratio of male authors of fiction being traditionally published – some 26% female to 45% male (Weinberg & Kapelner, 2018, p. 10) – and the female audience wanting to read female authors that opportunities open up for digital communities to develop around writing by female-identifying citizen authors which do not have a place in the traditional publishing industry. As female-identifying citizen authors occupy more space in the parts of the global village where groups gather around writing and sharing fiction, they are subverting the traditional publishing industry's hierarchy of gender by actively commoditising their connectivity with readers by creating feedback loops around their work, where "the effects of public self-disclosure on feeling connected are mediated by the received likes and comments" (Utz, 2014, p. 4). This interactivity, in turn, increases the cultural capital of the citizen author's work, bringing in more readers and the potential interest of the publishing industry, which may choose to traditionally publish the citizen author. In this way, the female-identifying citizen author is shifting the power dynamic of the traditional, and traditionally male-dominated,[6] publishing industry embracing the technology available in the digitally global village such as feedback loops, connectivity, and sharing.

Gender's disruption of the book and its relation to the wider industry

Female-identifying citizen authors who interact and develop their works in digitally social spaces can potentially influence non-discursive aspects of the wider industry.[7] In the traditional publishing model, the author's first audience is the gatekeeper of the industry: the agent or the publisher, who are in positions of power. However, part of the disruption the female-identifying citizen author brings into play is their use of the "imagined audience" (Litt & Hargittai, 2016, p. 1), which embodies who they believe they are speaking to when they write and share their works in a digital space and which may not be the same as the actual audience (Litt & Hargittai, 2016, p. 2). For the female-identifying citizen author, the imagined audience to which they write is a conflation of what Litt and Hargittai describe as two of the four types of audiences: "communal ties" and "professional ties" (2016, p. 6). The 'communal ties' are based around hobbies and communities of interest that the female-identifying citizen author actively involves themselves in within the global village, and they make up the bulk of the imagined audience. These communities can be based around styles of writing, genre, or subgenre fiction, to name a few.

The 'communal' audience of readers are those that will interact with the author and give feedback on a work, and they are most likely to be female, as seen in research by Shen et al. (2017) and in the comments on the chapter of Rebecca Sky's *Arrowheart* on Wattpad. At the back of the same female-identifying citizen author's mind is the imagined audience of the 'professional ties.' The audience of professional ties manifests itself as agents, publishers, or other cultural gatekeepers within the publishing industry that could potentially read an author's work in the digital community and pull it back into the hierarchy of the traditional publishing industry. Claire Askew discusses the professional audience she addresses using Twitter:

> on Twitter I definitely self promote. [...] it's one of the best ways to get people to look at my stuff. It's proved again and again to be really effective. And, I've also found a lot of jobs through Twitter. People have got in touch with me through Twitter and direct messages and said, do you want to come and read at Hillhead High School, or do you want to come and do a creative writing workshop with whoever? I get far more job-related stuff come to me through Twitter than I do through any other platform, including email.
>
> *(15 November, 2017)*

She goes on to say that on Twitter she took part in a hashtag submission day where authors were able to submit a small synopsis of their work to a group of gatekeepers consisting of unknown agents and publishers brought together by the Society of Young Publishers in Scotland. She says that "I wrote my 120 Character tweet #XPOB and then both Black and White Publishing and Jenny Brown Associates got in touch and said, 'we like the sound of this, send us your first 50 pages.'"[8]

Similarly, Janet Simpson[9] speaks of using social media to connect with a professional audience: "I run writing courses and consultancy and have probably gained 75–80% of my clients through social media [... M]y social media presence makes it easy for people to find out about my books, and I think it makes me more visible within the industry" (15 February, 2016). Both Askew and Simpson are able to envision and navigate the professional ties that exist in online community spaces and use them to further their careers in the offline world.

In the digital communities that the female-identifying citizen authors choose to inhabit, the 'imagined audience' is often expected, by the author and other members of the community, to be more open with self-disclosure and supportive of the work being shared within that community (Savicki et al., 1996). This support develops when the citizen author chooses an appropriate social platform and digital community in which to take part (such as writing fan fiction on FanFiction.net), and due to the group norms that work as sets of rules that govern how the group functions and delimit acceptable behaviours (Mazambani et al., 2015, p. 151). This adherence to group norms fosters a sense of trust, which itself is a conduct performed by the members, that manifests itself in the favourable environment of the digital community (Bialski & Batorski, 2010, p. 184). An element of writing in the digital community is taking the audience into account and developing relationships with those imagined and actual readers, which may inspire further writing to be developed. If the 'imagined audience' moves from lurking to posting and responding to works, the audience for the citizen author moves into a more tangible realm, and the author can build their digital identity as a writer around these interactions, performing for the known readers while keeping the 'imagined audience' in the back of their mind as an idealised version.

Even "minimal cues to gender are enough to elicit stereotyped responses" (Christofides, 2009, p. 898) in digital communities. Communities wherein members are majority female-identifying foster an openness and intimacy in the potential digital relationships, where "[p]eople cooperate and work reflexively on their identities by mirroring themselves in those around them" (Lindgren, 2017, p. 39), or as Rebecca Sky said in response to the conversation around editing her grammar "It's all love here" (30 June, 2016, see footnote 4).

Working across platforms, a female-identifying citizen author can create multiple accounts, websites, blogs, and connected fictions using hashtags and other linking devices built into the structure of the platforms. Female-identifying citizen authors share their work and interact with readers, who are often female-identifying, creating a "meta-text that evades being tied down by male-centric techniques of surveillance and viewing" (Lyons et al., 2016, p. 10). The ability to take control of their self-representation via social media provides female-identifying citizen authors a means of chipping away at the gendered hierarchy that exists in the traditional publishing industry, and as such they may be "harshly judged by their male peers" (Lyons et al., 2016, p. 10), as work published in digital communities may be marked as being of lesser value culturally than those works printed in paper form, leading to questions of whether 'publishing' means to make available or to make legitimate (Dietz, 2018, p. 125). This idea of online work being lesser or less legitimate is evident when Askew (15 November, 2017) points out that "a lot of people are still snobby about self-publishing [including on platforms such as Wattpad], and don't see it as being as good."

Women are more likely to be part of the 'labours of love' ethos: 'Women's work' and free labour in digital communities

The gendering of social spaces based around fiction creates a community that feels authentic and intimate to the female-identifying inhabitants. The perceived intimacy in a female-dominated sphere creates a safe space where the feedback that is developed is supportive and, to a degree, more personal between the author and reader, such as in the comments on Sky's *Arrowheart*, when Random_056[10] writes, "NEVER throw a girls book" (5 November, 2016) and Sky replies "I like you already! ♥" (5 November, 2016).

It is from this place in the global village that the citizen author changes the idea of what can be a book through "enterprising femininity" (Gray, 2003) that seeks to harness 'women's work' as a cultural and economic capital that exists outside the male-dominated publishing industry.

The idea of 'women's work' is not a new one. It relates to the domestic labour undertaken by women that comes with little cultural capital and rarely any economic returns. The concept of 'women's work' has recently been brought to bear on the idea of free labour and the feminine aspect of prosumerism in a digital realm (Jarrett, 2014), where not only is it performed by the female-identifying citizen authors in the creation of free cultural items but also in the fostering of community in these social spaces. In the role of the citizen author and reader, the work that women are doing relates to the "socially generative layer of value creation – the production of social relationships that reproduce the social order" (Jarrett, 2014, p. 21). While the 'social order' that Jarrett refers to relates to the patriarchal system of the wider global village, within these niche digital communities developed by the coming together of citizen authors and readers, the social order that is developed is specifically female and, as such, disrupts the "hegemonic masculinity" (Connell & Messerschmidt, 2005) of the traditional publishing industry.

By creating relationships that help redefine what a book can be in the digitally social sphere, citizen authors are normalising the place of women in the wider discourse as they actively step around the gatekeeping mechanisms of the industry. The more these disruptions are repeated, the more normalised 'women's work' becomes. This is seen in the way that agents and publishers have begun to actively move the work of the citizen authors away from their digital communities and pull them back into the conventional industry as with works like *Arrowheart*.

As in the traditionally domestic role of 'women's work,' much of the work done by the citizen author and reader is a labour of love, or free labour. Closely related to these concepts of labour of love and free labour is 'affective labour,' defined by Melissa Gregg to be "meaningful and productive human activity that does not result in a direct financial profit or exchange value, but rather produces a sense of community, esteem, and/or belonging for those who share a common interest" (2009, p. 209). The citizen author exists in the fuzzy area between the commercialisation of culture by the industry and the free/affective labour of those working in the digital public. Some citizen authors work in "hope labour" (Kuehn et al., 2013), where they write, share, comment, and build connections online in the hope of gaining some future opportunities related to the industry. These opportunities are not necessarily manifest in the traditional publication of the fiction they have shared online but can potentially be the promise of speaking engagements, paid writing, teaching, or other opportunities brought about by their exposure as a citizen author.

Though the citizen author could potentially receive economic payment for the writing they share via digital communities, many of them, much like the self-published authors identified by Baverstock and Steinitz, share their fiction in order to feel a sense of accomplishment and "socially recognized self-realization" (Arvidsson, 2008, p. 332). Or they do it for the "potential to build an audience" as Marcus Lopés noted in our interview (20 January, 2017). Part of this recognition comes from the interaction with readers, whether it's a reply or comment or just a like or retweet, and the perceived authenticity with which they interact. This all happens through the mediations of the platforms themselves, which can help the citizen author to consider incorporating reader feedback into the next iteration, or extension, of their work (Duffy, 2016, p. 449).

There are other ways that citizen authors thank their readers both online and when/if a book gets traditionally published. For instance, Sky ran a competition to get Wattpad reader reviews published in the print edition of *Arrowheart*. She shared the competition both in a chapter in her Wattpad novel and in a post on her Wattpad page. By engaging with her readers in the digital community, she encouraged them to have a vested interest in the printed version of the work that was originally published online for free, and in doing so as part of her regular interaction with readers, it makes the relationship feel all the more authentic.

Authenticity in digital communities

In the digital communities, verifying the authenticity of participants does not rely as much on matching the online and offline identities as it does on "narratives of authenticity" (Duffy & Hund, 2015, p. 3) presented by a user, which are articulated through the social platform's limitations and those limitations' association to the heteronormativity of societal gender roles. As "[w]e do not know how to behave in a gender-free environment" (O'Brien, 1999, p. 85), one of the ways that the citizen author seeks to create an authentic connection with readers is through the development of a gender identity and a personal narrative that is associated with that identity. Sky does this when she replies directly to reader comments with emojis, friendly words or acronyms like "Lol!" (12 March, 2017) and asks readers questions, as when she asked reader Dash how he left a gif as a comment (26 June, 2016), to which he replied, and they started a brief conversation. These personal narratives are what give the online persona a believability that is necessary for authentic, or perceivably authentic, interactions to develop. Profiles on the platforms facilitate the narratives of authenticity, where the citizen author can share personal details, flaws, favourite items such as books, style of writing, and 'guilty pleasures' that serve to perform a narrative of self to other members of the digital community that makes them more relatable.

Authenticity within social sites can be a part of the branding of a citizen author, a role that allows the author to choose which narratives are performed in relation to gender norms, genre, readers, platform, and the wider industry. This performance is a repetition that shapes the way the citizen author interacts with the digital community, subtly changing in order to more accurately reflect the ethos of that particular community (Shen et al., 2017; Lee et al., 2014). This is reflected, for example, in maintaining a professional author persona on a Twitter page. Author Rachel Thompson (@w_notebook) almost exclusively reviews books and does not interact with other users but used her Twitter page to write her short story "The Other Side of the Glass." This is different to the style of author Marcus Lopés (@MMarcusALopes), who again wrote on the platform (a science fiction thriller) but mostly retweets others who discuss reading and writing, sometimes retweeting tens of times per day. Simon Grant (@FSimonGrant) uses his account to write fiction and to promote his stories across platforms.

All three of these authors on Twitter and Sky on Wattpad keep the brand of the 'authentic writer' at the forefront of their communication online. This communication is part performance, part interacting with readers, and part playing to their imagined audiences of readers, where authenticity and branding become a culturally and economically productive narrative. It is this keeping the self-branding balance between the personal and the private that is "symptomatic of a highly gendered, forward-looking and entrepreneurial enactment of creativity" (Gatson, 2011, p. 224), and it manifests itself in the interactions within the digital community and those interactions' relationships to cultural capital.

If a reader moves from lurking and reading to posting about/commenting on the work of a citizen author, the social platform itself works as an active intermediary in the connectivity (Van Dijck, 2012). This discontinuous interaction mediated by the platform allows the citizen author the opportunity to craft a response that takes into account the reader, as well as the imagined audiences that could potentially read the interaction. In responding to a comment by a reader, the citizen author enters a feedback loop that can then allow for a relationship to develop wherein both participants work to perform themselves in an authentic, or real, manner, to "establish themselves as relatable" (Duffy, 2016, p. 447).

When readers and citizen authors have accepted the authenticity of the other and venture into a reciprocal relationship where the author posts, the reader comments, and the author reacts either by reworking the writing or speaking directly to the reader, sometimes both, the gendered nature of this communication is likely to be more positive and encouraging (Thelwall et al., 2010). In addition, the digital communities where female-identifying citizen authors and readers congregate are more self-revealing, fostering an intimacy between the members, which alters their authenticity and the power dynamics of the interactions (Sheldon, 2013; Shen et al., 2017).

Digital spaces facilitate an intimacy between citizen authors and readers

Performing narratives of authenticity, which are always gendered, in an online community encourages "users to become intimate – or at least simulate intimacy" (Reid, 1999, p. 113) as the open and public nature of the global village shifts the understanding of intimacy from a private to public connection

(Turkle, 2011, p. 172). Here the citizen authors and readers develop relation-ships that feel private and personal, which are played out, at least to begin with, in the public sphere of social platforms. The connections come through the comments sections of blogs, social posts, and reviews, etc., which facilitate a form of intimacy with the author and other readers in the global village and where "private and public messages on SNS [Social Networking Sites] can result in positive relational outcomes" (Utz, 2014, p. 1). In their study on 'circuits of value,' Skeggs and Wood found that:

> The realm of intimacy is one traditionally associated with the feminine private sphere, but various commentators have marked out how public worlds, insti-tutions, and market forces have marshalled the intimate terrain into public spaces for the operation of power.
>
> *(2008, p. 559)*

The varying digital mediums used by citizen authors allow different relationships to develop between the members of the community and the technology. When female-identifying citizen authors and readers come to occupy the same affinity spaces (Lindgren Leavenworth, 2015), the "common identity shared by members is enough to assure their functionality" (Grădinaru, 2016, p. 188). In the commu-nities that are developed around fiction that is written in online social spaces, this common identity around a work influences the way that expected behaviour is balanced with discussions of the work (Pfister & Soliz, 2011). This identity, connec-tion, and expected behaviour can be seen in the comments on the first chapter of *Arrowheart*, where two commenters argue over grammar and resolve their differences civilly. Others comment on the discourse "This was a beautiful conversation" (-,[11] 15 August, 2015) and "if only everyone would handle their problems this civilly" (___Naz,[12] 19 December, 2015).

It is the discussions of the works and the interactions around them that develop a sense of belonging and intimacy among members of a community (Ferreday, 2009, p. 35). Writing, for the citizen authors and the readers who often write to join in with a community online, becomes a social activity that brings into play a "sur-rendered intimacy" (De Certeau, 1984, p. 176) between those who share a space within the community. This sense of intimacy is directly related to the "quality of membership duration" (Lee & Suh, 2015, p. 389), where those who post content frequently may be less intimate than those who post less frequently but still use the interactions to grow relationships both online and off.

The intimacy in a digital community of female-identifying citizen authors and readers is quite different to the traditional industry set up, where the only interac-tion a reader had with an author was relegated to attending public events, where "the spaces we refer to as *public* are assumed to be male [... and s]pace was and continues to be largely defined as a male construct" (McFadden, n.d.).

But, looking at the levels of intimacy fostered in the global village, as opposed to the physical spaces of traditional book and literary events, it becomes apparent that the degrees of separation between author and reader are fewer here. Within the digitally social setting, readers can join in with online conversations with each other and authors. In these online spaces, readers can follow authors' social channels, leave comments, directly message authors, and interact with a community of likeminded readers through technological mediation tailored to the social platform.

By limiting any perceived awkwardness or hierarchical stance between citizen author and reader that may happen in face-to-face conversation, the use of technology allows for an intimacy and increased sharing among group members (Pfeil, 2010, p. 126). The connectivity of the global village "offers new possibilities for experimenting with identity" (Turkle, 2011, p. 152) and its relationship to authenticity, where on social platforms writers are able to take on a role of their avatar/username as they see it and can "end up being [...themselves] in the most revealing ways" (Turkle, 2011, p. 153). This enables the citizen authors to develop their identities as writers within the community. In their "surrendered intimacy", a citizen author has the freedom to test their writing among a dominantly female, supportive audience of readers that exist wholly outside of the traditional, masculine, publishing mechanism.

This can lead to feedback between citizen author and reader, which can be taken on board when the author edits and shares their work, such as when Sky takes on board grammatical suggestions in the user comments of her work. When readers notice that their suggestions and commentary on the work may be taken into consideration, either through direct interaction with the author or in seeing the changes in the work itself, the "readers gradually begin to reciprocate the [felt] intimacy as their comments move from being directed to the story" (Lindgren Leavenworth, 2015, p. 108) to include a wider range of content outside of strictly writing-based interplay.

The feeling of intimacy between citizen authors and readers induces feelings of comfort and camaraderie in the digital community, as Wellman and Gulia note, "[e]ven when online groups are not designed to be supportive, they tend to be" (1999, p. 173). Spaces like Wattpad, Facebook, Instagram, and Twitter enable readers to both ask questions and feedback positively on the work/section. In *Arrowheart*'s comments, a reader asked how many specific characters have a superpower and Sky replied that the reader would need to read to find out. The reader, DoNotFuryUS12,[13] replied, light-heartedly, "@RebeccaSky Lol I know your going to say that, I will by the way its a great book...probably the nist unique book I read so far in wattpad [sic]" (7 January, 2017).

The ability to speak directly to a reader and engage with them over a shared interest in a written work not only ties the citizen author to the reader but it has the potential to bring in others as the reader shares content that interests them. This links back to the technology-based focus on the end user and user design. In social repositories such as Wattpad and Medium, among many others, citizen authors interact with their readers, vying for view numbers, answering comments, and thrive on keeping "in touch with their audiences whilst writing their books and obtain[ing] feedback on material and plotlines" (Phillips, 2014). Which leads

Phillips to remark that "If a potential reader has been involved early on, they will be more likely to buy the final product" (2014) should a work of fiction written on a social repository site be picked up by a publishing company for a traditional release.

As Turkle notes, at some point "when technology engineers intimacy, relationships can be reduced to mere connections" (2011, p. 16), and in the digital environment, one can be intimate without being authentic. When these relationships become less than ideal, there is a safety net where the user can dismiss the digital community as "not really real" (Ferreday, 2009, p. 41) and retreat to the offline world (Fernback, 1997, pp. 37–38). This can happen when a citizen author goes outside the expectations of a reader, such as those authors who ignore the unspoken rules around genre fictions and how they should be structured. The potential tension inherent in the interactions within the digital communities brings to the fore questions about who in these communities has the authority to speak and from what position. This leads to questions of what can be said in these spaces that are not governed by the wider industry.

Exploration without boundaries in digital communities

Though the digital communities that are built on social platforms can be censored by the platforms themselves, female-identifying citizen authors are choosing to write and share fiction in these spaces due to their lack of governance from the publishing industry. Using social platforms to create and form relationships with readers allows citizen authors to develop a cultural economy that relies on connectivity (feminine) rather than economic (masculine) gain. When a citizen author is no longer actively seeking to join the wider industry, they have the freedom to create works that do not conform to the socio-economic discourse of publishing. Some of these works fall into genres that are often dominated by men, such as science fiction, while others, such as fan fiction, tend to be written predominately by women.

Within genres, generally, there are gender biases at work that influence the power dynamic within each subculture. Jenkins writes about fans' gendered reception of a work and in the writing of fan fiction, concluding that females involved with fan fiction get more invested in the world and the relationships built around it, while males focus more on the process and the movement of the narrative (1992, p. 110). "Authorship, publication, copyright, and paid writing [is thought of] as masculinized, commercialized, and 'legitimate,' and fan fiction, the 'gift economy,' and hobbies as feminized, free labors of love, that either reject or must fight for elusive (and undefined) legitimacy" (Flegel & Roth, 2014, p. 1094).

In actively avoiding the traditional publishing model, a female-identifying citizen author subverts the idea of 'legitimacy' as linked to paid authorship and ownership of copyright – which I argue are masculine traits – by using the digitally social technology available to them to write directly within the global village for an audience of readers who may also serve as a feedback loop. In doing so, the power dynamic of the publishing industry shifts away from the agents and publishers and moves to the readers and the citizen authors of genre fictions and the platforms on which these works are shared.

When looking at the three works that were located and tagged #Twitterfiction, the ratio of gender is of interest, as it supports the two-thirds male to female ratio as a base rate for the male/female split of traditionally published science fiction books. However, if we take into account the gender ratio of the citizen author, which is likely to be mostly female, then the gender of Grant, Thompson, and Lopés do not support this. Similarly, if we look at the nine authors who wrote prolifically with the #Twitterfiction hashtag in 2016, the ratio remains 2:1 men to women. However, in the context of Twitter, this ratio makes sense.

Looking at the content of their tweets in relation to gender, Thompson's story was concise, easy to follow, and fit most neatly into the genre tropes of science fiction. She also consistently tagged her works with #Scifi and #Twitterfiction in order to anchor the story in an identifiable stream and to give readers a sense of what to expect from the story. Thompson's use of the #Blog to highlight that she has other writing outwith Twitter shows that as a citizen author she is actively reaching out to readers and inviting them to explore more of her writing. Much like Thompson, Lopés was consistent in his tagging with the #Twitterfiction hashtag, but he did not tag his story with the genre, nor did he lead the readers to other locations to find his work, even though he has a writing-based Instagram account as well as a fan page on Facebook (20 January, 2017). Using the #Twitterfiction hashtag, Grant only directed his readers to the follow up to his work on Facebook once in 687 tweets, far less than Thompson, who linked readers to her blog four times in sixty-four tweets. Lopés only shared one link outward in the 629 tweets of his multi-part Twitter story. This link led to a short story on Facebook, one that had already been shared on Twitter.

Tweet for tweet, Thompson was the most active in seeking to invite readers to engage with her other in other ways, with 15% of her tweets mentioning or linking to her blog, whereas Lopés and Grant[14] had far less outreach with .001% and .002% of tweets linking elsewhere or mentioning other digital spaces to interact. This indicates that female-identifying citizen authors on Twitter are more likely to move their readers into a space that they as authors feel more comfortable and free interacting in, such as more 'intimate' blogs. In doing so, citizen authors like Thompson are directing how and where their work is shared and who has control over the work itself in a space that sits outside the publishing industry.

Other genres that have found wider audiences in digital communities are the areas of romance and erotica. Though romances are the "most widely read genre in commercial fiction" (Lois & Gregson, 2015, p. 460), they have a sense of shame and embarrassment attached to them in the printed format (Lois & Gregson, 2015). They are also genres that are traditionally associated with having female writers and readers. Those who are not fans of the genres often express disapproval of their stories, content, and styles, and they consider these genres open for derision (Lois & Gregson, 2015). Through the use of the digital communities that are built around common interests in erotica and romance, the mostly female-identifying citizen authors and readers can exist in safe spaces where their shared enjoyment of these genres and subgenres is allowed to grow and thrive.

In specialised communities and repositories, authors and readers can explore topics in these genres that would be unavailable and commercially unviable for the traditional industry to take on. In addition, highly specialised communities built around niche subgenres can be closed off, with access being granted to those community members who seek them out and have a claim to authenticity. The ability to build communities and to thrive in the global village allows citizen authors to harness the power to actively disrupt the hierarchisation of literature, which is built on a "gender-based hierarchy with men at the top [... where] men and masculinity are ascribed a higher value than women and femininity" (Pauli, 2015, p. 195).

Women have the authority to speak

As female-identifying citizen authors are actively moving beyond the hierarchy of the traditional publishing industry, they are able to bring new definitions of the book into existence. These new definitions are directly related to the female-oriented digital communities that have developed around commonalities between the citizen authors and the readers. It is in these spaces that the works written by citizen authors are reaching and engaging audiences beyond the discourse provided by the print or digital book.

Female-identifying citizen authors are the ones most likely to be marginalised by the publishing industry and to use social platforms to share their work and interact with readers. In their active bypassing of the author-agent-publisher route, they connect directly to their audience and often enter into feedback loops with the (mostly female) readers who can help them hone their work and potentially reach a wider audience. It is this active engagement with the digital community that gives the citizen author the power to create new understandings of the book and to decide which of those definitions get shared.

The rise of the citizen author and its relationship to the gender balance of social media and genre fictions highlights how the shifting of power dynamics within the publishing industry is being pushed through by those who are most often involved in the gift economy of writing and sharing online. By bypassing the gatekeepers of the publishing industry, with its surplus of male authors, the citizen authors are using innovative ways to reach their audience directly and in large numbers. Whether in general fiction, science fiction, fan fiction, or niche subculture writing, it is the connectivity and community that is developed around texts that are written and shared by citizen authors in a digitally social setting that creates relationships within the global village and helps to delimitate the framework of the genres, alters the power dynamic in the industry, and provides a place of development for what a book can be.

In these digital communities that exist outwith the traditional publishing model, it is the "presented gender that shapes the social interactions and dynamics" (Shen et al., 2017, p. 183). These dynamics play out in the communication between citizen authors and readers, in that those who present a female presence online, whether by avatar, name, or checked and visible box on a social profile, position themselves in a more accessible and supportive place in relation to a female-identifying citizen author.

Female-occupied spaces online can feel "very safe," says Askew (15 November, 2017). The different digital platforms enable female-identifying users to feel more or less safe in proportion to the gender balance in those communities, which Shen et al. note "affects the communication norms" (2017, p. 191). Those spaces that have more female-identifying members are more likely to take on the understood communicative norms of those members, and in turn will feel more supportive, intimate, and safe. This sense of safety allows for an openness of communication between readers and citizen authors around works of fiction.

The discussions that can develop between the readers and the citizen authors can influence the way a work progresses or is received by the wider community. By occupying a gendered role of advisor, reader, editor, and promoter, the reader has the potential to alter the trajectory of that work in the non-discursive industry by increasing the numbers of views and interactions that are of interest to the traditional publishing industry in relation to potential markets.

Notes

1 Researchers such as Pedersen and Smithson (2013) found that on popular social network Mumsnet "new forms of femininities are emerging online and a clear-cut binary divide between make and female behaviour can no longer be applied" (p. 97). However, they also note that there is a use of frank language, witty replies, and some abrasiveness – often seen as masculine traits in online spaces – have become something that Mumsnet is known for. This is an important forum in the study of gendered communities and communication in online spaces, but as the community is more closed off than those of Facebook, Twitter, Instagram, etc. (in that mumsnet has a very specific target demographic based in and around being mothers), they are not included in this research, but could be in future continuations of this study.

2 Female-identifying insomuch that their avatars, names, and their own Wattpad profiles, and linked social media and/or websites identify them as female.

3 This user has since deleted their account, but their earlier commentary reads as male: "I'm out, I need a manly story" (11 December, 2016) and "Lol yeah I think I'm outta here. This website is for girls and their... Romance (yuck)" (12 December, 2016). See https://www.wattpad.com/1497321-arrowheart-the-love-curse-one/page/5/comment/1392089621/replies/1799123303 [accessed 28 April 2018].

4 For this comment thread see: wattpad.com/1497321/comment/489392002/replies/495807961 [accessed 28 April 2018].

5 In 2020, Arkady Martine won the 2020 Hugo Award for Best Novel, Nnedi Okorafor won Best Graphic History or Comic, Ana Grilo and Thea James won Best Fanzine, and R.F. Kuang won the award for Best New Writer (not a Hugo).

6 This, much like the gender dynamics in science fiction, is beginning to change, with more females dominating the list of literary prizes and being published across the board. However, Juliet Lapidos notes in her article in *The Atlantic* that men are "abandoning the field of literature as its commercial prospects plummet" (2020).

7 While this research focuses solely on the gendering of digitally social spaces where authors and readers come together, it should be noted that other factors can and do shape online encounters. Sexuality, race, and socio-economic status, among other considerations, influence social media use and choice of platforms. Scholars such as boyd (2012), Hargittai (2012), and Wilson III and Costanza-Chock (2012) have shown that users of different ethnic backgrounds have varied experiences in online spaces – including what boyd called 'white flight' from social platforms. Similarly, Fekete (2019)

explores how platforms such as Foursquare leave African American tracts in cities virtually invisible. Hargittai further highlights the diversity in the way social platforms are used based on socio-economic backgrounds and the education levels of users and their families. Not only are ethnicity, socio-economic status, and education significant in the user experience and interaction in online communities, so too is sexuality. De Ridder (2017) and Davis (2018) both explore the ways an understanding of sexuality is shaped in digitally social spaces, while MacAulay and Moldes (2016), Cavalcante (2016), and Tan (2016) focus on aspects of representation of the LBGTQ+ digital communities.

8 Askew was successful in this and the book she pitched, *All the Hidden Truths*, was published by Hodder and Stoughton in August 2018.
9 Pseudonym of a bestselling, award-winning novelist.
10 Female identifying. See comment thread: https://www.wattpad.com/1497321-arrowheart-the-love-curse-one/page/7/comment/1293996630 [accessed 28 April 2018].
11 Dash. See comment thread: https://www.wattpad.com/1497321-arrowheart-the-love-curse-one/page/7/comment/489392002/replies/671334009 [accessed 28 April 2018].
12 Female-identifying. See comment thread: https://www.wattpad.com/1497321-arrowheart-the-love-curse-one/page/7/comment/489392002/replies/671334009 [accessed 28 April 2018].
13 Gender neutral. See comment thread: https://www.wattpad.com/1497321-arrowheart-the-love-curse-one/page/7/comment/2095974490/replies/1614919534 [accessed 28 April 2018].
14 Within the segment of his work collected for this book. In 2020–2021 Grant was using his Twitter feed to link to more works on Facebook and other platforms.

Bibliography

Arvidsson, A., 2008. The Ethical Economy of Customer Coproduction. In *Journal of Macromarketing*. Vol. 28, No. 4, pp. 326–338.

Askew, C., 2017. Interviewed by Miriam Johnson [email].

Bialski, P. & Batorski, D., 2010. In Zaphiris, P. & Ang, C.S. (Eds), *Social Computing and Virtual Communities* (pp. 179–204). Boca Raton: CRC Press.

boyd, d., 2012. White Flight in Networked Publics: How Race and Class Shaped American Teen Engagement with Myspace and Facebook. In Nakamura, L. & Chow-White, P. (Eds), *Race After the Internet* (pp. 203–222). New York and London: Routledge.

Cavalcante, A., 2016. "I Did It All Online:" Transgender Identity and the Management of Everyday Life. In *Critical Studies in Media Communication*. Vol. 33, No. 1, pp. 109–122. Available at: DOI: doi:10.1080/15295036.2015.1129065.

Christofides, E., Islam, T., & Desmarais, S., 2009. Gender Stereotyping over Instant Messenger: The Effects of Gender and Context. In *Computers in Human Behavior*. Vol. 25, pp. 987–901.

Connell, R.W. & Messerschmidt, J.W., 2005. Hegemonic Masculinity: Rethinking the Concept. In *Gender and Society*. Vol. 19, No. 6 (December), pp. 829–859.

Davis, S., 2018. Objectification, Sexualization, and Misrepresentation: Social Media and the College Experience. In *Social Media + Society*. Available at: DOI: doi:10.1177/2056305118786727.

DCMS, 2016. Taking Part Focus On: Social Media, Statistical Release. DCMS [online]. Available at: https://assets.publishing.service.gov.uk/government/uploads/system/uploads/attachment_data/file/519678/Social_media_-_FINAL.pdf. [Accessed 2017].

De Certeau, M., 1984. *The Practice of Everyday Life*. Berkeley: University of California Press.

De Ridder, S., 2017. Social Media and Young People's Sexualities: Values, Norms, and Battlegrounds. In *Social Media + Society*. Available at: DOI: doi:10.1177/2056305117738992.

Dietz, L., 2018. The Short Story and Digital Media. In Delaney, P. & Hunter, A. (Eds), *The Edinburgh Companion to the Short Story in English* (pp. 125–144). Edinburgh: University of Edinburgh Press.

Duffy, B., 2016. The Romance of Work: Gender and Aspirational Labour in the Digital Culture Industries. In *International Journal of Cultural Studies*. Vol. 19, No. 4, pp. 441–457.

Duffy, B. & Hund, E., 2015. "Having it All" on Social Media: Entrepreneurial Femininity and Self-Branding Among Fashion Bloggers. In *Social Media + Society*, pp. 1–11.

Elizabeth, 2014. Sex and Reading: A Look at Who's Reading Whom. Goodreads [online]. Available at: https://www.goodreads.com/blog/show/475-sex-and-reading-a-look-a t-who-s-reading-whom. [Accessed 3 October 2016].

Fan Fiction Statistics – FFN Research, 2011. Fan Fiction Demographics in 2010: Age, Sex, Country. In *FFN Research* [online]. Available at: http://ffnresearch.blogspot.co.uk/. [Accessed 3 October 2016].

Fernback, J., 1997. The Individual Within the Collective: Virtual Ideology and the Realization of Collective Principles. In Jones, S. (Ed.), *Virtual Culture: Identity and Communication in Cybersociety* (pp. 36–54). London: Sage Publications.

Fekete, E., 2019. Race and (Online) Sites of Consumption. In *Geographical Review*. Vol. 105, No. 4, pp. 472–491. Available at: DOI: doi:10.1111/j.1931-0846.2015.12106.x.

Ferreday, D., 2009. *Online Belongings: Fantasy, Affect and Web Communities*. Oxford: Peter Lang.

Flegel, M. & Roth, J., 2014. Legitimacy, Validity, and Writing for Free: Fan Fiction, Gender, and the Limits of (Unpaid) Creative Labor. In *The Journal of Popular Culture*. Vol. 47, No. 6, pp. 1092–1108.

Gamerman, E., 2017. These Guys Don't Care If You Think They're Women. In *The Wall Street Journal*, 18 July, p. A1.

Garcia, D., Weber, I. & Garimella, V., 2014. *Gender Asymmetries in Reality and Fiction: The Bechdel Test of Social Media*. Proceedings of the 8th International Conference on Weblogs and Social Media, ICWSM. Ann Arbor, Michigan.

Gatson, S., 2011. Self-Naming Practices on the Internet: Identity, Authenticity, and Community. In *Cultural Studies ↔ Critical Methodologies*. Vol. 11, No. 2, pp. 224–235.

Grădinaru, C., 2016. The Technological Expansion of Sociability: Virtual Communities and Imagined Communities. In *Academicus: International Scientific Journal*. Vol. 14 (1 July), pp. 181–190. Available at: doi:10.7336/academicus.2016.14.13.

Gray, A., 2003. Enterprising Femininity: New Modes of Work and Subjectivity. In *European Journal of Cultural Studies*. Vol. 6, No. 4, pp. 489–506.

Gregg, M., 2009. Learning to (Love) Labour: Production Cultures and the Affective Turn. In *Communication and Critical/Cultural Studies*. Vol. 6, No. 2, pp. 209–214. Available at: doi:10.1080/14791420902868045.

Hargittai, E., 2012. Open Doors, Closed Spaces? Differentiated Adoption of Social Network Sites by User Background. In Nakamura, L. & Chow-White, P. (Eds), *Race After the Internet* (pp. 223–245). New York and London: Routledge.

Jarrett, K., 2014. The Relevance of "Women's Work": Social Reproduction and Immaterial Labour in Digital Media. In *Television and New Media*. Vol. 15, No. 1, pp. 14–29.

Jenkins, H., 1992. *Textual Poachers: Television Fans & Participatory Culture*. New York: Routledge.

Johnson, J., 2020. Penetration of Social Networks in the United Kingdom (UK) 2018, By Gender. Statista. Available at: https://www.statista.com/statistics/611848/penetratio n-of-social-networks-in-the-united-kingdom-by-gender/. [Accessed 9 December 2020].

Kuehn, K., Newport, C., & Corrigan, T., 2013. Hope Labour: The Role of Employment Prospects in Online Social Production. In *The Political Economy of Communication*. Vol. 1, No. 1, pp. 9–25.

Lapidos, J., 2020. There is a Culture Industry that Gives its Top Prizes to Women. In *The Atlantic*, 14 January [online]. Available at: theatlantic.com/ideas/archive/2020/01/where-women-make-blockbusters/604867/. [Accessed November 2020].

Lee, J., Nass, C., & Bailenson, J., 2014. Does the Mask Govern the Mind? Effects of Arbitrary Gender Representation of Quantitative Task Performance in Avatar-Represented Virtual Groups. In *Cyberpsychology, Behavior, and Social Networking*. Vol. 17, pp. 248–254.

Lee, J. & Suh, A., 2015. How Do Virtual Community Members Develop Psychological Ownership and What Are the Effects of Psychological Ownership in Virtual Communities? In *Computers in Human Behavior*. Vol. 45, pp. 382–391. Available at: doi:10.1016/j.chb.2014.12.002.

Lindgren, S., 2017. *Digital Media & Society*. London: Sage Publications.

Lindgren Leavenworth, M., 2015. Reader, Please Follow Me: Fan Fiction, Author Instructions, and Feedback. In *Human IT*. Vol. 13, No. 1, pp. 100–127.

Litt, E. & Hargittai, E., 2016. The Imagined Audience on Social Networks Sites. In *Social Media + Society*. (January–March), pp. 1–12.

Lois, J., & Gregson, J., 2015. Sneers and Leers: Romance Writers and Gendered Sexual Stigma. In *Gender & Society*. Vol. 29, No. 4 (August), pp. 459–483.

Lopés, M., 2017. Interview on Publishing and Social Media. Interviewed by Miriam Johnson [email].

Lovell, B., 2016. Friday Essay: Science Fiction's Women Problem. In *The Conversation*. Available at: https://theconversation.com/friday-essay-science-fictions-women-problem-58626. [Accessed 1 December 2020].

Lyons, A., Goodwin, I., Griffin, C., McCreanor, T. & Barnes, H.M., 2016. Facebook and the Fun of Drinking Photos: Reproducing Gendered Regimes of Power. In *Social Media + Society*. (October–December), pp. 1–13.

MacAulay, M., & Moldes, M.D., 2016. Queen Don't Compute: Reading and Casting Shade on Facebook's Real Names Policy, Critical Studies. In *Media Communication*. Vol. 33, No. 1, pp. 6–22. Available at: DOI: doi:10.1080/15295036.2015.1129430.

Mazambani, G., Carlson, M., Reysen, S., & Hempelmann, C., 2015. Impact of Status and Meme Content on the Spread of Memes in Virtual Communities. In *Human Technology*. Vol. 11, No. 2, pp. 148–164.

McFadden, P., n.d. Why Women's Spaces Are Critical to Feminist Autonomy. In *Isis International: International Feminist Advocacy Organisation*. Available at: http://www.isiswomen.org/index.php?option=com_content&view=article&id=630:why-womens-spaces-are-critical-to-feminist-autonomy&catid=127&Itemid=452. [Accessed 1 June 2020].

Messud, C., 2014. Gender and Fiction: A Turning Point in the 21st Century. In *Radcliffe Magazine* [online]. [Link unavailable].

Miller, D., Costa, E., Haynes, N., McDonald, T., Nicolescu, R., Sinanan, J., Spyer, J., Venkatraman, S., & Wang, X., 2016. Gender. In *How the World Changed Social Media* (pp. 114–127), 1st ed., vol. 1. London: UCL Press. Available at: www.jstor.org/stable/j.ctt1g69z35.15. [Accessed 15 June 2020].

O'Brien, J., 1999. Writing in the Body: Gender (Re)Production in Online Interaction. In Smith, M. & Kollock, P. (Eds), *Communities in Cyberspace* (pp. 75–106). London: Routledge.

Pauli, K.S., 2015. Gender Theory and the Family Business. In Nordqvist, M.*et al.* (Eds), *Theoretical Perspectives on Family Businesses* (pp. 191–210). Cheltenham: Edward Elgar Publishing.

Pfeil, U., 2010. Online Support Communities. In Zaphiris, P. & Ang, C.S. (Eds), *Social Computing and Virtual Communities* (pp. 121–150). Boca Raton: CRC Press.

Pfister, D.S. & Soliz, J., 2011. (Re)Conceptualizing Intercultural Communication in a Networked Society. In *Journal of International and Intercultural Communication*. Vol. 4, No. 4, pp. 246–251.

Phillips, A., 2014. *Turning the Page: The Evolution of the Book*. New York: Routledge.

Publishers Association, 2019. *UK Publishing Industry Diversity and Inclusion Survey 2019* [online]. Available at: file:///Users/miriamj/Downloads/Diversity-Survey-of-Pu blishing-Workforce-2019.pdf. [Accessed November 2020].

Ramdarshan Bold, M. & Wagstaff, K., 2017. Marginalia in the Digital Age: Are Digital Reading Devices Meeting the Needs of Today's Readers? In *Library & Information Science Research*. Vol. 39, No. 1, pp. 16–22.

Reid, E., 1999. Hierarchy and Power: Social Control in Cyberspace. In Smith, M. & Kollock, P. (Eds), *Communities in Cyberspace* (pp. 107–134). London: Routledge.

Savicki, V., Kelley, M. & Lingenfelter, D., 1996. Gender and Small Task Group Activity Using Computer Mediated Communication. In *Computers in Human Behavior*. Vol. 12, No. 2, pp. 209–224.

Sheldon, P., 2013. Examining Gender Differences in Self-disclosure on Facebook versus Face-to-Face. In *Journal of Social Media in Society*, Vol. 2, No. 1, pp. 89–106.

Shen, K., Zhao, F., & Kalifa, M., 2017. Dural Identity Process for Virtual Community Participation and Impact of Gender Composition. In *Internet Research* [e-journal], Vol. 27 No. 2, pp. 182–198. Available at: https://doi/10.1108/IntR-06-2015-0166/full/html.

Simpson, J. 2016. Interview on Publishing and Social Media. Interviewed by Miriam Johnson [email].

Skeggs, B. & Wood, H., 2008. The Labour of Transformation and Circuits of Value 'Around' Reality Television. In *Continuum: Journal of Media & Cultural Studies*. Vol. 22, No. 4, pp. 559–572.

Tan, J., 2016. Aesthetics of Queer Becoming: Comrade Yue and Chinese Community-Based Documentaries Online. In *Critical Studies in Media Communication*. Vol. 33, No. 1, pp. 38–52. Available at: DOI: doi:10.1080/15295036.2015.1129064.

Thelwall, M., 2017. Reader and Author Gender and Genre in Goodreads. In *Journal of Librarianship and Information Science*. Vol. 51, No. 2, pp. 403–430. Available at: https://doi. org/10.1177/0961000617709061.

Thelwall, M., Wilkinson, D. & Uppal, S., 2010. Data Mining Emotion in Social Network Communication: Gender Differences in Myspace. In *Journal of the American Society for Information Science and Technology*. Vol. 61, No. 1, pp. 190–199. Available at: doi:10.1002/asi.21180.

The Vida Count, 2019. The Vida Count. Vida: Women in Literary Arts. Available at: http s://www.vidaweb.org/the-count/2019-vida-count/. [Accessed 8 December 2020].

Turkle, S., 2011. *Alone Together: Why We Expect More from Technology and Less From Each Other*. New York: Basic Books.

Utz, S., 2014. The Function of Self-Disclosure on Social Network Sites: Not Only Intimate, but Also Positive and Entertaining Self-Disclosures Increase the Feeling of Connection. In *Computers in Human Behavior* [online]. Available at: http://dx.doi.org/10.1016/j.chb.2014. 11.076. [Accessed 19 November 2016].

Van Dijck, J., 2012. Facebook and the Engineering of Connectivity: A Multi-layered Approach to Social Media Platforms. In *Convergence: The International Journal of Research Into New Media Technologies*. Vol. 19, No. 2, pp. 141–155.

Weinberg, D., & Kapelner, A., 2018. Comparing Gender Discrimination and Inequality in Indie and Traditional Publishing. In *PLOS One* [online]. Available at: https://doi.org/10. 1371/journal.pone.0195298.

Wellman, B. & Gulia, M., 1999. Virtual Communities as Communities: Net Surfers Don't Ride Alone. In Smith, M. & Kollock, P. (Eds), *Communities in Cyberspace* (pp. 167–194). London: Routledge.

Williams, M., 2017. Wattpad Insights. In *The New Publishing Standard* [online]. Available at: https://thenewpublishingstandard.com/2017/10/27/wattpad-insights/. [Accessed 24 March 2021].

WilsonIII, E. & Costanza-Chock, S., 2012. New Voices on the Net? The Digital Journalism Divide and the Costs of Network Exclusion. In Nakamura, L. & Chow-White, P. (Eds), *Race After the Internet* (pp. 246–268). New York and London: Routledge.

6

GENRE FICTION IS LEADING THE WAY

The concept of genre is useful as a taxonomy that provides a framework to explore the relationship between power and the authority to define a book, or a genre. Some of the most useful genres to focus on are science fiction and fan fiction. These genres both have a slightly subversive nature that creates a push and pull in the power dynamic within the industry. Both science and fan fictions are considered less privileged than literary fiction (Roberts, 2007). As such, they enable the writers in these genres to benefit from the invisibility within the industry that the genre provides, allowing more freedom in writing when they do not need to appeal to the traditional gatekeepers.

Defining genre

In order to understand what is meant by genre here, it is important to first situate genre studies in the wider discourse of the book. To do this, we must go beyond the categorising of texts as based on historical and repetitious constructs (Owen, 2007, p. 1391) and explore the ways a text can move and change with the accumulation of the knowledge of the reader, where it exists in history, as well as the rhetorical and structural repetitions that help to classify it as a particular genre.

As citizen authors write genre fiction on social platforms, they are developing their own structural guidelines to how those genres may be used in that social sphere, at that particular point in time. Building on this, we should consider genre to be a dynamic framework that shifts according to its series of recurrences and its relationship to the writer, reader, and the definition of the book. Furthermore, genres can be considered "'*historical families*'" (Frow, 2007, p. 1629) and as such are historical values that are rooted in the time they are developed, changing according to the social structures around them which allow certain characteristics of genres to be repeated and canonised into a particular genre, such as science or fan fictions.

DOI: 10.4324/9781003186649-7

It is through retrospective framing that the constructs of a genre within a historical period can be recognised and applied. New genres that benefit from the rise of the citizen author and the use of social technology continue to rely on the recognisable features of traditional print-based genres in order for them to be classified and understood within new platforms. Retrospective framing as a way to move traditional genres into a new, digitally social format provides the authors, readers, and the industry itself, with the understanding of where genre fits in relation to a traditionally recognisable canon. This provides inexplicit guidelines for those within the industry to create, share, and market works based on historically accepted frameworks that carry over into new technology. However, it must be noted that genres are not necessarily stable and can "evolve and decay" (Collin, 2012, p. 80) over time. It is this use of retrospective framing that allows a work to be seen at a particular point, within the context that surrounds it.

How genre works in discourse

The use of tropes, themes, terminology, etc. creates the frame of a particular genre through their repeated use. According to Miller, the "typified rhetorical actions based in recurrent situations" (1984, p. 159) define the properties of a genre. Its "repeatable materiality" (Foucault, 1989, p. 102) informs how a text gains its status as a book within a genre, how it is limited by the other books around it, the domain in which it can circulate, and by what roles it can perform within those limitations imposed by the framework of a particular genre (Foucault, 1989, p. 103).

Genres are not closed systems impervious to change. They do not have hard edges that define the outer limits of what can be included within them, and there are several different components that are used to define the generic properties of a text, which depend on the reader's perception and the text's acceptance into a literary canon. Instead of prescribing to a set of guidelines as to what constitutes particular genres, it is useful to engage with what Rieder calls a "fuzzy set" (2010, p. 194) that includes elements across a range of characteristics, where some texts may have all the characteristics and others only a few. However, this use of "fuzzy set" identification of genre elements could be impossible to exhaust, lumping in texts with all or only one element that is identified with a particular genre. As such, the width of the fuzzy set will be tempered by structures that identify how a text gained its status within that genre, how it interacts with those around it, the domain it inhabits, and what roles it can perform.

Though it is useful to know what characteristics allow a text to be included within a genre in a particular slice of history, it is, perhaps, more important to understand which texts have been excluded from a genre classification and why. It is this point of exclusion where changes begin to occur that allows new genres to develop.

The point of rupture, the rise of genre

Although there are numerous ways that we can map the breadth of genre fiction, the focus here is on the places where citizen authors are writing works of genre fiction on social media and the way that challenges what is traditionally considered to be a book. Broderick defines science fiction as "that species of storytelling native to a culture undergoing the epistemic changes implicated in the rise and suppression of technical-industrial modes of production, distribution, consumption and disposal" (1995, p. 157). This is also relevant for fan fiction. The growth of digitally social technology and the low barriers of entry into the publishing process for a citizen author who wishes to use these new modes of "production, distribution, consumption and disposal" in the global village develop into a new way of writing and connecting in the digital age that bypasses the traditional publishing industry and allows these often marginalised genres to flourish.

Across social platforms, there are more genres and subgenres represented than there are within the traditional publishing model (Khan, qtd. in Herman, 2014). This is due to the publishing industry having a series of gatekeepers in the form of self-censoring, agents, publishers, and to an extent, marketers and booksellers. Compared to the standard process of getting a text published via traditional publishers, which could take up to three years if it goes into hardback production first, and a minimum of a year for straight to paperback editions, the connectivity of the global village, and social media platforms in particular, allows for nearly instantaneous sharing of work with a wider audience (Clark & Phillips, 2008, p. 17).

Unlike the traditional publishing model, writing on digitally social platforms has a low barrier of entry. As such, this highlights the rise in certain types of fictions that have traditionally been marginalised by the gatekeepers of the publishing industry. To address the questions around which genres do *not* come into being in these new communities, the focus here remains on science and fan fictions, both of which have found a niche market online in social spaces and proliferate in the absence of more 'literary' fiction. This invisibility of being outside the gates of the industry allows these two genres to be more malleable and wide-reaching, leading to a large variety of texts that can be included in the fuzzy set of the genres and potentially pulled back into the publishing hierarchy.

One such place where the rise of genre fiction is noticeable is on Twitter, with the hashtag #Twitterfiction. When scraped in 2016, there were 7,879 total tweets with that hashtag. And of the three authors who were found to have written complete and unique works of fiction on the social platform, all three were of the science fiction genre and followed tropes such as space travel, aliens, or the super-powers of the characters. Likewise, on Wattpad, there are 211,000 stories tagged 'science fiction,' 113,000 'sciencefiction,' 202,000 'scifi,' 929,000 'fantasy,' and 242,000 tagged 'future.' By contrast, there are only 3,300 stories tagged 'literary fiction' and 107,000 for 'literaryfiction.'[1]

The second genre of interest, which has come into its own as the "advent of the internet has broadened its reach" (Johnson, 2016, p. 1646) is fan fiction. Fan fiction often finds itself "unauthorized but tolerated" (Tushnet, 2007, p. 137) as a subgenre of fiction that uses worlds, characters, themes, and other elements of a previously published work (any form of media such as print, audio, or video, etc.) to create additional storylines based around those works. Fan fiction thrives online due to its place in a shared community built around fandoms of published works. Tushnet points out that such "Creative fan cultures developed along with mass media entertainment over the course of the twentieth century" (2007, p. 138). A citizen author's access to, and connection within, the global village has enabled fan fiction to develop into a large, barely monetised facet of the publishing industry; one that succeeds most when the works are just below the radar of the wider industry and where the citizen authors have direct feedback from their readers.

The industry's relationship to science and fan fictions

In order to understand the publishing industry's relationship to the communities that are developing around the common interest of genre fictions, one must look at genres' past relationship to publishing. This includes examining the industry's snobbery around genre fictions (Roberts, 2007, p. 3), which is apparent in the lack of canonised works of science fiction that are embraced by the mainstream industry and the hidden nature of fan fiction. Genre fiction is often considered as a pejorative term which brings to mind certain tropes that must be brought to bear in the text for it to live up to its genre. Krystal goes further to relate the format of genre writing to 'commercial' writing, which is meant to sell a particular style that the readers seek out, knowing what they will get when they pick up a work (2012). This is a type of branding of a genre that allows the industry to dictate the output that reaches a wider audience of readers. However, the branding of science and fan fictions by the industry and its gatekeepers only works if control is maintained over the brand, or genres. The citizen author seeks to subvert the control of the brands of science and fan fictions that are approved and sold to the reading public by finding new outlets and audiences in digital social spaces, where they can create a community with their readers.

If published genre fictions exist somewhere in the fuzzy sets below literary fiction, then works of genre fiction written online endure a place one level below as fiction that is hidden away in the depths of the internet, in repositories, on social platforms, or actively avoiding the spotlight, in the case most fan fiction. The history of science fiction and fan fiction and their relationships to the publishing industry could have taken innumerable path. Scholars have disagreed on the genesis of science fiction, but there is a clearer notion of when fan fiction developed.

Fan fiction, roughly defined as texts that have been written based on works from popular culture, came into its own with the emergence of science fiction fandom in the late sixties (Coppa, 2006, p. 43). In the 70s, 80s, and early 90s, much fan fiction was written as zines and hard copies were sent around via mailing lists and shared face to face (Coppa, 2006; Tushnet, 2007; Johnson, 2016). However, coinciding with wider access to the internet and the global village, fan fiction surged as it moved online, enabling new forms of fan fiction reader and author relationships. As fan fiction grew in the digital realm, it remained thoroughly embedded in the structures of the subculture, which are based on staying out of the industry's way while trying not to draw the attention of the original writer or publisher as they enter into reader and fan communities.

Throughout the history of fan fiction, the driving force has been about connectivity and tapping into a feedback loop of a "reader's active participation in meaning-making" (Lindgren Leavenworth, 2015, p. 103) as when readers comment on characterisation or plot devices, etc. However, an active feedback loop can be a double-edged sword where a publisher is concerned. While a traditional publisher might be pleased with the prospect of having access to a work that has a ready-made fan base, as in Wattpad works, there is often a saturation point for a work within a given audience. If millions of people have already read the work for free, the publisher is still gambling that enough would be willing to now pay to read that work and to own it for themselves. Publishers here would be tapping into the value of ownership of a particular work, based on the intrinsic value applied to the traditionally printed book as an item. One of the ways that publishers can tap into this is to involve the readers directly in the printed book.

Many of the stories written on FanFiction.net and Wattpad are published as chapters or short stories that can be read together to make a complete work. This develops an ongoing relationship between the authors and readers who return to read and comment on the serialised work. As evidenced on the Wattpad chapters of *Arrowheart*, these comments can be positive, "I am so excited ⊕⊛ And Cover is beautiful ⊚⊛♥" (_Anjali, 15 February, 2018), or negative, as when Dash wrote "I need a manly story" (–, 11, December, 2016). This allows readers to voice opinions or advice on topics that range widely, from the characterisation to the plot, to the way the work may, or may not, fit into a wider canon. This interaction creates a sense of ownership over the work and how it is shared in both the citizen authors and the readers.

Blurring the 'high' / 'low' literature differential

The power relationship developed between the genres of science fiction and fan fictions creates new strategies when citizen authors choose to strike out on their own, using digitally social technology to write and share their works and develop a dialogue directly with their readers, while the industry seeks to harness that power by using gatekeeping mechanisms as a way to present traditional publication as a desirable objective for any author. If the publishing industry cannot harness the rise of citizen authors and genre fictions, they "must be represented as 'other,' must be held at a distance so that fannish [or sub-genre] taste does not pollute sanctioned culture" (Jenkins, 1992, p. 19).

The industry relies on repetitions of tropes and recognisable features to define a genre, but genres are not stable and react to the culture in which they are derived as a social construct (Mittell, 2001). The act of labelling a subset of literature as a 'genre' positions a text in the discourse and influences how it will be received and embraced by the readers. Generic labels are often provided by the industry as a way to direct "how it will be printed, where it will be sold, and by whom it is most likely to be read" (Rieder, 2010, p. 200). It is the ability to label genre that the rise of citizen authors question and challenge by taking back the term and applying it to modes of writing and texts that are outliers, well beyond what the traditional industry would acknowledge as publishable.

In his book on the history of science fiction, Roberts discusses the 'ghettoisation' of the genre and how the literary establishment and publishing industry privileges almost any other genre over that of science fiction (2007, p. 3). The same, or worse, can be said of works of fan fiction written in subculture communities online. One reason this hierarchy is in place is highlighted by Jenkins when he says that the "[citizen authors'] transgression of bourgeois taste and disruption of dominant cultural hierarchies ensures that their preferences are seen as abnormal and threatening by those who have a vested interest in the maintenance of these standards" (1992, p. 17). The ghettoisation of the works that disrupt the current publishing model pushes the citizen authors and readers into a closer relationship, as they find refuge in the global village. Ghettoisation and growth of genres does not happen in a vacuum, and other media formats echo these changes with the development of genre-specific television (top-down), YouTube channels (peer sharing), and website and dedicated social spaces (bottom up).

The growth of digital technology has expanded the readership of genre fictions by making the ghettoised texts more mainstream due to the physical invisibility of the digital book (Dunneback, 2013; Howell, 2014). Reading genre texts with a low cultural currency on a tablet, phone, or on another personal, handheld device, removes the book cover, allowing a reader to be simply reading without worrying about the judgement of others. The equalising anonymity of the internet, where readers and citizen authors can share as much or as little about themselves as they choose, begins to close the differential between 'high' and 'low' texts; not because the industry and readership believes these differences no longer exist but because the readers and citizen authors now have the choice of whether or not they develop relationships with these texts in a fashion that is sanctioned by, and visible to, the industry itself.

As the dynamic framework of genres shifts, the power may begin to migrate away from the traditional publishing model and instead move to the citizen authors who choose to work within these genres, taking advantage of new social technology to push the definition of a book in new directions. As they move towards the edges of genre, "more prestige accrues to violating these boundaries than to conforming to them [...] where every work constructs its own unique genre" (Rieder, 2010, pp. 198–199).

It is not only the publishers who seek to exploit the rise of genre fiction and its relation to the citizen author and the concept of high and low literature. The authors of fan fictions are beginning to insist that their work be accepted more widely in the digital sphere and in the traditional publishing model as well, causing a disruption where new groups have formed. The Organization for Transformative Works (OTW) is one such group that was created as a non-profit, fan-activist organisation to help writers push back against their "position of weakness" (Jenkins, 1992, p. 20): pitted against the top-down power and suppression of the wider media and cultural industries. The OTW believes "that fanworks are transformative and that transformative works are legitimate" (Organisation of Transformative Works, 2017). With this in mind, they established the *Transformative Works and Cultures Journal* to legitimise the study of fan writing through its relationship to academia and have developed a fan archive which currently holds nearly 7 million works across 40,380 fandoms.[2] Though OTW is not actively trying to change the law of copyright, they are raising awareness of fan fiction, a move which some fan fiction authors see as "dangerously exposing their subculture and forcing the hand of the copyright holders" (Flegel & Roth, 2014, p. 1093).

The place where fan fiction resides in relation to copyright is unclear at best, and the nature of the texts and the disruptive modes of writing of the citizen authors challenges the industry's hold on copyrights of 'popular narratives' (Jenkins, 1992, p. 285). Some works, like Todd's *After* and James' *50 Shades* series, were fan works which had overtly recognisable names and attributes of their fandoms altered by publishers to consider them original works and monetise them. As a result, some fans felt that "James had taken advantage of the fan community" (Johnson, 2016, p. 1652). Authors such as J.K. Rowling support fan fiction of their works (with the exception of erotica), while Neil Gaiman and Stephenie Meyer have no qualms with fans using their characters or worlds as long as they don't commercialise it, but canonised authors George R.R. Martin, Diana Gabaldon, and Orson Scott Card are vehemently against any use of their published writing, even in non-commercial fan fiction. Though some authors are against fans using their works, this doesn't mean that citizen authors obey, and at least they disobey as a community.

Notes

1 Wattpad search done December 2020. These numbers are up dramatically from February 2017, when the same searches recorded 109,000 stories tagged 'science fiction,' 11,500 'sciencefiction,' 13,800 'scifi,' 141,000 'fantasy,' and 21,100 'future,' 1,300 stories tagged 'literary fiction,' and 35,300 for 'literaryfiction.'
2 December 2020. This number is up dramatically from 2017, when there were 2,881,000 works across 24,110 fandoms.

Bibliography

_Anjali, 2018. On Arrowheart, Book One of The Love Curse. Wattpad. https://www.wattpad.com/1497321-arrowheart-the-love-curse-one/comment/3758663113. [Accessed 28 April 2018].
Broderick, D., 1995. *Reading by Starlight: Postmodern Science Fiction*. London: Routledge.
Clark, G. & Phillips, A., 2008. *Inside Book Publishing*. 4th ed. Abingdon: Routledge.
Collin, R., 2012. Genre in Discourse, Discourse in Genre: A New Approach to the Study of Literate Practice. In *Journal of Literacy Research* [e-journal]. Vol. 44, No. 1, pp. 76–96. Available at: http://dx.doi.org/10.1177/1086296X11431627.
Coppa, F., 2006. A Brief History of Media Fandom. In Hellekson, K., & Busse, K. (Eds), *Fan Fiction and Fan Communities in the Age of the Internet* (pp. 41–60). North Carolina: McFarland & Company, .

Dunneback, K., 2013. Erotica's Full-Frontal Shelving. In *Library Journal*. Vol. 138, No. 3, pp. 20–24.

Flegel, M. & Roth, J., 2014. Legitimacy, Validity, and Writing for Free: Fan Fiction, Gender, and the Limits of (Unpaid) Creative Labor. In *The Journal of Popular Culture*. Vol. 47, No. 6, pp. 1092–1108.

Foucault, M., 1989. *The Archaeology of Knowledge*. Translated from the French by A.M. Sheridan Smith. Routledge: London.

Frow, J., 2007. "Reproducibles, Rubrics, and Everything You Need": Genre Theory Today. In *PMLA* [online]. Vol. 122, No. 5, Special Topic: Remapping Genre (October), pp. 1626–1634. Available at: http://www.jstor.org/stable/25501811.

Herman, B., 2014. What is Wattpad? The 'YouTube for Stories' is Transforming Book Publishing. In *International Business Times* [online]. Available at: http://www.ibtimes.com/what-wa ttpad-youtube-stories-transforming-book-publishing-1710151. [Accessed 9 September 2016].

Howell, V., 2014. E-Books and Reading Experience. In *The Journal of Publishing Culture* [online]. Vol. 2. Available at: http://journalpublishingculture.weebly.com/uploads/1/6/ 8/4/16842954/howell.pdf.

Jenkins, H., 1992. *Textual Poachers: Television Fans & Participatory Culture*. New York: Routledge.

Johnson, B., 2016. Live Long and Prosper: How the Persistent and Increasing Popularity of Fan Fiction Requires a New Solution in Copyright Law. In *Minnesota Law Review*. Vol. 100, No. 1645, pp. 1645–1687.

Krystal, A., 2012. It's Genre. Not That There's Anything Wrong With It! In *The New Yorker* [online]. Available at: http://www.newyorker.com/books/page-turner/its-genre-not-tha t-theres-anything-wrong-with-it. [Accessed 30 March 2017].

Lindgren Leavenworth, M., 2015. Reader, Please Follow Me: Fan Fiction, Author Instructions, and Feedback. In *Human IT*. Vol. 13, No. 1, pp. 100–127.

Miller, C.R., 1984. Genre as Social Action. In *Quarterly Journal of Speech*. Vol. 70, pp. 151–162.

Mittell, J., 2001. A Cultural Approach to Television Genre Theory. In *Cinema Journal*. Vol. 40, No. 3 (Spring).

Organisation of Transformative Works, 2017. What We Believe. Available at: http://www. transformativeworks.org/what_we_believe/. [Accessed 27 February 2017].

Owen, S., 2007. Genres in Motion. In *PMLA* [online]. Vol. 122, No. 5, Special Topic: Remapping Genre (October), pp. 1389–1393. Available at: https://doi.org/10.1632/pm la.2007.122.5.1389.

Rieder, J., 2010. On Defining SF, or Not: Genre, Theory, SF, and History. In *Science Fiction Studies* [online]. Vol. 37, No. 2. Available at: http://www.jstor.org/stable/25746406.

Roberts, A., 2007. *The History of Science Fiction*. New York: Palgrave MacMillan.

Tushnet, R., 2007. Payment in Credit: Copyright Law and Subcultural Creativity. In *Law and Contemporary Problems*. Vol. 70, No. 2, pp. 135–174.

7

THE ROLE OF COMMUNITY IN WRITING FICTION ONLINE

Social platforms as places where authors and readers meet

Identifying communities

Relationships that have developed around writing and reading fiction have been liberated of the traditional, geographical constraints of place (Aroles, 2015, p. 7), allowing new communities with malleable boundaries to develop within a global village. These are delineated by the digital space used and the repetition of contacts dictated by social exchanges, which can include shared objectives, properties, identities, or interests through the mediation of IT artefacts and technology (Lin & Huang, 2013, p. 135; Shen et al., 2017, p. 183). Communities that have developed around the writing and dissemination of fiction represent the coming together of citizen authors and readers in a digital place of shared ideas, communications, and values based around reading and writing fiction, where the development of the interchange between the members and the writing is a process (Ferreday, 2009, p. 25) and a "matter of becoming" (Hall, 1996, p. 225).

This 'matter of becoming' is a form of continual disruption to the discourse of the book, composing new statements that are situated in the changing forms of connectivity and interaction in digitally social spaces. The communities that are developed here take advantage of the lack of geographical boundaries and the role of the platform as a catalyst for the citizen author's identity formation as a writer, the expression of their work, and the feedback potential of the connectivity. It is within these communities that works develop that directly relate to the rise of the citizen author. They embrace new social technologies not only as places to build networks but as communities where they can write and market their work using cross-platform techniques.

Interaction between authors and readers is not a new area of study, but the changes in the ways authors and readers communicate in a digital community has just starting to gain ground. Murray takes into account these digital interactions in

DOI: 10.4324/9781003186649-8

her research, noting that "The digital domain offers authors the possibility of rapid or even real-time interaction with readers irrespective of their geographic location, and publicly accessible archiving of such interactions" (2018, p. 30). As the internet develops as a "new frontier in social relationships" (Zaphiris & Ang, 2010, p. vi), so do the relationships of the citizen authors and readers evolve among differing digital communities.

The context through which interactions between the citizen authors and readers in the global village take place is key to understanding the reflexive nature of the relationships, the potential for future interaction within the community (Vrasidas & Veletsianos, 2010, p. 3), and how these interactions can create changes in how the book is defined. The way users interact in different digital communities alters depending on the social platform where the communities exist and how/if these communities also exist in physical spaces. Authors Claire Askew and Janet Simpson have found that through Twitter several employment opportunities and clients have come their way, and they find social platforms, as Askew says, "less formal and frightening" than other forms of reaching out to other members of a community. Here Askew actively takes on the persona of a writer, as she perceives it to be, within the community online; whereas she says that "with Facebook, it's much more a personal thing" because that is where her family and friends virtually reside (15 February, 2016).

The collapse of context between digital and physical communities

The places where the citizen author as both writer and reader collapse the context of digital media is where the "tension between the public and private meet the double standards of the user – content producer and spectator" (Grădinaru, 2016, p. 187). Here, the citizen authors and readers form feedback loops that serve to strengthen their bonds in a communal space formed around (often) unspoken rules of behaviour and engagement within that particular social space, where "technology redraws the boundaries between intimacy and solitude" (Turkle, 2011, p. 11). These interactions between users can combine online and offline environments, as the citizen author may find offline work or be approached by an agent or other publishing gatekeeper to take their work into a more traditional publishing model. This helps to remove the 'us and them' dichotomy where the reader reads the book the author writes and there is never interaction.

The digital communities that form around writing fictions have four aspects of belonging, identified by Lee and Suh (2015) as the ability to use the technology, the accountability of interaction, "belongingness," and a "self-identity" directly linked to membership of a particular group. These four characteristics allow a user to cultivate an attachment to the community, and in forming that attachment they situate themselves at a place where these connections allow for new relationships between communities of readers and authors to develop. Going further, combining these four characteristics with the technical scaffolding and the feedback loop that social platforms provide, the communities allow for relationships to be developed between citizen authors and readers that can play a role in the editing and adoption of a work in both the digital and physical realm. If the reader has a hand in the citizen author's process of writing in the global village, where they feel their membership is valued, this value is likely to transfer into the reader sharing the work and potentially more sales should the work be brought to market in a traditional sense.

The digital community, facilitated by the social platforms and their ability to enable and grow relationships, is where new understandings of the book come into being. These relationships provide new ways of understanding the book by taking it out of the power mechanism of the traditional publishing industry and putting the control into the hands of the citizen authors and readers who use the social platforms outwith the socio-economic publishing model.

Citizen authors are sharing their writing even without the promise of a publishing deal. Rebecca Sky, Rachel Thompson, Marcus Lopés, and Simon Grant write for the sake of sharing work and community. They may hope to get a publishing deal or have received one, but this is not their sole goal of writing. Lopés says, "I chose to share my work on Twitter simply to get it out there" (20 January, 2017). Likewise, Grant states that "For me, publication is secondary to gaining readers, and merely a means to that end" (8 February, 2017). Making connections and finding readers in the global village is key to these authors' decisions to write and share work in online communities.

What communities exist?

Within the global village, the communities exist around fictions, where the citizen authors "seek to build communities of interest in cyberspace because we might not be able to build them elsewhere" (Fernback, 1997, p. 40). This can include those marginalized subgenres such as fan and science fictions, among others.

The dominant social platforms where the citizen authors find and grow communities are Facebook, Twitter, YouTube, Blogs, Instagram, Wattpad and Medium. Much like the citizen authors, publishers also heavily use Facebook and Twitter, and to a much lesser extent Instagram, YouTube, and other platforms. Small publisher Tatterdemalion Blue highlights the company's engagement with Facebook and Twitter as its main social platform, while authors tend to use these platforms to create connected hashtag stories and seek to write on platforms that lend themselves to longer-form writing, such as blogs.

Popular social media platforms, blogs, fiction repositories, reviews, audio platforms, websites, etc. are all locations that appeal to the citizen author. The different sites of inquiry where the citizen author chooses to write challenge the industry's understanding of where an author can produce work and how they bypass human gatekeeping systems.

Though not all citizen authors are born into the digitally connected, global village, many are. The demographics of these new authors differ from that of self-publishers around the concept of digital natives (Prensky, 2001). This is due to factors that have an impact on how we allow people to define a book, including a citizen author's age, education levels, and socio-economic status – which relates to access and their physical location within the world – and the citizen author takes this continual flow between internal and external media into the process of where and how they write and what is meant by the idea of the book.

Writing and sharing fiction on Twitter

It is the within communities developed on social platforms that the understating of what we consider a book to be is disrupted by those who use these platforms to write and share works. Whereas Matt Stewart used Twitter as a place to release his novel before it was published in the traditional paperback format, Thompson, Lopés, and Grant actively wrote and shared works on Twitter with the #Twitter-fiction hashtag in order, as Lopés says, to get their "writing out there and to, perhaps, slowly build an audience" (20 January, 2017). Three of the four authors tend to focus their Twitter accounts more on sharing work and not interacting with readers. This is evident from their lack of speaking directly to their readers, as well as the rare retweet or 'hearting' of any number of their tweets. While Grant posts continual links to other social media platforms (mostly Facebook) and all of Thompson's tweets reaching back into September 2016 are based on her blog, Lopés is slightly more interactive with his Twitter account, posting comments and occasionally engaging with others. In fact, Lopés is the only one of these three citizen authors who uses his Twitter account as a 'real' person on a regular basis. Lopés' choice to stay involved in his chosen community on Twitter enables him to continually draw attention to himself and his writing.

Thompson says in her blog that her follower numbers only went up slightly during her time writing "The Other Side of the Glass." Lopés tweets about his growth of followers on a regular basis, even claiming that his follower numbers grew in the final week of publishing his Mann brothers story on Twitter (@MMarcusALopes, 21 September, 2016). Though he has few readers who interact with him on a regular basis, in our interview, Grant stated that he has confidence in the readers he does have and that he has hopes of creating a dialogue between himself and those who read his works.

Romance author Simpson goes further than simply posting and hashtagging her work by regularly collaborating in what she calls "Twitter role play" with a role-playing partner. She goes on to say that "as it's regularly updated we have regular readers both on Twitter and on A03 [Archive of Our Own], who actively follow for updates" (15 February, 2016). Likewise, Askew, as an author and reader, finds herself looking for other writers' works on Twitter and is interested in how followers interact with works of poetry and fiction on the platform.

These authors who are publishing on Twitter, by hashtagging their work, are inserting it into a searchable database of tagged tweets that will appeal to a wider range of readers who follow certain hashtags, expanding their reach beyond their own personal Twitter feed, where they must be followed to show up. Ninety-two per cent of writers and 70% of publishers who took part in the survey are using Twitter as a place to read and interact, and 50% of authors said Twitter was their go-to platform should they choose to write fiction in what Janet Simpson calls "real time." This uptake of Twitter is juxtaposed with the 50% of publishers who use social communities as a place to source new materials or find these citizen authors. Reaching new audiences in this way allows the citizen author to challenge the traditional industry model by bypassing the gatekeepers to share works and entering potential feedback loops with readers.

Fiction repositories

Medium, Wattpad, and FanFiction.net are three large, online, English-language repositories. As mentioned previously, they have low barriers of entry, which makes them ideal places for a citizen author to hone and test their writing, interact with readers, and get feedback, all of which increase the quantity and quality of their relationships in the global village. To gain access and expand their relationships around their writing, all the citizen author needs is a device that has connectivity to the internet and an email address with which to register with the digitally social platform.

The citizen author discriminates between social platforms and digital communities based on their own interests and needs. Lopés states: "I currently use Twitter, Facebook, Instagram and LinkedIn. [...] My preferred platform is Twitter because it's fairly stable" (20 January, 2017). This differs from Grant, whose choice of social media platform is "driven almost entirely by aesthetic concerns" (8 February, 2017).

Interestingly, the consideration of what social platforms to use is influenced by gender and the gender of the communities within them. Askew "self-protect[s] as a female social media user" and limits her use of Facebook to family and close friends, even going as far to say she doesn't like it but "feel[s] beholden to it." She uses Twitter the most and feels "most at home on [it]" but also censors her approach in relation to the community on the platform, where she "feel[s] the most need to alter [... her] behaviour" (15 February, 2016).

In making a choice to use or not use particular platforms, citizen authors take on the roles traditionally enjoyed by "professional media workers" (Deuze et al., 2012. p. 5). They alter the available social spaces to accommodate their needs as writers and producers of works of fiction. In fact, we find again and again that those authors who do not find a suitable place in the digitally connected global village to write their fiction often create one themselves. This can be seen most evidently in the proliferation of writers creating blogs and building websites to house their works. This not only gives the author more control over the formatting, delivery, and dissemination of their work, but it also allows them to return to it again and again to edit the work, often based on feedback from readers, which can be facilitated by comments and author contact forms.

The different communities of interest attract a particular type of author. Each platform has its own niche, with Wattpad's being the widest and most open to a variety of genres, but they all remain free and open to readers and authors, who could just as easily post their works as a Kindle eBook or on Smashwords and sell them online. However, the communities these platforms are built on thrive by making books and stories social, and it is here that the creative opportunities exist for writing, feedback, and encouragement on a mutual level between those who read and those who write, allowing them both to be "socially present in a situation that is mediated via technology" (Vrasidas & Veletsianos, 2010, p. 9). Certainly, the authors who write on these platforms would like to monetise their work, but of more importance is the feedback, in-line commentary, and constructive and encouraging notes they can receive on each segment they post, drawing them further into the community.

As many citizen authors have worked their way from social networks to social writing platforms, and from self-publishing on to traditional publishing deals, the sociality of online networking sites is the link across their trajectory. Social networks such as Facebook, Twitter, Instagram, FanFiction.net, Medium, and Wattpad brush aside the silence of the publishing model and its curatorial gatekeeping by allowing writers and readers to engage with one another, develop works, and build a following, which, in turn, challenges the traditional publishing model and is slowly requiring it to shift to accommodate the rise of the citizen author.

As to the question of which social platform or communities are best for the citizen author, it depends on what a particular community offers a writer or a reader and perhaps what their reputation for 'fame' (of authors/readers) is. A citizen author starting out might find more support and community in Wattpad or Fan-Fiction.net, where even a small amount of engagement may be enough. A better known author might notice that posting on Twitter gets more interaction from a wider array of readers. As for the publisher, they are more likely to find repositories with easy-to-understand user metrics the most valuable.

Genre writing in digitally social communities

There is a direct link between the new places where the author chooses to write and the types of fiction that are embraced within those digitally social spaces. The link between the 'vibrant subcultures,' the citizen author, and the power play within the publishing industry is best explored through the genres of science fiction and fan fiction, as they often do not pass the gatekeeping criteria of the industry, and authors often seek out other modes and places for their expression, such as in digitally social spaces. Here it is the community among citizen authors and readers that "represent[s] a vibrant subculture, one that inspires passion among thousands of people who find creative outlets in shared universes" (Tushnet, 2007, p. 138). The connected individuals care about their preferred genres, developing the cultures around those genres in an "active, engaged and creative way" (Roberts, 2007, p. 17). Askew noted in an interview that several "genre people have ditched traditional publishing [...] in order to go with publishing in social media" (15 February, 2016).

This engagement with the subcultures of science fiction and fan fiction manifests itself in the creation of texts that adhere to the generic frameworks approved of by the social constructs in which they are situated (Lindgren Leavenworth, 2015, p. 107; Stein & Busse, 2009, pp. 196–197). Simpson suggests that it is precisely because of these well-known structures that genre fiction flourishes in social spaces online, making it "easier to consume in the non-traditional format." She goes on to say that "unlike literary fiction, the writing in genre fiction tends to be more transparent than literary fiction" and would be "easier to consume on a more distracting platform" (15 February, 2016) Gatekeeping by the communities of readers and authors draws on the gatekeeping mechanisms of the traditional publishing industry and previously developed tropes on what a book is, which provide a lens through which they understand and categorise works of science and fan fictions. However, instead of simply being turned away, the authors who embrace these new digitally social places to write and share their works have the opportunity to enter into a dialogue with the readers in order to gain entry into the subculture community. Genre fiction that utilises the freedom to write on social platforms has come into its own, as the "advent of the internet has broadened it reach" (Johnson, 2016, p. 1646).

Authors of works of fan fiction will often read, participate, and finally post their creative works within approved fan fiction communities such as FanFiction.net, Archive of Our Own, and Wattpad, among others that are dedicated to more canon-specific digital repositories that focus on *Harry Potter, Buffy the Vampire Slayer*, and Jane Austen Fan fiction, etc. Citizen authors writing science fiction often have more opportunities to disrupt the traditional discourse around the book in how they present and share their works due to the nature of the freedoms granted to them by the genre. Whereas an author of fan fiction is more likely to go unnoticed by the wider industry and post in a specific location in order to engage with their chosen communities and avoid the issues of copyright, the authors of science fiction can experiment with the way they write and share their work among communities by posting across platforms with links from Twitter to Facebook, Wattpad to YouTube, Oolipo,[1] and more.

Grant is one such author who has entered the community of science fiction on social media. He writes works of fantasy science fiction across multiple platforms, often juggling seven or more serialised stories at a time, which are released on Twitter and Facebook. He says of this mix, that:

> [s]ince the beginning of my experience with social- media first drafting, I've gone back and forth between Facebook and Twitter, and I've spent much of the time simultaneously posting, whether I post the same story on both platforms or have particular stories for the different platforms which I am presenting in parallel serialization.
>
> *(8 February, 2017)*

Grant embraces the complicated structures that social platforms allow to develop around genre fiction, saying that "publication is secondary to gaining readers and developing relationships" (8 February, 2017). Though authors disagree on the amount of complication of genre fiction that is acceptable in a social space, there is something to be said for both points of view. It is the genre itself, with its tropes and inherent understanding of another world or genre feature of some description, that allows readers to take any complications with the plot or platform in their stride as a feature adding to, not detracting from, the story itself.

In science fiction, and, indeed, by the very nature of fan fiction, most authors begin as fans (Roberts, 2007, p. 18). From their fandom, the citizen author moves on to create new texts using social technology to share their works digitally with specific groups. It is this interaction within what Lindgren Leavenworth calls the "affinity space" (2015, p. 102) that allows for a relationship to develop between the way a reader engages with a text and the citizen authors themselves.

Within fan fiction communities, authors, readers, and the texts (both the original work and the derivative) play off one another; the author can get direct feedback on specific aspects of their work and the way it relates to the canonised original (Lindgren Leavenworth, 2015, p. 107). This can help develop the text and author in a way that will bring the text more in line with the expectations of the prevalent discourse within the community. Some social platforms, such as Wattpad, provide in-line comments that serve to give readers a way to feedback on specific lines of a text. This feedback can encourage an author by creating statements praising the text, giving guidance on making it better, or even suggesting places where it can be shared further. The citizen author can take the feedback on board, can change the text if required, and further develop the story based on direct interactions with their readers. This creates a "relatively safe environment where ideas can be tested and debated" (Lindgren Leavenworth, 2015, p. 102), which in turn creates a more tightly knit community that will stand behind an author and happily share and promote their favourite works.

Much like in the dynamics of fan fiction, "[f]ans are integral to the way contemporary SF operates: numerous fan-created magazines, websites and conventions generate much of the energy on which the continuing vitality of the genre depends" (Roberts, 2007, p. 17). Unlike fan fiction readers and writers, who usually stay out of the spotlight of the traditional publishing industry, or if they come into it, they alter their works so they are no longer recognisable as fan fiction, the fans and the authors of science fiction who develop relationships are more likely to exist in real-world communities as well as online, when the contexts collapse. Fans and authors will attend conventions and gatherings to share their affinity for the genre and particular works. This is seen in the long-standing World Science Fiction Convention (WorldCon), which was first held in New York in 1939 and included writers such as Ray Bradbury. It is based on recognising the role of the fans in supporting writers. Another example of fans and authors of science and fan fiction coming together in an offline setting is at comic book events (comic-cons) and science fiction and fantasy events (dragon-con), which have been ongoing since 1970 and 1987, respectively.

Readers of science fiction and fan fiction alike take courage in the connectivity that social technology has given them; it makes them a group who has more authority on what a book can be in the spaces they inhabit, both on- and offline. They can now "speak from a position of collective identity, [and] … forge an alliance with a community of others" (Jenkins, 1992, p. 23). This identity as part of a community not only fosters relationships between readers, writers, and genre-specific works, it also allows the separation between readers and writers to relax, enabling the rise of the citizen author as a prosumer who is both familiar with their audience and willing to enter into conversations with readers, making science fiction "a community, not an elite" (Roberts, 2007, p. 18).

Genre in #Twitterfiction

Part of growing the community of the citizen author involves the role they play in inserting their writing into specific areas of association by using hashtags. The growth of these communities outwith the publishing industry gives members both connectivity with one another and a certain amount of power.

Authors are beginning to realise the power of connecting with readers in the social spaces. Twitter user @FSimonGrant wrote and shared six stories during 2016. Each tweet that made up a story was tagged with the #Twitterfiction hashtag, a separate identifying hashtag, and the sequential number of the tweet. Each story was set in a different world, with no overlap between them. In addition, Simon Grant also wrote 10 stories with the hashtag #Metacarpals, which he described as "the story of Asher Jacobson, whose fingers contain ten separate & distinct worlds with their own heroes, villains, & epic adventures" (Grant, 2015), and he created a Metacarpals fiction Facebook page that was a space dedicated to sharing new chapters.

All Grant's stories had elements of fantastical science fiction and/or horror coming through, with elements such as "red rain" (#Orkney), the "Living Moon" as a character (#Fader), and a murderous real estate agent named Landon (#LandK), just to name a few. By creating works of genre fiction, Grant harnesses the freedom of the genre, which by its very nature allows him to test the "tight-rope walk, balancing between order and chaos" within a new digital setting. The use of fantastical science fiction in Grant's works on Twitter allows him to nest stories inside one another and create elaborate, if limited in scope and scale, worlds that the reader is invited into. In doing this, Grant, from the position of citizen author, is using the fuzzy edges of genre to push the boundaries set by the industry's gatekeepers.

Rachel Thompson's "The Other Side of the Glass," shared from May 25, 2016 to May 29, 2016, used the hashtag #Twitterfiction for 65 tweets, which included promotional tweets around the story that enticed readers to check out her blog posts about it, or to await the next instalment. Much like her published work, *Beneath the Surface* (Vanguard Press, 2006), the short Twitter story was a work of science fiction. Written in first person point of view, "The Other Side of the

Glass" tells the story of a boy and his love, Megan, who has just returned from a mission to a colony where humanity will move to in the near future. However, there are sinister beings called Stalkers living outside the colony on Jupiter, something the teachers and those in charge are trying to keep under wraps in order to continue to send people out, to get them away from Earth, which has to be evacuated. Megan is the only returning crew member to dare speak out, but she is taken away, unseen, and at the end of the story the reader discovers that she too has become a Stalker.

The story itself is fully contained but has the potential to be expanded into a larger work and could be of interest to publishers who seek out works written on social platforms to effectively reinsert them into the traditional publishing model. Thompson's background as a published science fiction author shows through in the pacing and writing of the story. She soon found that without writing the story out beforehand she was unsure of how the story might end and suggests that writing the tweets in advance might work to the author's advantage, though this might lose some of the rawness that adds an edge to a work of short science fiction, making it feel excitingly present when published live on a social platform.

Thompson shows how a traditionally published author can go outwith the industry model and share a new work as it's being written. Though she gained only six new followers, she readily admitted on her blog that to her "that is a lot" (2016), and that those few new followers might go on to seek out her other, published works, read her blog, or even contact her directly to discuss what they did or did not like about her short story. Regardless of their motivation, Thompson's connectivity was expanded through the life of the story on Twitter.

Where Grant used Twitter to share his fantastical science fiction during a five-month spree and Thompson utilised it to write a self-contained science fiction story over a few days, Marcus Lopés used the hashtag #Twitterfiction to consistently write and share a longer work of science-spy fiction. Lopés tweeted consistently throughout the data collection period, beginning on 27 November, 2015. His tweeting pattern was consistently one to two tweets per day, shared between 17:00 and 20:00 until 22 January, 2016 at 17:00:10, when he began to tweet his story of the Mann brothers every few seconds, using the Tweetcaster app. Each tweet was numbered to allow the reader to follow them sequentially. This particular segment of the story recorded in the data was sixty tweets long and was told entirely within the hour on 22 January, 2016.

The story of the Mann brothers is just under 13,000 words in length and tells of the adventures of Jacob and Sam Mann, brothers with powers to read minds and teleport. The brothers are part of an elite organisation called The Agency, which is charged with helping maintain peace in Canada. It is led by PM Jacob Mann. New characters were added and others died as the story progressed, and, for the most part, it made use of the elements of science fiction to underscore the characters' abilities to be world leaders and top spies.

Lopés said of the story: "I had to cut down on description and move the story along mostly through dialogue. I learned to keep dialogue tags to a minimum, i.e., he said, she said. I had to always make sure that each tweet had 140 characters or less" (20 January, 2017). This short, sharp writing lends itself to the medium, which can be refreshed at the touch of a button. Author Janet Simpson said that the issue with sharing longer fiction on social media such as Twitter is exactly this need to be concise and fast: "If you see it happening in real time, it's great, but the time frame is limited" (15 February, 2016).

Lopés utilised the form of the medium to concentrate his story, and the resulting pace of the tale is fast, with much action, gun fire, and twists along the way. An example of this high-intensity storytelling is a scene where the Prime Minister is calling for his brother's death.

> 3 Sam barked his orders. "This is not a drill. Jacob Mann's alive and in the city. Find him. I want him taken in 24 hours." 4 'What do you mean by 'taken?" a croaky voice asked. Sam spoke calmly. 'In 24 hours I want Jacob Mann in a body bag!' 5 Ten minutes later, Eric walked back into Sam's office. 'It's too risky.' Sam folded his arms. 'There's no other choice.' 6 Eric closed the door to Sam's office. 'He's your brother. There's got – "Blood doesn't matter. Just stop him.' Sam said. 7 The door to Sam's office burst open, a thin-face blond shaking. 'It's him. 5 minutes ago at Union Station. What do we do?' 8 Eric looked wide-eyed at Sam. 'He's coming here.' Sam grabbed the phone. 'I want a Level-One lockdown. No one in or out.' 9 Sudden darkness. A deafening, incessant siren erupted, ricocheting off the walls. Sam grasped the Glock 17 in his holster. 10 Eric watched as Sam depressed the trigger safety. "Sam, you can't—"Sam raised a hand. "It's him or me. It won't be me." [All use of mixed single and double quotes are Lopés'.]

In writing these stories, Lopés numbers the tweets so that they are sequentially read. The numbers in the extract above show how the author is choosing to guide the reader through the disjointed threads and timelines of Twitter.

Lopés writes with a conciseness akin to that of Thompson, who worked to tell a complete story within the medium. Also, like Thompson, Lopés is a published author, whose work, *Freestyle Love*, is a work of fiction that has slight echoes of the story of the Mann brothers in character names and the themes of a gay male love story, which makes both works part of a minority canon in their respective genres. Creating a community around genre and subculture in a digital setting enables the readers and authors to develop a closer bond that comes from a growing connection based on the writing itself.

Who has the authority to write fiction in online spaces?

When authors – such as Rebecca Sky, Simon Grant, and Marcus Lopés – and readers – such as Guest, PhatBasset, and Serendipity2909 – are able to speak from within the communities they develop and populate, they confront the status quo of the publishing industry's hierarchy and allow a dialogue to develop at the level of their own community: author to reader, author to author, and reader to reader: moving from a traditional model (Figure 7.1) to a new model of connectivity (Figure 7.2).

In order to understand the authority of those in the digital communities to say what is or isn't a book, we can look more closely at the wider industry as the place where this authority is derived. Naming individuals and organisations is less important here than understanding how their roles relate to the knowledge-power complex that influences the socio-economic and political structures that crossover in the discourse of the book, and how their unique positions give them the authority to say what a book is to them, in their space.

When citizen authors join social networks, they present themselves by means of an avatar (be it a name or an image) as an intermediary between themselves as real people and others – readers and publishers – who present and interact online. This separation between online identity and real-world identity decentres the subject of

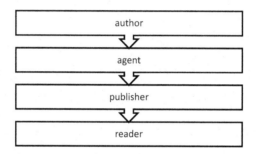

FIGURE 7.1 Traditional publishing model

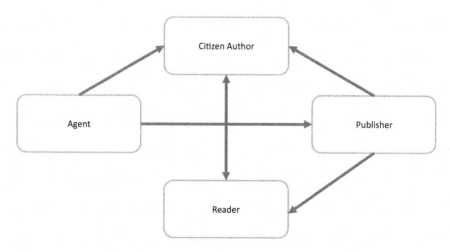

FIGURE 7.2 A new hierarchy of publishing

the work from the work itself, by presenting it as separate from the author. This separation allows for works to be evaluated within the "historical framework" (Foucault, 1989, p. 117) without necessarily tying together the author and their work in a single trajectory or genre.

By actively engaging with their real and potential audiences on social networks – that is, by following and being followed and replying to comments on their works – the citizen author actively fosters relationships with readers. In doing so, the citizen author, much like the self-published author, decentres themselves from their work so that they can both speak as the author of that work and speak about it as a work separate to themselves. It is this role as both subject and speaker that allows them to challenge the author-agent-publisher-reader hierarchy that the industry currently, and historically, relies on.

The reader's role in saying what a book can be

It is the push and pull relationship between the readers and the authors within the digital communities they inhabit that allows the reader to say what a book can be. Their place as members of the community where digitally social works are shared relies on their relationships to the works, the authors who create them, and other readers. As readers who, generally speaking, seek out particular communities that reflect their own interests, they are able to interact with the works as a reader who is invested, a reader who is actively choosing to join the citizen author in a place outside of the traditional publishing model.

As readers often dictate publishing trends through their socio-economic choices, "new titles are inherently risky products." However, a successful title can produce a "Bandwagon effect" (Gaffeo et al., 2006, p. 5) among publishers, who will see the success and move to emulate it with books that are similar in content, genre, or style. By using their position as prosumers, readers can also influence what the author creates. They seek out and consume works that are of interest to them by joining digital communities, and then produce feedback and comments and make relationships based on and around these works. They are perhaps most influential when they disagree with an author on aspects of their work, such as the representation of canonised characters in fan fiction, or if there are hard to follow hashtag overlaps, which, in the case of Grant, led to a backlash.

Readers who so love the original work/band/cultural phenomenon that gave rise to a work of fan fiction often have an "aggressive Doberman loyalty that is tinged with cultural paranoia" (Roberts, 2007, p. 343) and that comes from an extreme sense of ownership and privilege over a text that is both "liberating and restrictive" (Lindgren Leavenworth, 2015, p. 101). This loyalty can raise its head when an author puts a character in a situation or has them act in ways that a reader considers unrealistic, where the balance between the canonised and fan fiction representations of the character hasn't been achieved for the fans (Lindgren Leavenworth, 2015, p. 112). This creates a tension and ruptures between the readers and citizen authors, who both feel ownership over the canonised text and how the new supplementary fan fiction relates to it.

However, their influence is not all negative. In fact, much of the influence a reader has is based around a shared, and then surrendered, intimacy, where the relationship between author and reader is a nurturing one for both parties. As the recipients of the works of the citizen author, readers are able to occupy the space as editors, advisors, friends, and publicists.

The publisher's role in saying what a book can be

Publishers often seek to return the power developed in digital communities to the traditional publishing industry. For the most part, with the exception of locked and private groups, the locations where the communities develop are freely accessible to those who have access to the platform. This open access to most digital communities allows for publishers to observe the interactions between authors and readers and peruse the resulting writing with an eye towards pulling it offline into a traditional, and traditionally monetisable, format. In lurking on social sites, publishers are coming from the institutional site of the industry and bringing with them institutional economic and marketing aspects.

When a work reaches a 'critical mass' of interactions, likes, 'hearts,' readers, etc., they can step in and take that work into the traditional format. Coming from the place of industry, they seek out the kind of intimacy between authors and readers that will lead readers to be more likely to purchase a more traditional version of a work from within their community (Phillips, 2014, p. 18). In addition, once publishers make their presence known within a digital community, they must be careful not to overly disrupt this intimacy between the citizen authors and readers. For example, when Anna Todd published her work of One Direction fan fiction to Wattpad, the first book had ninety-nine chapters. Each of these chapters was available for commentary on Wattpad, and many fans took advantage of this. In fact, Todd's editor at Simon & Schuster was quite "careful to edit the book without taking out the parts the *After* family was particularly attached to" (Odell, 2014).

One interesting aspect of the interaction between publishers and readers is the ability for publishers to take on the persona of a writer in order to insert a work they publish into the global village and speak about a work in a community which the publisher would normally only observe.

In an interview with John King of Tatterdemalion Blue, he said that though he has "asked Noreen and Lorna [authors] to actually go in and do things, to write things, it's me that does it. I'm Mr Tilly"[2] (25 February, 2016). He speaks on behalf of the authors themselves and interacts with readers as if he is the writer. This links back to the identity of the members of the digital communities and how those identities are shaped, in part, by the groups to which they are attached. The publisher speaking from this position as false author seeks a different sort of interaction with the readers, often working a marketing angle. However, this does not preclude publishers taking on the role of false author in order to gain valuable community feedback on a work or series.

The citizen author's role in the digital communities they inhabit enables us to understand the real and potential relationships that exist between them, the readers, and the wider industry. The relationships may not always develop into fruitful publishing deals or reader feedback that generates new elements in the author's work, but they open up spaces within the discourse that require the connectivity developed by the interaction of the author and reader on a social platform to be acknowledged by those involved in the industry. Those citizen authors, readers, and publishers all have the authority to say what a book is, or can be, and in doing so new definitions of the book are developed as they overlap, creating new strategies of power.

Notes

1 Now defunct.
2 A character in one of the children's book series the company publishes.

Bibliography

Aroles, J., 2015. Performance and Becoming: Rethinking Nativeness in Virtual Communities. In *Games and Culture* [e-journal]. Available at: doi:10.1177/1555412015616714.

Askew, C., 2016. Interview on Publishing and Social Media. Interviewed by Miriam Johnson. Edinburgh.

Deuze, M., Blank, P., & Speers, L., 2012. A Life Lived in Media. In *Digital Humanities Quarterly*. Vol. 5, No. 1 [online]. Available at: http://digitalhumanities.org/dhq/vol/6/1/000110/000110.html.

Fernback, J., 1997. The Individual Within the Collective: Virtual Ideology and the Realization of Collective Principles. In Jones, S. (Ed.), *Virtual Culture: Identity and Communication in Cyberspace* (pp. 36–54). London: SAGE Publications.

Ferreday, D., 2009. *Online Belongings: Fantasy, Affect and Web Communities*. Oxford: Peter Lang.

Foucault, M., 1989. *The Archaeology of Knowledge*. Translated from the French by A.M. Sheridan Smith. Routledge: London.

Gaffeo, E., Scorcu, A., & Vici, L., 2006. *Demand Distribution Dynamics in the Book Publishing Industry*. WEHIA 2006 Conference. Bologna, Italy, 15–17 June 2006.

Grădinaru, C., 2016. The Technological Expansion of Sociability: Virtual Communities and Imagined Communities. In *Academicus: International Scientific Journal*. July, No. 14, pp. 181–190. Available at: doi:10.7336/academicus.2016.14.13.

Grant, S., 2015. Metacarpals Fiction. [Facebook page] December. Available at: https://www.facebook.com/MetacarpalsFiction. [Accessed 3 January 2017].

Grant, S., 2017. Interview with Simon Grant. Interviewed by Miriam Johnson [email].

Hall, S., 1996. Cultural Identity and Diaspora. In *Frameworks: The Journal of Cinema and Media*. No. 36, pp. 222–327.

Jenkins, H., 1992. *Textual Poachers: Television Fans & Participatory Culture*. New York: Routledge.

Johnson, B., 2016. Live Long and Prosper: How the Persistent and Increasing Popularity of Fan Fiction Requires a New Solution in Copyright Law. In *Minnesota Law Review*. Vol. 100, No. 1645, pp. 1645–1687.

King, J., 2016. Interview on Publishing and Social Media. Interviewed by Miriam Johnson. Stirling.

Lee, J. & Suh, A., 2015. How do Virtual Community Members Develop Psychological Ownership and What are the Effects of Psychological Ownership in Virtual Communities? In *Computers in Human Behavior*. Vol. 45, pp. 382–391. Available at: https://doi.org/10.1016/j.chb.2014.12.002.

Lin, F. & Huang, H., 2013. Why People Share Knowledge in Virtual Communities: The Use of Yahoo! Kimo Knowledge + as an Example. In *Internet Research* [e-journal]. Vol. 23, Issue 2, pp. 133–159. Available at: https://doi.org/10.1108/10662241311313295.

Lindgren Leavenworth, M., 2015. Reader, Please Follow Me: Fan Fiction, Author Instructions, and Feedback. In *Human IT*. Vol. 13, No. 1, pp. 100–127.

Lopés, M., 2017. Interview on Publishing and Social Media. Interviewed by Miriam Johnson [email].

Murray, S., 2018. *The Digital Literary Sphere: Reading, Writing, and Selling Books in the Internet Era*. Baltimore: Johns Hopkins University Press.

Odell, A., 2014. This Twenty-Five Year Old Turned Her One Direction Obsession into a Six Figure Paycheck. In *Cosmopolitan* [online]. Available at: http://www.cosmopolitan.com/entertainment/books/a32330/after-author-anna-todd-interview/. [Accessed 2 March 2017].

Phillips, A., 2014. *Turning the Page: The Evolution of the Book*. New York: Routledge.

Prensky, M., 2001. Digital Natives, Digital Immigrants Part 1. In *On the Horizon*. Vol. 9, No. 5, pp. 1–6.

Roberts, A., 2007. *The History of Science Fiction*. New York: Palgrave MacMillan.

Shen, K., Zhao, F., & Kalifa, M., 2017. Dural Identity Process for Virtual Community Participation and Impact of Gender Composition. In *Internet Research* [e-journal]. Vol. 27 No. 2, pp. 182–198. Available at: https://doi.org/10.1108/IntR-06-2015-0166.

Simpson, J. 2016. Interview on Publishing and Social Media. Interviewed by Miriam Johnson [email].

Stein, L. & Busse, K., 2009. Limit Play: Fan Authorship Between Source Text, Intertext, and Context. In *Popular Communication: The International Journal of Media and Communication* [e-journal]. Vol. 7, No. 4. Available at: http://dx.doi.org/10.1080/15405700903177545.

Thompson, R., 2016. A New Writing Technique. A Writer's Notebook [blog], 1 June 2016. Available at: https://awritersnotebookblog.wordpress.com/2016/06/01/a-new-writing-technique/. [Accessed 2017].

Turkle, S., 2011. *Alone Together: Why We Expect More from Technology and Less From Each Other*. New York: Basic Books.

Tushnet, R., 2007. Payment in Credit: Copyright Law and Subcultural Creativity. In *Law and Contemporary Problems*. Vol. 70, No. 2, pp. 135–174.

Vrasidas, C. & Veletsianos, G., 2010. Theoretical Foundations of Social Computing and Virtual Communities. In Zaphiris, P. & Ang, C.S. (Eds), *Social Computing and Virtual Communities* (pp. 1–20). Boca Raton: CRC Press.

Zaphiris, P. & Ang, C.S., 2010. Preface. In Zaphiris, P. & Ang, C.S. (Eds), *Social Computing and Virtual Communities* (pp. v–viii). Boca Raton: CRC Press.

8

THE POWER RELATIONSHIPS OF THE BOOK

The idea of the book is changing

There is an ongoing shift in the concept of what a book can be based on who has the authority to say what these new definitions are and where they can appear. This movement is taking place in the spaces between citizen authors, traditional publishers, and the digital communities and social platforms that provide locations to host the 'new' book. The rules for inclusion in these locations differ from those of the traditional publishing model in that they provide spaces and gaps for the citizen authors to develop new writing outwith the gatekeeping mechanisms of the industry, which are more deeply embedded with the role of commerce and the marketability of a work.

Books have come to be understood as content that can be re-formatted into different marketable outputs. These can take the form of printed editions, eBooks, or audiobooks, with the occasional foray into testing new technology, which more often than not comes from an initiative by a smaller company which is seeking legitimisation from the industry (as seen in the Futurebook awards for the Booktech Company of the Year).

Publishers such as John King from Tatterdemalion Blue said that they continue to see "the book as an item […] because it's a real thing […] in a real form somehow" (25 February, 2016).

This highlights the role of the publisher in promoting a hierarchy that elevates the book as a printed, physical object above other existing and potential formats. However, publishers are not alone in buying into the idea that a real book is a physical item. Authors Tracey Emerson, Claire Askew, and Janet Simpson believe that the physicality of a work of fiction, in this case a novel, is key to its definition. Askew stated in an interview that "when people say book I think of printed fiction, a printed novel, basically a traditionally published, printed novel" (15 November, 2017).

DOI: 10.4324/9781003186649-9

Emerson echoed this when she said, "I'm old and old school, so in my mind a book is primarily the printed paper, bound object" (8 February, 2018).

Askew went on to differentiate between the word 'book,' as a work of printed fiction, and a 'novel,' as something she can imagine taking on different formats, such as an eBook version.

Emerson, however, differed in her comprehension of how a book can be understood in relation to new formats when she stated:

> I have just recently purchased a Kindle to use when travelling and I am now beginning to see e-books as actual books as well. I don't think I see audio-books as books because to me they are usually an abridged version and I think of them as more akin to a radio play. They are certainly a way of experiencing a book, but I don't think of them as a book itself.
>
> *(15 November, 2017)*

Simpson connected the term book to its perceived economic value in saying that "a book implies a commodity, rather than a freely accessed piece of fiction" (15 February, 2016).

The authors and publishers in this book have differing definitions of what a book is and can be, and all the definitions are independent of one another. The varied ways that each of the authors understand a book is directly related to their position within the wider industry and what it says are books. Publishers and some authors define a book as an object that has the authority to permit the repetition of its materiality, so the identity of the book itself is never changed even if the format does change.

Askew, Emerson, and Simpson, as authors with agents and publishing deals who can speak with authority from a specific place within the gates of the traditional industry's hierarchy, have an alternative understanding of the book from that of the authors who use social media as places to write and share their work among a community of like-minded readers and writers. Grant simply stated that "a book need only be what the writer intends it to be" (8 February, 2017).

Being an author of Twitter fiction, Grant places himself in a position of authority as an author who chooses to write in online spaces outwith the traditional industry, making his work part of the wider community of science fiction citizen authors who write fiction on social media platforms. In this role, he is able to define his own understanding of what a book is or can be. As such, Grant believes that a book can exist in different, digitally social formats, and that these 'books' also have a place, and value, within the wider discourse. He went on to say that by:

> Forcing [... the writers] to be beholden to traditional notions of what a book can be would undermine the discovery process and the structural freedom that gives social media composition such rich potential.
>
> *(8 February, 2017)*

Grant's position as a citizen author puts his understanding in opposition to how the publishing industry traditionally defines a book as a work that can be developed and sold in formats that are usually limited to print, eBook/app, or audio-based.

The gatekeepers of the industry enact their positions of power by taking on roles as arbiters of what traditionally constitutes a book and therefore dictate what authors should strive towards: a book deal with a publisher, a printed edition, and the cultural currency that comes with being published by a traditional publisher. This systematic hierarchy of the industry exists in relation to the resistance against it, which itself proliferates what Askew called a "snobbery about self-published books," where "authors would rather be published by a real publisher" (Baverstock, 2015). This develops a strategy of power where gatekeeping mechanisms are seen by those in the industry as a means of developing what is understood as a book and, to some extent, the author.

The gatekeepers of the industry and their power to define authors and books

Each of the gatekeepers in the publishing industry have different roles that define their position to and within the hierarchy of the industry and how that positioning enables them to speak, or not, with authority on defining a book. There are several ways these gatekeepers have claimed the power to pronounce what a book is and can be. The authors themselves, aware of the hierarchy of the industry, self-regulate the work they share and become their own gatekeepers – the first gatekeepers – both granting themselves the power to pronounce what a book can be and limiting their power to do so, as they try to fit into the traditional publishing model. The growth in popularity and necessity of having a literary agent provides a second level of gatekeeping to the traditionally published book, with the publishers, the third level of gatekeepers, having the power to choose what will be published, often based on what Askew characterised as "a package that is more than just the words in the book," which in many cases has to do with the author's status both on and offline, previous works, awards won, and other factors that make the author part of the marketing package for the work itself (Baverstock, 2015).

This is not to say that all publishers have the same standards or submission processes, and, in fact, these will vary widely between the individual publishers. The fourth gatekeepers are the bookstores, which have a hand in giving a shop window to the publishers. Finally, the last, and perhaps most contentious, gatekeepers are those readers who have sway over others. These can be social media groups and influencers or people from a celebrity culture that have an influential say in what other readers should pick up or put down. Such people, as well as the bookstores, essentially act as cultural curators, narrowing down the already (relatively) narrow stream of books being published. The "[g]atekeepers – persons or institutions able to confer visibility or legitimacy to cultural products [in this case, books] – occupy an intermediate position between production and consumption" (Merriman, 2017, p. 442), and here they hold the power to develop a definition of a book, or novel, that is taken up in the wider discourse.

Authors like Askew are aware of the tension created by the need to be accepted by the gatekeepers of the industry. She said that "I have far more respect for people who read poetry on Twitter than I do for people who subscribe to *Poetry Review*." She goes on to say that sometimes particular works "are only stocked in certain bookstores and some of them are only in London, and you just kind of think, it's like a gated community" (15 November, 2017). She shows an awareness of the hierarchy of the industry as those that require writers to be accepted into an 'exclusive' community of those who have been published in a traditional fashion in order to progress in their career as authors.

Authors are the first gatekeepers

Authors are the first gatekeepers of the publishing industry. They choose what work to send where and match their writing to what a particular agent or publisher prefers to represent or publish. When an author creates a written work and decides they want to publish it in a traditional fashion (meaning the creation of a printed book/eBook by a physical publisher), they need to have an understanding of which agents and publishing houses are best suited to the style of writing they have produced. For instance, if the writer has written a work of literary fiction and sends it to a publisher of poetry they will be likely be rejected outright, as a large part of what an agent or publisher can sell depends on their speciality, authority to decide what becomes a book in that area, and a knowledge of the market. If the content and themes of the work do not match what the agent or publisher knows and can sell, they will not take up the work and press for traditional publication.

Authors such as Emerson were keenly aware of the need to choose carefully where they sent their work. She said:

> I always made sure I approached only agents who I thought might have an interest in my genre/subject matter. The reason I approached my now agent [...] is because he'd represented [a novel], which had tackled the controversial subject of sex-workers. Thus I figured he wasn't bothered by a bit of controversy!
>
> *(8 February, 2018)*

The self-sorting process begins with the author themselves. They develop an understanding of how the industry works in a hierarchical fashion and who has the authority to accept certain works into the system – to allow these works to become 'books' as understood by the industry. This gives the author a means of self-regulating their writing and the ability to best match their work with the gatekeeper who is in the most likely position to accept it and sell it on to a publisher.

Likewise, Askew says that she doesn't "really post my writing online anywhere because I am aware that that counts as publication" (15 November, 2017). This shows self-censorship in a way that is beholden to what the industry accepts as publishable and published content. This differs between publishers and is beginning to alter. This shift in the power dynamic of what is pulled back into the traditional publishing industry highlights the productivity of power that runs through the discourse of the book (Foucault, 1980, p. 119). The flow of power can be seen in the move to traditional publication of the works by Rupi Kaur and Matt Stewart, whose works were first published on Instagram and Twitter, respectively. However, it should be noted that though Stewart's novel was not a commercial success, Kaur's poetry is; driving the Instapoet movement, she has sold over three million copies of her poetry book *Milk and Honey*. [1]

The larger publishers, notably the recognisable brands of the industry such as Harper Collins, Penguin Random House, etc., from their place at the top of the hierarchy often forgo taking on unsolicited submissions directly from an author, thus limiting access to the highest level of gatekeepers and keeping a top-down framework of power in place. This can be seen from the submission guidelines on the HarperCollins UK site, which advise authors that "We recommend that you consult your local bookstore or library for sources that can direct you in locating an appropriate agent" (Harpercollins, 2020). In this case, authors are denied the power to say what they have written is a 'book' and must first approach and retain the services of a literary agent, who has more authority to speak to the traditional industry than an author does. Much like the process of the author self-selecting the publishers they wish to approach based on how their work might fit into the publisher's list, they perform a similar task in locating and selecting an agent.

The agent is the second gatekeeper

In specifically seeking out agents with an interest in what she writes, Emerson shows not only that she, as an author, is aware of the need to self-censor what she sends and to whom but also that she is aware of how the gatekeeping mechanisms of agents work in the role they play in the complex strategies of how a traditional book gets published.

This inclusion of the literary agent as a part of the gatekeeping mechanisms of the industry evolved along with the growth of rights, complex royalties, and negotiations (Finkelstein & McCleery, 2013, p. 95). With publishers working for readers and agents working for writers, they have both come to occupy different spaces within the hierarchical structure. As such, they have the power to play an exclusionary role in deciding which authors and works get taken on board and published as books.

In the later part of the nineteenth century, the role of agents grew out of authors wanting to take more control of their position in the hierarchy of the industry. With the complexities of contracts and negotiations, authors employed agents for two main tasks: to handle "the extra economic capital an agent could acquire for writers" (Gillies, 2007, p. 25) and to "add to a writer's social status" (Gillies, 2007, p. 26), where the necessity of an agent imbued the author with social capital. This social capital was beneficial in enabling the agent to secure better publishing deals and more recognition for their author; with the aid of an agent, social capital could translate into economic capital, reaffirming the author's place as 'accepted author' in the hierarchy of the industry.

The wrangling of economic capital is something that Askew mentions in her interview, saying of the technical issues of dealing with contracts is "the reason I'd be keen to have one [an agent], because I'm not really confident with that sort of thing" (15 November, 2017).

This echoes what Simpson believes: "you as an author need an agent, because publishers are not looking out for their author's best interests" (15 February, 2016). This understanding of an agent as a key player in both sorting out the contractual details and getting the book to print showcases how some authors have come to feel they need the experience and command of the agent to help unlock the third gate, manned by the publishers themselves.

Today in the UK, there are agents who work as the second level of gatekeepers for an author trying to access the traditional industry. From their area within the hierarchy of the industry, the literary agent is able to decide what is a book in their role as cultural curator. As an intermediary between authors and publishers, their unique position gives them the knowledge and power to ascribe value to a work and to move it to the next level of gatekeepers. They do this with their exclusive selection of the works that authors bring to them. This selectivity can be based on their interests as readers, on previous knowledge of what sells in the industry, or on existing relationships the agent may have with particular publishers, among other factors. The agent has a role in deciding what becomes a book by choosing to represent works that they believe have a mix of cultural and economic capital that will benefit authors, publishers, readers, and the agents themselves.

It is the disruption of this hierarchical process that is of interest when exploring the role the agent has in deciding what a book can be. The author has access to most publishers only via an agenting system, but in turn publishers have little access to the authors except via the agents. Likewise, in this process the author is at a distance from the end reader: the people they are supposed to connect with in the most immediate fashion through their writing. Having a work chosen by the agent originally altered the power dynamic between author and publisher, and as the industry advanced, publishers began to rely more heavily on the agent's role in ascribing a work's value as it relates to its viability as a traditionally published book.

Publishers are the third gatekeepers

The publishing industry itself is one of the largest gatekeepers, and arguably the most powerful. It retains the authority to have the final say about what rules and criteria must be met before a work is allowed to be considered a book. Their position of power at the top of the hierarchy enables the publisher to maintain a conservative definition of the book which does not substantially deviate from its longstanding position. This position of power is not one that is possessed by the publisher; instead, it is one that is formed in relation to the resistance from those outside the hierarchy. This resistance comes in the form of the push for more say by the agent, on behalf of the author, and more recently from the rise of the citizen author.

As for the author, after they find an agent, the agent must 'sell' the work to the publisher before the work can be crafted into the form of a book, as defined by the industry and accepted by the booksellers, both physical and digital. However, even within the publishing houses, there are different rules that relate to what can be a book. These are often based on the economic viability of a work, or the saleability of an author to a wider reading public, and as such, within the publishing houses there is a tension between the editors and the marketers (and more and more these days, the rights team), which can create a power struggle in deciding what books are produced.

Emerson makes reference to this internal hierarchy in the industry when she discusses her path to publication through the traditional author – agent – publisher route. She talks about the way sales and marketing play a large role in the decisions around what gets through the gatekeeping mechanisms of the industry itself:

> [I]t seems the sales and marketing are the final gatekeepers with the ability to say no to something the rest of the team may like. [...] Sales and marketing folk are, I imagine, objective gatekeepers. It is down to potential sales and past sales and figures are figures. [...] Several editors were keen to work with me, but their marketing departments felt the subject matter of abortion was a no-go topic in the way I had approached it and they said it was too risky.
>
> *(8 February, 2018)*

Even within publishing houses there is a push-pull dynamic of the knowledge and power of the different teams in the publishing house, where the necessity of keeping up the editorial standards of the organisation must be balanced with the economic viability and marketability of the work.

Deciding which books a publisher chooses to publish is not based solely on a work's perceived cultural value as an object as it comes from the agent (Merriman, 2017). Instead, there are many constraints within the publishing house that come into play in the gatekeeping process, such as economic restraints that alter depending on the publishing house's particular position and how this position might evolve based on economic successes or failures. A marketer has a key position within an organisation as a voice in selecting a work for publication and so has a thorough understanding of their target audience.

It is through the tension imbedded in the process of its creation as an object that cultural legitimacy is granted to the book when it is published as a physical or digital item with the stamp of approval on it in the form of a publisher's logo. Definitions of what a book is within the publishing industry are held in traditional ways and directly tied to this physical structure and nature of the book, even when it is produced as a digital object.

Citizen authors such as Grant believe that:

> Our concept of publication is still shaped by and stuck in the technological advance of the printing press [and as such authors] dogmatically treat [...] the

novel as a necessary form with its own myriad, seemingly intrinsic necessities instead of a form designed to fit a practical structure.

(8 February, 2017)

What Grant stresses is the need for strategies that loosen the bonds of the rigid structures of the novel as a form that must follow the conventions put into place by the definition of what a book can be. He draws attention to the role that social media plays in allowing that structured format of the book to be played with, stretched and left behind in order to tell a story that fits different mediums where it can be shared.

It is this interaction between the gatekeepers and the citizen authors that is changing ideas about the nature of the book and what it means to be published in spaces outside the institutional role of the publishing industry and its hierarchical structure. Authors, such as Grant, when faced with a rejection from the second gatekeeper, the agent, are spurred on to "challenge [themselves] to write a full novel" (8 February, 2017) and to develop it within the communities of the global village, showing that they can circumvent the gatekeepers and share their works directly with an interested readership, creating a new statement of the book in the process.

The role of the bookstore as gatekeeper

"Making a new book meaningfully available to consumers has traditionally required the assistance of one of the major world publishing houses" (Waldfogel & Reimers, 2015, p. 48), and these publishing houses now often distribute to bookstores, both on and offline, and do not sell books themselves. As a main point of access to buying books, bookstores, especially brick and mortar shops, continue to play a role in how people seek and find books, especially in demographics that are older, female, and have more expendable income (McCabe, 2013). Bookstores are embedded in the exclusivity of the publishing process and access to a readership in the conventional marketplace. The space a bookstore has is constrained by the physicality of the location and the dimensions of the book as an object, defined even in size and shape by the publishing mechanism. The limitations of the bookstore have changed due to the growth of the internet and online shops, which can better utilise a long tail strategy.[2]

Amazon aside, book retailing has been dominated by a handful of chains. Barnes & Noble and larger retail chains and supermarkets accounted for 81% of sales in the USA (Waldfogel & Reimers, 2015). In the UK, the highstreets are dominated by Waterstones, WHSmith, and The Works. In 2018, Waterstones purchased the large, central London flagship independent bookshop Foyles, bringing it into a wider chain management. And in 2019, the hedge fund that owns Waterstones[3] also acquired Barnes & Noble, the largest US bookstore chain. In addition to these changes, Waterstones centralised distribution and ordering early in the 2010s and opened unbranded shops across the country that look and feel like independents but are owned and run by Waterstones.

What this meant for the publishers is that they could no longer purchase premium real estate in the Waterstones shop fronts, and sometimes they could no longer send out sales reps to the shops. For the book-buying customer, this translates into a more niche shopping environment, where, for example, branches may contain more area-specific books – say, those that deal with local history or are written by a local author. What this means for the bookstores themselves is that they have regained a large amount of buying power to stock their shelves and have become more powerful local gatekeepers of which books get in front of customers.

This isn't to say that all bookshops work in the same way as Waterstones. There are many different ways shops choose and display stock. But each store has limited shelf space, even if we take into account the eight miles of shelf space at Waterstones Piccadilly[4] or the Norrington Room at Blackwell's in Oxford.[5] A quick Nielsen Bookscan search shows that there were 255,942 books published in the UK in 2019, far too many to shelve.[6]

Part of the joy of going into a physical bookshop is to browse titles, see what cover jumps out at you, or to be guided by the advice given by employees on what books to read, or what table specials to pick up. The 2017 Centre for Economics and Business Research report on Bookshops asserted that "Bookshops provide a physical interface that can trigger different and unpredictable exploration of themes and topics beyond what was intended when entering the shop" (CEBR, 2017, p. 6). It is part of the bookseller's job to choose what will sell – what window displays, sales, or events will draw customers in. There is no purpose in the bookseller stocking titles that will only be returned to the warehouses.

"Physical retailing added a second filter between creators and consumers" (Waldfogel & Reimers, 2015). Booksellers, both chains and independents, gatekeep what comes into their shops and what consumers have access to purchase. Their stock can be based on a variety of considerations, location, bestsellers, what kinds of customers come into the shop on a regular basis. All of these things influence what bookshops will order, and, in the grand scheme of things, not many make the cut.

> If one or more of the bookselling chains decides not to stock a particular title, then that title will find it very hard to achieve substantial sales and [it will] be virtually impossible for a title to be on the best seller lists if it's not stocked by most of the major chains.
>
> *(Blake, 1999, p. 119)*

New research into the diversity of books has shown that though publishers used to be the key gatekeeper who made BAME and diverse books available, now it's the booksellers. Brandes of Jacaranda Books noted in June 2020 in a conversation with Anamik Saha, a co-author of the Rethinking 'Diversity' in Publishing report, that most booksellers and sales reps are white and middle class and tend to stay in their lane when choosing which books to sell (Chandler, 2020). Likewise, the buying process for large grocery chains, which can help sink or swim a title, are centrally purchased and shipped to stores often with an eye on the same audience: white, middle class, and likely female. This isn't to say that booksellers are intentionally marginalising diverse voices, as Alex Call said in *The Bookseller*, it's likely that they are catering to the people that always come through their doors and are simply not trying to get new audiences into the shop (Chandler, 2020).

Readers as gatekeepers in a connected world

Ramdarshan Bold found in her research on Wattpad that "Readers, especially the most dedicated kind, are most affected by the confines of traditional publishing" (2018, p. 126). Because they are the ones who are most affected by the hierarchy of the industry, they have the power to help change this dynamic, as the power lies with the choice and voice of the reader.

Word of mouth marketing, social media shares and influencers, and cancel culture: all of these are ways that readers have direct influence as gatekeepers of not only books but media. The journalism industry was one of the first to consider the audience of readers as a form of gatekeeper.[7] Research in the area has shown that since we've had data, newsrooms have been interested in using it to better reach their audience and influence their editorial decisions (Vu, 2014). In order for a story to make it to the public, that public must be engaged in the story more broadly than in a traditional media environment (Singer, 2011). This creates tension in the questions of who has control over a story and who can participate in its telling.

Not unlike the changes that have come to bear on journalism, social media and prosumerism allow readers to engage with a work and to gatekeep whether or not it gets shared more widely or shut down. Readers can do this in a variety of ways, three of which are worth looking at more closely: via being influencers, writing reviews, or participating in cancel culture.

Though every reader has the potential to influence another reader, often their reach is limited. According to PEW Research Center, the median number of followers for US users of Twitter (the country with the highest number of Twitter users) is 19 for 90% of users, and 387 for the highest 10% of users (2019). On Instagram, the average number of followers is around 150 (Erin, 2020). In 2014, Pew Research Center also found that the average number of friends on Facebook is 338 (Smith, 2014). As can be seen here, the numbers differ for each platform as to what an average user's reach is. This is not to say that a user can't buy followers, boost their posts, or use other methods to extend their reach, but the base reach that the average user has is not very high.

This relatively small reach from user accounts allows for the rise of influencer culture. Those who have more followers are able to command more of the attention economy on their chosen platform. Generally speaking, the more friends you have, especially on Facebook, the more likely the profile is seen as popular (Kleck et al., 2007). When readers recommend to their friends/followers that they read/not read a particular book, they often come across as genuine to those that know them, but even if all those people decide to boycott a book or buy it, it won't make much of a dent in the sales of a title. This is where the role of the influencer comes in.

Micro-influencers are those 'normal' users who have between 1,000 and 10,000 followers, though there is no consistent measurement regarding opinion leader status (Kay et al., 2020, p. 251). Who we call micro-influencers often relates back to what Carolan and Evain (2013) suggested about self-publishers, in that these people are the bigger fish in a smaller pond of people interested in particular types of content. Micro-influencers are often a key focus of media agencies, as they have that more personal touch and still feel like authentic, accessible people that other users can connect with and relate to. In fact, in a 2020 study, Kay et al. found that "less is more" when it came to follower numbers and brand relationships, highlighting the more persuasive elements of micro-influencers and their ability to feel more authentic than a macro-influencer.

In 2019, Caroline Duong wrote an article for *The Bookseller* on the rise of the micro-influencer in bookselling, quoting that "49 per cent of consumers depend on influencer recommendations." That number goes way up if we look at the rate that women take on such recommendations – up to 86% use social media for purchasing advice (Digital Marketing Institute, 2018) and 53% of women made purchases based specifically on influencer posts (Morrison, 2016). Duong mentions the success stories of Alison Carmen and John Churchman, who both self-published works and used micro-influencers to get the word out: a strategy that paid off in terms of making bestseller lists and getting offers from publishers. Another interesting angle to the role of the micro-influencer is the element of disclosure, making them more authentic to their audiences. Kay et al. found that those micro-influencers who disclosed that they were doing paid advertisements or working in collaboration with a brand actually had higher levels of purchase intentions among their audience (2020). This could be linked to the perceived honesty of the influencer and the way they present themselves as just trying to make a living by sharing their favourite items with their followers. This really shows through when it comes to booktubers and bookstagrammers, who are some of the key micro (and in some cases macro) influencers of the bookish web that have been well researched by Hughes (2017), Anderson (2020), and Thomas et al. (2019).

However, micro-influencers are not the only influencers. There are the macro-influencers such as the Oprahs and Reese Witherspoons of the world that play a particular role in influencing others to pick up a book. Oprah is well known for her talk show that aired 1986–2011. She has a book review club that has reached the pinnacle of publishing PR. Getting your author on Oprah guarantees exponential sales. "The all-powerful Oprah Book Club is not so much a club as a ruthlessly influential marketing vehicle, with the power to fundamentally alter bestseller lists, Amazon rankings and royalty payments" (Pickert, 2008). For instance, when Oprah was in her classics phase and recommended *Anna Karenina*, Penguin ordered 800,000 more books ready to hit the shelves (Pickert, 2008).

Over the years, Oprah has personally chosen and reviewed 86 books in her book club on her TV programme and on an Instagram account. She has recently joined forces with Apple to have even more reach when it comes to selling the books she recommends. On an arguably lesser-known scale globally is Reese Witherspoon's book club, for which she reviews books with women at the heart. It has 1.9 million followers on Instagram, which is where the book club began. Witherspoon also posts the books on her own profile, which has 24.8 million followers. You can follow her conversation across social media, including Goodreads. Author Ruth Ware suggested in a 2017 article in *Publishers Weekly* that Witherspoon has now recommended three books for her book club, the third of which was also influenced by PR from Simon and Schuster. In addition, notably, Ware admitted that she didn't see any noticeable sales jumps based on these inclusions (Boog, 2017) but that she "had so many readers tell [her] that they picked up the book specifically on [Witherspoon's] recommendation" (Boog, 2017).

Other macro-influencers with celebrity status also play a part in introducing a new book to readers. Celebrities like Kim Kardashian and Emma Watson each have their own book clubs. Mariah Carey posted a photo of a stack of her favourite books on her Instagram (2020) with the caption "2020 essential reading." At the top of the stack was her book *The Meaning of Mariah Carey*, which Nielsen Bookscan shows sold roughly 300 more copies in the UK in December after her post. Though images on social media of celebrities pictured with books and carefully curated shelves are relevant in that their audience could want to emulate the celebrity's reading habits, what followers are often attracted to more, both at the micro and macro-influencer level, are the reviews.

A history of institutionalised reviews in the academic field can be dated back to the mid-1600s in European cultural centres like Paris and Bologna, but reviews of works go back much further to Athens BCE (Obeng-Odoom, 2014). Books and manuscripts have always been reviewed, and people always have an opinion. In academia, it's getting harder for time-poor lecturers or PhD students to justify writing book reviews when book reviews rarely count in the world of 'publish or perish.' But in the world of fiction, reviews have thrived and are part of how readers become gatekeepers in the digital era.

In 2019, of the 39 literary magazines that the Vida Count reviewed for gender balance of reviewers, only 15 published more reviews by women and non-binary people than men. In the main count, only 3 publications published reviews by women and non-binary authors more than 50% of the time (The Vida Count, 2019). If we look more closely at the UK market of established publications that review books, *London Review of Books* only managed 32.64% inclusion of women reviewers. To address the poor showing in equality, it's worth quoting the response *London Review of Books* gave to the Vida Count in 2014 (quoted in the 2019 report) in which they cited a 2001 interview:

> When [...] Mary-Kay Wilmers, gave an interview [...] in 2001, she put it this way: 'I think women find it difficult to do their jobs, look after their children, cook dinner and write pieces. They just can't get it all done. And men can. Because they have fewer, quite different responsibilities [...] They're not so frightened of asserting themselves. And they're not so anxious to please. They're going to write their pieces and to hell with the rest. And I don't think women think that way.'

The publications considered by the Vida Count are important in how they influence the industry and what certain readers will purchase, but the growth of digital communities has allowed for a more democratic spread of reviews of works in online spaces.

When we think of online reader reviews, Goodreads often comes to mind. Goodreads launched in 2007 with a mission to "help people find and share books they love" (Goodreads, 2020a). In 2013, it was purchased by Amazon and has grown to over 90 million reviews in 2019 (Clement, 2020). The platform, much like other community-driven platforms, has low barriers to entry. This allows for any reader to create an account and leave stars and comments on a work. Whether a user is a reviewer or lurker, Goodreads can still be considered elitist. The platform invites advertisers to use their advertising programmes to reach an "affluent and educated audience" (Goodreads, 2020b). This audience also happens to be 75% female (Thelwall & Kousha, 2017). This links back to the gatekeeping booksellers, who believe their target audience is mostly white, middle class, and often female.

Readers generally are "well educated and with a high proportion of females" (Griswold et al., 2005), especially in developed nations (Thelwall, 2017), and like to share their views on Goodreads. Thelwall found that star ratings for books written by authors of the same gender as the reviewer are more favourable, but the reviews themselves often aren't (2017). And that women tend to prefer male-authored reviews, perhaps for the more information-driven way that the book is reviewed, which links to how men and women communicate in digital settings differently (2017).

Gender differences aside, authors and readers alike believe that reviews matter. A quick Google search for 'do book reviews help sales' turns up 1,690,000,000 results on the topic of why reviews matter or how to get your book reviewed in the best places. On Goodreads, there is a discussion with 48 comments that argues over the usefulness of reviews for sales, or if good sales lead to more reviews. The 'which comes first' question can be argued repeatedly,[8] but what matters most here is the way readers review books and if those reviews hold sway with the purchasing power of other readers.

Research by BrightLocal revealed that in 2019

> 79% of consumers say they trust online reviews as much as personal recommendations from friends or family. These days, word of mouth can come from outside a consumer's social circle, with an online review having a ripple outside of a happy (or unhappy!) customer's peers.
>
> *(Murphy, 2020)*

Kathryn Brown, writing for IngramSpark, states that when it comes to consumer reviews, what matters most is quantity over quality (2017). She goes on to say that book reviews by professionals (like the writers counted in the Vida Count) are valuable for a book's success in establishing "credibility and competence" in the market, "set[ting] the tone for reader interaction" and supporting the author by giving the work the validation of the publishing hierarchy (2017).

In an article in *The Millions*, Natalie Bakopoulos leads with the story that Alexander Maksik's debut novel *You Deserve Nothing* was praised by professional reviewers in *The New York Times* and other outlets only to be castigated by *Jezebel* for being a bit too close to the author's personal experiences (2013). She states that "Amazon and Goodreads readers retracted their stars and updated their reviews to show their disgust and moral outrage" (2013). Subsequently, Bakopoulos notes, the reviews for Maksik's second book have hovered around that literary 'scandal,' tainting the tone.

Bakopoulos goes on to say that

> when as reviewers we ignore the created experience and instead focus on the author and his or her 'right' to create, or not create, we never even enter the conversation. Nothing is revealed. The map is blank and therefore useless.
>
> *(2013)*

This questioning of the author's right to create leads directly into another area where the reader has become more powerful in recent years, that of cancel culture.

We hear the term 'cancel culture' being batted around the internet with various meaning and moral obligations attached to it. It can be, as Clark notes, "an expression of agency, a choice to withdraw one's attention from someone or something whose values, (in)action, or speech are so offensive, one no longer wishes to grace them with their presence, time, and money" (2020). But more colloquially it has come to mean a silencing of individuals or groups or the removal of their public platform to hold them to account for what could be seen as 'immoral' behaviour (Henderson, 2020). There is a growing pool of scholarship around cancel culture,[9] but here we will focus on how it comes to bear on the publishing industry, specifically on readers as those who have the power to cancel books and content.

According to Clark, being cancelled has its roots in the queer communities of colour (2020, p. 89), and was then taken up by journalists, where it took on a different meaning of censorship and silencing. 'Being cancelled,' according to Clark, should be the last resort for justice in the face of the transgressions of those who are out of reach of the average person – celebrities, authors, etc. (2020, p. 89). Regarding cancel culture in literature, we can look at both sides of the argument: there are those like Lionel Shriver who bemoan cancel culture and the lack of 'free speech,' and those like Amélie Wen Zhao who choose to remove their book from publication due to 'sensitivities.'

The role of cancel culture is most prevalent in YA literature, where both authors and publishers are making more use of sensitivity readers to indicate if a work treats a specific group of characters, often minorities, in a negative light. With Zhao, her hotly anticipated first book of a fantasy trio was castigated on Twitter for being racial insensitive, and she was accused of harassing reviewers who did not like her work. What started out as a few tweets from a single book reviewer on Twitter, who has less than 900 followers, snowballed until Zhao asked for her book to be pulled, prior to publication.

Likewise, Laurie Forest's *The Black Witch* was accused of being racist and homophobic by a book blogger, Shauna Sinyard, who ripped the book apart in a long review. Twitter threads damned the novel, and the author of the review called out the publisher, asking why they were publishing it and why no one had commented officially. Furthermore, there was a coordinated effort to give the book low Goodreads reviews and to ask readers of the book why they would support such a work. Importantly, this was all before publication.

This sort of suppression of a work and those associated with it goes deeper than the calling out of the author and publisher and the coordinated Goodreads reviews. Journalist Kat Rosenfield was accused of bullying and having a vendetta when she tried to approach Sinyard for an interview about her *Black Witch* review for an article challenging cancel culture within the realm of Young Adult fiction titles. Rosenfield's publisher, *Vulture*, was also harassed over why they enabled her to write this piece. Likewise, most of the people Rosenfield spoke to refused to give their real name for fear of backlash from those readers and authors with influence (2017).

In 2019, another author, Kosoko Jackson, also pulled his book from publication due to backlash that started on Goodreads and moved to Twitter. Early on, his book, *A Place for Wolves*, was lauded due to its portrayal of a gay love story against the backdrop of the Kosovo War. But as soon as the commentary snowballed over social media, Jackson pulled the book from publication. The irony in this is that Jackson himself is a sensitivity reader and also took part the above-mentioned Zhao controversy online. As Singal sums it up: "The guy who helped contribute to a stifling climate of plot-policing and paranoia received the same treatment he had doled out to others" (2019).

However, it should be noted that the ripple effect went further, with another successful YA author, Heidi Heilig, apologising for writing a good review of the book on Goodreads. Her updated review is quite short and now reads, in part "I'm editing my review in light of recent critiques, as it reads as flippant and disrespectful. To those I've hurt by my blurb, I apologize. I'm always working to do better, clearly i need to work harder [sic]" (2018).

This isn't to say that only YA books are affected by cancel culture, or that no cancelled books ever make it to publication. In fact, *Blood Heir*, *The Black Witch*, and *A Place for Wolves* have all been published. In 2020, because of such reader and, in this case, employee backlash, Hachette cancelled their publication of Woody Allen's autobiography *Apropos of Nothing*, just four days after it was announced. A small American indie snapped it up and published the book in March 2020. Natasha Tynes tweeted to shame someone who was eating on the underground in D.C. (no, they weren't supposed to be eating), and it took off on Twitter. Because of the backlash, her publisher Rare Bird Books cancelled her contract for her upcoming novel *They Called me Wyatt*.

There are numerous examples of the power of readers on social media to cancel authors and works.[10] While some of these works would, indeed, benefit from a read through, it does beg the question, as raised by Shriver in her article in *Prospect Magazine*, of who gets to say who can write fiction and why those that dare to write outside of their lived experience are cancelled.

The power of the citizen author's role in the publishing industry

The power that the industry has in defining a book is fragile because the industry does not own this power exclusively. The strategy of pulling new definitions of the book back into the hierarchy is a means of wielding the power to keep the traditional definition of the book as the visible, prominent one.

In the traditional publishing model, there are different levels of gatekeeping, with the publisher at the top, the agent in the middle, and the author at the bottom. The author must move up the hierarchy and adhere to the elements of inclusion put forth by the industry in order to have their work produced by a publisher and released to the market in the traditional fashion. This movement sits alongside, and relates to, the audience of readers, who are involved in the subtle push and pull between telling the publishers what to publish (by their purchases) and buying what the publishers introduce to the market and heavily promote, highlighting that power does not always come from above and that its transience depends on what position the person speaking holds within the industry (or adjacent to it).

In this model, the author is the one that is left powerless, as author Matt Stewart, author of the Twitter-shared novel *The French Revolution*, suggested, stating that "in the end, you are just waiting [...] and there's really nothing you can do. It's just a completely emasculating feeling [...] I had no power" (1 June, 2016). With the advent of, and access to, the internet in the mid-nineties and the rise of the citizen author, who creates as well as consumes what they find online, the power that is predominantly held by traditional publishers is shifting.

The citizen author is driving this shift in the power hierarchy by forming resistance in three key ways: by going directly to the reader within their communities, by gaining power within these communities through reader numbers and interactions, and by working with the platforms themselves to bring their writing into the marketplace as a traditionally published book. At first glance, this is a shift which empowers the author, and it does, but looking more closely, these disruptions alter and reaffirm that there are always power structures in place, as power does not come from a top-down position but exists in all relationships.

Firstly, the citizen author challenges the power structures of the publishing industry and their gatekeepers by simply "circumvent[ing] the traditional publishing gatekeepers to make their products directly available to the consumer" (Waldfogel & Reimers, 2015, p. 48). This takes place within the communities developed in the global village, where we begin to see the disruptions to the discourse of the book that come from places such as Twitter, Facebook, Medium, Wattpad,

FanFiction.net and others where different formats are regularly accepted. As these disruptions take place, citizen authors gain more authority in terms of who has the ability to say what a book is.

Citizen authors such as Grant, Lopés, and Thompson are pushing back against gatekeepers by choosing to write in a digitally social space where they can connect directly with potential readers. Grant says "[t]he internet and social media represent the ultimate democratization. I'm not enchanted by the romance of big publishing house[s] and physical books, but I am excited by the creative possibilities of this new medium" (8 February, 2017).

These authors are all using the medium of Twitter to tell stories. They are doing this by using the #Twitterfiction hashtag and inserting their stories into a stream of fiction on the social platform, and they approach this in different ways.

Grant says he "purposefully did [as] little planning as possible [and approaches] planning as a very loose guideline for characters to organically play out, the less consciously planned the better" (8 February, 2017). In the spaces where he writes, Grant's choice to forgo the planning of his stories differs greatly from the strict planning, writing, and production process required by the traditional industry, where there can be a long lead time between delivery of manuscript and publication, with many levels of editorial and marketing oversight in-between. Likewise, Simpson takes part in Twitter roleplay, where she writes in reaction to the content published by her writing partner. She then moves this content into Archive of Our Own, publishing it on the repository as a work of fan fiction, where she says it was "translating remarkably well into connected prose […] I think that if this weren't a fan work, it would be publishable after some editing" (15 February, 2016).

Not all authors who work on social platforms spontaneously write and share their works, but doing so makes them subversive in the eyes of the traditional publishing industry. Grant takes advantage of his ability to write spontaneously within the constraints of the platforms, while Lopés and Thompson are able to establish themselves by choosing a writing and publishing timeline, with both approaches being outside the traditional publishing mechanism. Lopés and Thompson both wrote out and scheduled the Tweets in advance, which Lopés calls "[t]he one, surefire [sic] way to make sure […they] don't exceed the 140-character limit" (20 January, 2017).

The transfer of power from the publisher to the author was first pushed by the modern, self-published author. Grant is one such author and took his polished Twitter works and put them on as many other platforms as he could and then to online digital book retailers such as Smashwords and Scribd.[11] For him, the goal is to gain readers, not traditional publication.

Specialist companies have cropped up to help the self-publishing author edit, format, market, and sell their books. Amazon, the home of the long tail strategy of bookselling, has branched out into self-publishing. Others such as Smashwords, Lulu, and more raise questions of power relationships in the marketplace in stepping in and providing authors a service and thus actively helping them to move around the traditional publishing mechanism.

In some cases, it is only after the citizen author has gained power that is measured in connectivity (such as followers or views) that publishers are willing to pay attention. This is the second key way that the citizen author is disrupting the traditional hierarchies of the publishing industry. An example of this is Stewart's novel, which was published in its entirety on Twitter prior to being picked up and published by a traditional publishing company, because, as he says about the process and gaining readership, "it can't hurt, all there is, is upside" (1 June, 2016). The novel on Twitter began to garner interest in the digital community and was then published in a traditional format by Soft Skull Press in 2010. Likewise, though Grant's original goal was to gain readers, since our first interview in 2016, he has published one of his novels, *The Upholstery Man*, with small publisher Thurston Howell and has another collection of short stories in the making. All of his published works began as works of fiction written on both Twitter and Facebook.

This move to pick up works written on social platforms by the second and third level of gatekeepers can be seen on both a large scale, where publishers solicit work from social media influencers such as Rupi Kaur (poetry) and Hulin's novel *Hey Harry, Hey Matilda*, and on a smaller scale, where publishers such as Unbound seek out middle-range Twitter writers to collaborate on a traditionally published work. The process of allowing the citizen author to create their own connections within the global village, which are then exploited by the publishing industry, brings into play a strategy of hierarchisation where those who have the most connections and power within their online communities are the ones sought after by the publishing industry. By harnessing the power of the citizen author, the publisher benefits from their digitally social connections. This, for publishers and agents, cuts out some of the guesswork that the publishing industry is notorious for and can give them a formula for publishing successful books (Anders, 2011, p. 326). Though authors such as Askew "don't think [...agents] are a necessity at all," the agenting system is not likely to end, and, indeed, Askew has an agent herself that has helped her place several books (15 November, 2017).

Social platforms are taking a more active role in selling and promoting the citizen authors who choose to share their work within them. This, in turn, is being driven by the author's move back to the centre of the publishing model, which is a third way that authors are challenging power structures. The author creates and shares a work of fiction when and where they choose, and the publishers, agents, and even the platforms themselves are moving to accommodate the best of them and pull them back into the fold of traditional publishing. This is not to say that all authors will be read by millions, sought after for publishing deals, and sign contracts on their own terms; instead, the pool of citizen authors, like self-publishers, will grow as the use of social platforms increases.

The citizen author is at the centre of new technology and expanding digitally social spaces which have imbedded power dynamics based on who has admittance to and use of these spaces. Publishers generally have access to social platforms and technology, but publishing is reactionary when it comes to digital technology and social spaces. In the coming years they will catch up with the rise of the citizen author and will actively seek to shift the power dynamic back in their favour by potentially leveraging the power of reader numbers, views, and the cultural economy of a printed book more definitively in their publishing strategy.

The dual role of power and quality in the production of a book

A part of authors leveraging the power of publishers relates to the role of what a book is and who has the power to say what a book can become. As gatekeepers, the author, agent, publisher, booksellers, and readers can make a decision on what works will reach a wider, traditionally published status and therefore what will be accepted as a book. The position of a conservatively created printed item as an arbiter of quality and good writing holds weight with authors who want their works to become part of the read canon of literature, which almost always means having a work in printed format. Askew acknowledges that she is:

> aware that a lot of people are still snobby [and that she has] ambition for [... her] novel and if it comes off [... she wants] people to kind of respect it and think it's good and [that this is not] just someone who shoved a pdf on Amazon and hasn't really thought about it.
>
> *(15 November, 2017)*

It is this understood hierarchical power of the traditional publishing industry that directly allows agents and publishers to embody the status to decide what reaches a wider reading audience. From their position of authority as gatekeepers, publishers have an overview of what books have performed well both culturally and economically. Even within their own organisation, marketers, editors, and slush pile-reading interns will all have different amounts of authority to ascribe value to a work. The hierarchy of the publishing industry directly drives the understanding of value and quality, as it employs strategies to promote specific works that have been accepted, published, and marketed within their hierarchical structure.

They do this through their selection process, which is based on more than perceived quality and links unequivocally to the socio-economic potential of the work, insomuch that the book must be economically viable in order for it to be worthwhile for the publisher to produce it. This is not to say that all publishers only publish works that are of great literary merit, or that all focus only on money-making ventures. It is instead often a balance between creating cultural capital and creating socio-economic capital that drives the publishing industry to include or exclude authors.

John King at Tatterdemalion Blue said that:

> Because sometimes I know the process of trying to make that next step and sometimes you feel you want to help others to make that step and you're not taking on a book that is going to be a bestseller. You're taking on a book to inspire someone to make the next step.
>
> *(25 February, 2016)*

Some publishers, such as Tatterdemalion Blue and Unbound, have business models that enable the publisher to produce works that may not be million-copy bestsellers but which allow for the economic pressure to sell to be reduced as a driving force in choosing which works deserve to be created as printed, bound, and shared works. For Tatterdemalion Blue, the impetus is less on making financial gains with a publication and more on supporting burgeoning authors at a local level. This variety of traditional publishing has grown in the last year, where small publishing houses have taken advantage of markets that are often underrepresented by the larger publishing houses (the big five[12]).

According to John King, a part of the power of the publisher and their position in the making of cultural and socio-economic capital is the editorial role they provide, where they can "offer guidance" (25 February, 2016).

Within the wider industry, there is a struggle to conserve the established order, which exists in the competition between the gatekeepers, especially publishers, who already hold the power, and those who work to create new concepts of the book. Publishers have a vested interest in continuing to maintain the status quo of the author – agent – publisher – reader model of the traditional industry. Not only does keeping the current system allow publishers to accrue the cultural capital of publishing renowned authors, whose agents will seek them out for publishing deals, but this same share of the cultural capital feeds back into the socio-economic capital that publishing a bestseller can provide the company.

Mittell sums up the relationship between texts and the hierarchy that produces them in saying that "Texts only exist through their production and reception, so we cannot make the boundary between texts and their material cultural contexts absolute" (Mittell, 2001, p. 7). This is evident when Askew speaks of publishing work in journals such as *Poetry Review*, which she says are:

> read by largely old, largely white, largely conservative [readers, where] it's like a gated community [...] yet it's necessary to be approved of by that gated community in order to keep going.
>
> *(15 November, 2017)*

Askew feels that Twitter is comprised of "a democratic, open, honest, diverse community" that is not found so much among the industry's high-art literary journals, even if those gatekeepers are the tastemakers of the industry.

The gatekeeping mechanisms in place in the publishing industry inspire self-perpetuating forms of resistance and capitulation, where an author may choose to publish in online communities where readers are but still might want offline validation and so needs the approval of the gatekeepers in order to gain wider access to those offline communities.

Emerson found that she spent "a lot of time in the dark" working within the traditional publishing model: "you get through the gatekeepers and then you have to fall back on yourself again" and trust your work is good enough for the readers (8 February, 2018).

Response from readers can be improved by avoiding the traditional publishing model and sharing work directly with interested communities online.

In our conversation, Askew points out that she:

> wouldn't be relying on a publisher to tell [... her] that [... her] novel was any good because [... she knows] that publishers are not always interested in what's good. They are interested in what fits with their lists or what will sell, or what is trendy.
>
> *(15 November, 2017)*

Here, Askew shows a clear understanding of her novel's relationship to publishers and the value that she ascribes to it as opposed to the value she ascribes to what the wider industry might see as fitting into their list or as saleable. This sort of knowledge facilitates a pushback against the tastemakers of the traditional industry, where authors are relying less on the cultural value ascribed by these tastemakers and more on that ascribed by the readers. However, the industry itself, and its role in creating cultural and socio-economic capital, still presents a strong model, which the global village has begun to emulate.

The sidewinders reproducing some aspects of the industry's traditional hierarchy and their contradictions

The citizen author's and the traditional industry's models of publishing are taking on more and more aspects of one another as new understandings of what a book can be have surfaced in the expanding publishing environment. In this way, it is useful to look at the "extent and form of the gap that separates them" (Foucault, 1989, p. 152) and how this gap is altering. Where there appear to be contradictions between the hierarchy, these contradictions are either those "of appearances" (Foucault, 1989, p. 151), which are resolved in the overarching unity of the wider discourse, or those that reach a more foundational level, which gives rise to an entirely new discourse (Foucault, 1989, p. 151). And one may lead into the other.

The trickle-down gatekeeping mechanisms that support the hierarchy of the publishing industry become evident not only in the way that authors and agents approach and value the potential cultural capital of a work but also in the way that the authors have come to reproduce some of the hierarchical attributes of the industry in a global context. The industry itself finds what the citizen authors consider a book to be challenging to their hierarchy and power structures, but they also seek to harness this power. Likewise, the citizen authors, who are writing from within these digital communities, begin to see the value of the gatekeepers and start to reproduce some of the processes the gatekeepers have in place.

Simpson recognises the usefulness of gatekeepers in the industry when she says "[b]eing rejected by gatekeepers was very good for me and for my work and made me improve my writing" (15 February, 2016). The idea of an author using the gatekeeping mechanism as a means to improve their writing is a theme that is echoed by Emerson, who says "I was keen to see if any of the advice that was given could make my book better" (8 February, 2018). This shows how authors are open to embracing some of the benefits that working with a gate-keeper can provide, especially as it relates to editorial guidance. In this we see the acceptance and normalisation of some of the hierarchical elements of the traditional industry model.

The readers themselves have a role in the power distribution in digital settings and can provide editorial guidance. As such, they take on the role of gatekeeper in their communities. This move to readers as editors is evident in the feedback that takes place in digital communities, where readers are able to interact with authors and have belief in their authority to do so. This is a democratic process, as there are no guidelines on commenting in a particular digital space beyond how those interactions play a role in establishing normative behaviours within that community (Barnes, 2018, p. 83).

The interactions and feedback can be as simple as reinforcement from readers in the form of "a like or retweet on Twitter," as Lopés says (20 January, 2017), or much more complicated and in-depth as seen in Book One of *The Love Curse, Arrowheart* by Rebecca Sky. In the work by Sky, the interactions between the author and readers play out in the in-line comments that are enabled by the plat-form. The first chapter alone has received two million views and has some 1,700 comments.[13] Not all of these comments require interaction between the reader and author, such as when user TheGeekyMe comments on the first paragraph of the work, "I'm ready. Here we go" (14 August, 2016). Other comments are more detailed, and Sky responds to many individually.

One example of this is in the first chapter, where reader Serendipity2909 writes, "Mariss here is [sic] seems far alike from Marissa in [CC, a different work by the author]" (10 April, 2017a). To this, Sky responds in a friendly and inviting manner saying:

> haha they are polar opposites. I wrote cc Marissa to apologize to anyone named Marissa after making their name look bad with this Marissa ?????.
>
> *(10 April, 2017)*

Serendipity2909 wrote back the same day saying, "Haha! That's nice of you" (10 April, 2017b). What is important to note about this interaction between a reader and the author is that it is happening in a way that allows for the citizen author to explain their choices in a work and for a reader to make suggestions that may or may not be taken on board by the author. Likewise, unlike the power held by those within the industry, a reader who takes on the role of editor (either upon request of the author or unsolicited) cannot halt the process of publication of a work. In fact, many of the works that the readers edit and make suggestions on are already in the digital community. However, if an author does choose to accept the suggested edits, the work can be edited live or a new version can be instantly uploaded; there is no need to halt the process of publication.

Other repositories that hold works of fan fiction, such as FanFiction.net, have numerous examples of readers imposing gatekeeping mechanisms for entry into the wider canon of certain genres of fiction and what can be considered a book within that field. One such example of this is in the commentary to the Jane Austen Fan Fiction (JAFF)[14] *Dangerous Curves*, which was written by PhatBasset (2005) and posted on FanFiction.net. Though most of the commentary on this nearly 51,000-word work is positive, there are readers who refuse to allow the work into the canon of Austen literature and the fan fiction that surrounds her writing. Reader Guest writes negatively about the adherence to the traits of the original characters in *Pride and Prejudice*, and it is worth quoting in its entirety:

> I have really liked the story up until this chapter. I didn't think the story line adhered very closely to traditional Pride and Prejudice, but I also don't think that is necessary, and your story was good. However, I think this chapter presents a silly, one-sided view of life. In giving up his old life, William would be giving up not only his money but also his home, family, and friends. He would presumably be able to talk to Richard, but he would have to leave Georgiana, Christopher, Bingley, Jane, and Mrs. Reynolds behind, perhaps without even saying goodbye. Love may be more important than being rich, but wealth wouldn't be the only consideration in this decision, and I don't think this chapter acknowledges that properly.
>
> *(29 October, 2013)*

In their commentary on the works published in digital social communities, readers themselves become the gatekeepers to a wider canon where the work by the author may or may not be accepted and therefore more widely read.

This echoes the gatekeeping mechanisms in the traditional industry in three ways. The first is the level of self-editing and censoring what they write and where they share it, as can be seen with authors such as Thompson and Lopés actively choosing to plan out their writing prior to posting it on a social platform in order to make the storyline fit with the platform and the potential readers. Grant discusses how he chose to focus more on embracing what made his work so unsuitable for inclusion in the traditional industry's consideration of a book.

The second way that we can see the hierarchal gatekeeping system coming into play is with reader dialogues with an author that comment on writing style, grammatical errors, or the organisation of the work. In acting as those who want to better the author's work, readers function as an unsolicited editorial service, similar to what an agent would provide if a work was accepted for representation. Not all readers choose to comment on elements of an author's work; in fact, many choose to ignore minor errors as part of the normal fabric of a work that has been published in a digitally social setting. Others simply choose to retweet, like, 'heart,' or provide short, positive messages on works to encourage an author to continue to write.

The third way the digital community echoes hierarchical gatekeeping mechanisms is in readers admitting a certain genre of writing into a cannon themselves.

The readers who have the most power in a digital setting can review a work in a way that markets the work to a wider audience, echoing marketers in the publishing industry. As seen in the quote by Guest above, some works do not reach the expectations of the reader, and as such, this creates tension where the reader may chastise the citizen author in the commentary, thus publicly refusing the work's entry into the established canon. This refusal of entry does not mean that the work will not find an audience; it is, in fact, already published in the global community of writers and readers. However, it can affect how widely a work is shared. The "aggressive Doberman loyalty" (Roberts, 2007, p. 343) discussed earlier highlights the sense of ownership some readers have towards a work. This loyalty does not only apply to works of fan fiction but all forms of writing in digitally social spaces.

The power of the platforms' mediation

"Twitter is the platform I a) use most, b) like most but also c) feel the most need to alter my behaviour on," says Askew (15 November, 2017). As an author who lives 'as an author' in her Twitter community, she has an understanding of how the platforms allow for different mediations and connectivity, both wanted and unwanted. This relates back to the first level of gatekeeper being the author themselves, as they alter their behaviour and writing to better inhabit the communities of their choice. It also deals specifically with the gendering of digitally social spaces, where the mediation of platforms plays a role in how gender is portrayed and censored, which specifically affects the citizen author, who is more likely to be female and to go to these spaces to circumvent censorship and gatekeeping.

With authors having conceived notions of the digitally social spaces, another consideration relating to the power dynamic is the role the platform plays as a mediator in what can and cannot be done where the citizen authors and readers come together, where "social media sites and search engines are the main arbiters of what gets communicated" (Heins, 2014, p. 325) and where "Western platforms such as Facebook or Google is algorithmically mediated, often resembling 'echo chambers'" (Srinivasan & Fish, 2017, p. 13).

Though a user often feels they have control of their profile and communications online, "platforms run on account of coded protocols that appear to 'mediate' people's social activities, while in fact steering social traffic" (Van Dijck, 2012, p. 145). Every interaction is mediated via a platform that is based on underlying code and algorithms. Each like, comment, post, or retweet is performed in the way that the platform itself is designed to allow, and though many platforms now allow for posting across writing, video, sound, etc., this connectivity is still performed under strict platform guidelines.

Askew says that "I'll sometimes mis-spell deliberately in order to prevent namesearches [sic] (e.g. G4merG4te), or I'll do what I've noticed many other female Twitter users do and use a nickname for a person you don't want to name and draw fire for talking about (e.g. Nigel Garage or Nigel Garbage, etc)."

She goes on to speak about how:

> these self-preservation measures are implemented to a greater or lesser degree on all platforms except Instagram. I find Instagram feels very female, very safe, and very benign. I call it my social media 'happy place,' as it's the only place on social media where I haven't experienced abuse or harassment (thus far… touch wood).
>
> *(15 November, 2017)*

The choice and 'personalities' of the platforms used by authors show that the way the sites are moderated in regard to their commentary and interactions around a work (or social media post) can impact on the behaviours of those who participate on them (Barnes, 2018, p. 78). While this mediation is often not felt directly by the users, it is a form of power relation that develops between the user and the designer through the interface of the platform (Cirucci, 2017, p. 2). It must also be noted that there may be inequality of access to these platforms, where the benefits provided by the platforms are "disproportionately enjoyed by those already in positions of privilege" (Srinivasan & Fish, 2017, p. 29). This echoes McLuhan's concerns about those in positions of privilege having the power to authoritatively state what a book can be in the new digital locations.

Through platforms' interfaces, the gender of a user is specified through the options available on the site, and many, though not all, are designed to replicate the hegemonic ideal of the offline world, which is predominantly run by white men (Cirucci, 2017, p. 5). In addition to the gendering of digital spaces, there is an element of marketing and capitalism that underlines the choices that are provided by the platforms. Those which offer two or three options of gender, or none, can sell marketing data of a much less specific nature than those platforms that provide many options, or allow a user to enter their own interpretation of gender.

Not only are the authors and readers required to adhere to the platforms' policies and use them within the limits of the digital structures imposed, so are the publishers, who use digitally social platforms for marketing, sharing information with readers, or for seeking out new works of fiction. There are limits to the length of messages that can be posted, with the most well-known being Twitter's 280-character count. There are similar guidelines around imagery and content which cannot be sexually charged, or overtly violent, or threatening (Facebook, Twitter, Instagram, Wattpad, 2020). While this may not have much of an effect on publishers, who can tailor their content to suit the platforms, it can have a direct effect on the way that the citizen authors interact with the site and how communities develop on it.

Another area where the mediation of the platforms moves beyond facilitation of writing and sharing is where it could potentially censor the content by citizen authors who are writing on sensitive or volatile topics, such as Emerson, who deals with sensitive topics related to abortion. A close look at Facebook and Wattpad shows that they have clauses in their Terms of Service allowing them to remove any content or information posted that doesn't fit in with their terms, effectively censoring some forms of work and creating a unique power dynamic between users and the sites. In fact, the large platforms have been considered to have "more power in determining who can speak and who can be heard around the globe than any Supreme Court justice, any king or any president" (Rosen, qtd. by Helft, 2010).

If Facebook deems something to be in violation, they have the authority to remove the content (such as that dealing with violence or exploitation, hate speech, or infringement of copyright), and sometimes the user's account is terminated. Similarly, on Wattpad, the company has the authority to remove offensive material and, uniquely, works that are of excessive length. Generally speaking, large-scale social networking sites (See Litt, 2013 and Breslawski, 2014) lend themselves to "subjective and unpredictable censorship of literature, art, and political discussion" (Heins, 2014, p. 326).

For authors using social media sites as places to write works of fiction that deal with graphic scenes or sensitive topics, there will always be a worry that the platform they've chosen to write on will remove their posts and potentially red-flag or terminate their accounts. This could lead to female-identifying citizen authors censoring themselves and their work as a trade-off for being able to utilise the platform as a creative outlet with a ready-made audience of social connections. While this form of front-end prevention by Facebook and other sites exists to protect their users, generally, it is somewhat ironic that "Facebook has a [...] right to censor whatever it wants in order to maintain the kind of social space it wants" (Heins, 2014, p. 326).

Though the platforms likely do not purposely gender their censorship of content they deem unacceptable; they do censor it according to the guidelines of the heteronormative and masculine discourses of the offline world.[15] In relation to the citizen authors and the digital community on social media, these spaces are used predominately by women, who are actively bypassing the traditionally male industry, and the censoring of their work is gendered, if not by design then by execution. Gendered censorship relates to the fiction, sometimes graphic, written and read by female-identifying citizen authors and readers which can be suppressed both by the wider industry and by the social platforms.

For those who are writing fictions on visual platforms, the censorship moves beyond the wording and use of hashtags, shares, and comments to the censorship of visible female bodies (Olszanowski, 2014). However, it should be noted that among the niche fiction repositories, there can be much more freedom to write and share controversial works that a more 'public' social platform might deem unacceptable. Repositories such as Literotica, FanFiction.net, and many more allow for the relatively ungoverned exploration of fictions that might be considered taboo or commercially unviable in the wider publishing industry.

The new role of platforms and how publishers are trying to reclaim the power of the citizen author

The main power to pronounce what a book is and can be is located in the publishing industry and supported by the hierarchy involved in the author – agent – publisher model. However, new players are the platforms themselves, who have developed innovative strategies that work with the citizen author to build concepts of social books and build a (sometimes) vast readership outwith the traditional publishing model.

Social platforms such as Wattpad are actively taking a role in promoting their most popular authors to agents and publishers who operate in the traditional industry. Though their role brokering publishing deals is not unusual for Wattpad's international arms, it is only beginning to take hold in the United Kingdom and America and represents an external force of power to the traditional writer – agent – publisher – reader model. Wattpad also has their own publishing arm, mentioned previously, and implements a 'ranking' system across the site that is the reader-facing results of a complicated, malleable algorithm determined by the amount of support a work gets in the Wattpad community – meaning the more views and stars/votes a story has, the higher it appears in the Wattpad rankings. While the rankings may be of use to readers who want to find the best fiction without having to trawl through over 200 million stories, it is also a valuable tool to publishers. The ranking system allows Wattpad and publishers to follow stories and approach authors at the point that the fiction reaches critical mass, defined by the number of followers and votes – that is, at the point that makes approaching the author to publish their work in a traditional fashion worth the risk.

Part of this shifting power dynamic is the role that the gatekeepers of the traditional industry are taking on in order to pull the newer discourse of citizen authors back into the traditional publishing model. Citizen authors such as Lopés, Grant, Stewart, Thompson, Sky, and others actively choose to forgo the traditional author-agent-publisher route to the market by sharing their work on social platforms, but all of these authors have now also had works that have been published as part of the traditional publishing model.

Though some authors, such as Askew, state that they think they would "want it [their book] to be published by a publisher" (15 November, 2017) and link ambition and the quality of a work to the cultural capital that has been developed in the creation of the book, others resist this drawing-in from the gatekeepers. Even if the market deals in cultural capital instead of economic capital, as in the case of most small publishers and the small royalties that an author can usually expect to make, citizen authors are usually aware of and keen to embrace a traditional publishing deal should it be offered. This is most easily seen with the publishing deals with authors such as Anna Todd and Rebecca Sky, who first found sizeable reader numbers on Wattpad (Published Samples, Wattpad, 2017). In fact, many publishers and agents now visit repositories such as Wattpad and Medium to seek out authors who are doing well digitally to offer them a traditional publishing deal.

This links directly to McLuhan's concept of the rear-view mirror, where we look to objects of the past, such as the physical, printed book, as we head towards the future (McLuhan & Fiore, 2008) of more connected media. The closer a work moves to becoming a book as defined by the publishing industry, the more conservative it becomes in relation to format, content and shareability. Another downside of moving from a new publishing model to the traditional one is the restrictions that the physical item of a book places on and around the text. Often works on social platforms that have been pulled back into the publishing industry are removed from their digital spaces, such as *The Intimate Adventures of a London Call Girl*, which began as a blog and was closed down once the book was published. Likewise, versions of Anna Todd's *After* are frozen in Wattpad after she signed a several-book deal. On Todd's Wattpad page for *After*, people are still commenting, but Todd herself no longer interacts.

As the shift of power towards the citizen author encourages the traditional industry to move the author back into their realm of marketing and commerce, the connectivity between these authors and their readers wanes, or becomes more market-related, with authors pushing readers to buy their books/follow their social feeds/come to their events in real life. This removes the perceived intimacy of these digital communities and restricts the interaction between readers and authors that allows the citizen authors to gain power in spaces not occupied by the industry.

It is not only Wattpad or blogs that play a role in pushing citizen authors up the new hierarchy of the social publishing mechanism – before they can tip back into the traditional model – but also platforms such as Twitter. Publishers and agents regularly have days where they invite authors to pitch their works via a tweet with particular hashtags, such as #XPO. Askew took part in a Twitter pitch with her novel, using the hashtag with an extra letter on the end to indicate genre. The tweets were seen by what Askew calls a "collective of various publishers, various publishing organisations and various agents in Scotland, who got together in their room on their tablets, laptops, etc." and read the tagged tweets (15 November, 2017). Askew was then approached by both a publishing house and a literary agency asking to see more of her work and was subsequently offered representation and granted access past the gatekeepers.

Traditional publication is not something that all citizen authors seek. For the majority, the potential to be a part of a specific community that reads and interacts with their work is the most valuable part of the process. This allows the gatekeepers the opportunity to observe the communities and the readership, giving them an understanding of how popular a work is, and would likely be, if it were published traditionally. The publishers can then leverage that knowledge to pull the citizen author's understanding of the book back in line with their own, developing a new power dynamic where the citizen author no longer has to seek access to the publishing model but is sought out in their own communities.

Not all citizen authors will desire to be published in the traditional sense, nor will they want to potentially alter their works to fit into the industry's definition of the book. As such, the power dynamic will not shift fully back to the gatekeepers as sole arbiters of cultural and socio-economic capital. The micro-instances of disruption, where the citizen author creates a new work and builds a community around it, will continue to push back against the mechanisms of the industry within the confines of platform mediation and in new and innovative ways.

Notes

1 As of February 2018.
2 When books are sold in shops they have a limited shelf time before they need to be replaced by new books. The long tail strategy allows for those sales to continue indefinitely, as online shops do not have shelf space to clear.
3 It's worth nothing that prior to Elliott Advisers purchasing Waterstones, it was owned by Lynwood Investments, a Russian investment firm.
4 200,000 titles.
5 2.5 miles and 160,000 volumes.
6 142,509 from Jan to Dec 15th, 2020.
7 For more information on journalism considering the audience as a new form of gatekeeper, see Lewis, 2012; Singer, 2011; and McKenzie et al., 2011.
8 In 2010, Goodreads did a blog post that showed the correlation between different types of media marketing and PR and spikes in Goodreads activity regarding particular books. (https://www.goodreads.com/blog/show/232-goodreads-stats-show-which-media-outlets-really-sell-books).
9 For more information on cancel culture, see Eve Ng (2020) and Gwen Bouvier (2020).
10 Julie Burchill, G.G. Lake, Milo Yiannopoulos, and Alexandra Duncan are among a few of the authors in recent years that have faced the wrath of cancel culture and had their novels pulled or dropped.
11 It is interesting to note that Knowles did not publish his work via Amazon, a move that would be interesting to explore in further research.
12 Soon to be the Big Four, when PRH purchases Simon & Schuster.
13 As of January 2018.
14 Jane Austen Fan Fiction has a wide range of readers and is often referred to as JAFF.
15 See campaigns such as #freethenipple, where on most social platforms visible male nipples are considered okay but images with female nipples (when the gender is identifiable via names, backend data, etc.) are removed and the account occasionally suspended. An interesting case of this was in 2016, when Facebook censors removed the iconic Vietnam War Photo of 'Napalm Girl' for being offensive. It soon, after much criticism, reinstated the photo.

Bibliography

Anders, G., 2011. *The Rare Find: Spotting Exceptional Talent Before Everyone Else*. London: Penguin Books.

Anderson, Tara., 2020. A Book Club for the 21st Century: An Ethnographic Exploration of Booktube. Thesis. University of North Carolina. Available at: https://doi.org/10.17615/r4aq-e587.

Askew, C., 2017. Interviewed by Miriam Johnson [email].

Bakopoulos, N., 2013. Particular Ways of Being Wrong. In *The Millions*. Available at: https://themillions.com/2013/11/particular-ways-of-being-wrong.html. [Accessed 8 December 2020].

Barnes, R., 2018. *Uncovering Online Commenting Culture: Trolls, Fanboys and Lurkers*. Switzerland: Palgrave Macmillan.

Baverstock, A., 2015. *How to Market Books*. New York: Routledge.

Blake, C., 1999. *From Pitch to Publication*. London: Macmillan.

Boog, J., 2017. Bookstagrammers Gain Influence in a Diffuse Marketplace. In *Publishers Weekly*. Available at: https://www.publishersweekly.com/pw/by-topic/industry-news/bookselling/article/74795-bookstagrammers-gain-influence-in-a-diffuse-marketplace.html. [Accessed 8 December 2020].

Bouvier, G., 2020. Racist Call-outs and Cancel Culture on Twitter: The Limitations of the Platform's Ability to Define Issues of Social Justice. In *Discourse, Context, and Media*. Available at: https://doi.org/10.1016/j.dcm.2020.100431.

Breslawski, T.M. 2014. Privacy in Social Media: To Tweet or Not to Tweet?, In *Touro Law Review*. Vol. 29, No. 4, Article 16.

Brown, K., 2017. The Value of Book Reviews for Indie Authors. In *IngramSpark*. Available at: https://www.ingramspark.com/blog/the-value-of-book-reviews-for-indie-authors. [Accessed 14 December 2020].

Carey , M., 2020. Instagram Post. Instagram, 1 December 2020. Available at: https://www.instagram.com/p/CIPFziGAnXL/?utm_source=ig_web_copy_link. [Accessed 17 December 2020].

Carolan, S. & Evain, C., 2013. Self-Publishing: Opportunities and Threats in a New Age of Mass Culture. In *Publishing Research Quarterly*. Vol. 29, No. 4, pp. 285–300.

CEBR. 2017. Bookselling Britain: The Economic Contributions to – and Impacts on – the Economy of the UK's Bookselling Sector. A Report for the Booksellers Association. Available at: https://www.booksellers.org.uk/BookSellers/BizFormFiles/dea8bb9d-a0a4-440d-9e7e-5de5f836eb88.PDF.

Chandler, M., 2020. Booksellers are the Gatekeepers for Titles by People of Colour, Says Brandes. In *The Bookseller*. Available at: https://www.thebookseller.com/news/booksellers-are-gatekeepers-now-brandes-tells-diversity-report-author-1207928. [Accessed 14 December 2020].

Cirucci, A., 2017. Normative Interfaces: Affordances, Gender, and Race in Facebook. In *Social Media + Society*, pp. 1–10. Available at: DOI: doi:10.1177/2056305117717905.

Clark, M., 2020. DRAG-THEM: A Brief Etymology of So-called "Cancel Culture". In *Communication and the Public*. Vol. 5, No. 3–4, pp. 88–92.

Clement, J., 2020. Number of User Generated Reviews on Goodreads 2012–2019. Statista. Available at: https://www.statista.com/statistics/252998/number-of-user-generated-reviews-on-goodreadscom/. [Accessed 12 December 2020].

Digital Marketing Institute, 2018. 20 Surprising Influencer Marketing Statistics. In *Digital Marketing Institute*. Available at: https://digitalmarketinginstitute.com/blog/20-influencer-marketing-statistics-that-will-surprise-you. [Accessed 12 December 2020].

Duong, C., 2019. The Rise of the Micro Influencer. In *The Bookseller*. Available at: https://www.thebookseller.com/blogs/rise-micro-influencer-983566. [Accessed 15 December 2020].

Erin. 2020. Instagram Followers: How Many Does the Average Person Have? In *Hastagsforlikes*. Available at: https://www.hashtagsforlikes.co/blog/instagram-followers-how-many-does-the-average-person-have/. [Accessed 14 December 2020].

Emerson, T., Interview on Publishing and Social Media. Interviewed by Miriam Johnson [email].

Finkelstein, D. & McCleery, A., 2013. *An Introduction to Book History*, 2nd ed. Oxon: Routledge.

Foucault, M., 1980. Truth and Power. In Gordon, C. (Ed.), *Power/Knowledge: Selected Interviews and Other Writings 1972–1977* (pp. 109–133). Translated from the French by C. Gordon, L. Marshall, J. Mepham & K. Soper. New York: Pantheon Books.

Foucault, M., 1989. *The Archaeology of Knowledge*. Translated from the French by A.M. Sheridan Smith. London: Routledge.

Gillies, M.A., 2007. *The Professional Literary Agent in Britain: 1880–1920*. Toronto: University of Toronto Press.

Goodreads, 2020a. About Us. Goodreads. Available at: https://www.goodreads.com/about/us. [Accessed 15 December 2020].

Goodreads, 2020b. Advertisers. Goodreads. Available at: https://www.goodreads.com/a dvertisers. [Accessed 15 December 2020].

Grant, S., 2017. Interview with Simon Grant. Interviewed by Miriam Johnson [email].

Griswold, W., McDonnell, T., & Wright, N., 2005. Reading and the Reading Class in the Twenty-First Century. In *Annual Review of Sociology*. Vol. 34, No. 1, pp. 127–141.

Guest, 2013. Comment. Fanfiction.net [link unavailable]. [Accessed on 24 April 2018].

HarperCollins. 2020. Submit a Manuscript. HarperCollins. Available at: https://www.harp ercollins.com/pages/corporate-for-authors-submit-a-manuscript. [Accessed 15 December 2020].

Heilig, H., 2018. Book Review: A Place for Wolves. Goodreads. Available at: https://www. goodreads.com/review/show/2278677186?book_show_action=true&from_review_pa ge=1. [Accessed 20 December 2020].

Heins, M., 2014. The Brave New World of Social Media Censorship. In *Harvard Law Review Forum*. Vol. 127, No. 325, pp. 325–330.

Helft, M., 2010. Facebook Wrestles with Free Speech and Civility. In *The New York Times* [online]. (Last updated 12 Dec. 2010). Available at: http://www.nytimes.com/2010/12/ 13/technology/13facebook.html?_r=2. [Accessed 20 October 2015].

Henderson, R., 2020. What Propels Cancel Culture: Human Nature May Lead People to Magnify Moral Transgressions. In *Psychology Today*. March/April 2020, pp. 36–38.

Hughes, M., 2017. BookTube and the Formation of the Young Adult Canon. In *Book Publishing Final Research Paper*, 24. Available at: http://archives.pdx.edu/ds/psu/21235. [Accessed 17 December 2020].

Kay, S., Mulcahy, R., & Parkinson, J., 2020. When Less is More: The Impact of Macro and Micro Social Media Influencers' Disclosure. In *The Journal of Marketing Management*. Vol. 36, No. 3–4, pp. 248–278. Available at: doi:10.1080/0267257X.2020.1718740.

King, J., 2016. Interview on Publishing and Social Media. Interviewed by Miriam Johnson. Stirling.

Kleck, C.A., Reese, C.A., Behnken, D.Z., & Sundar, S.S., 2007. *The Company You Keep and the Image You Project: Putting Your Best Face Forward in Online Social Networks*. Annual Meeting of the International Communication Association, San Francisco (2007, May), pp. 172756–172761.

Lewis, S., 2012. The Tension Between Professional Control and Open Participation. In *Information, Communication & Society*. Vol. 15, No. 6, pp. 836–866. Available at: DOI: doi:10.1080/1369118X.2012.674150.

Litt, E., 2013. Understanding Social Network Site Users' Privacy Tool Use. In *Computers in Human Behaviour*. Vol. 29, No. 4, July 2013, pp. 1649–1656. Available at: https://doi. org/10.1016/j.chb.2013.01.049.

Lopés, M., 2017. Interview on Publishing and Social Media. Interviewed by Miriam John-son [email].

McCabe, D., 2013. Why Bookshops Matter. In *The Bookseller* [online]. Available at: https:// www.thebookseller.com/blogs/why-bookshops-matter. [Accessed 9 January 2018].

McKenzie, C.T., Lowrey, W., Hays, H., Young Chung, J., & Woo, C., 2011. Listening to News Audiences: The Impact of Community Structure and Economic Factors. In *Mass Communication and Society*. Vol. 14, No. 3, pp. 375–395. Available at: DOI: doi:10.1080/ 15205436.2010.491934.

McLuhan, M. & Fiore, Q., 2008. *The Medium is the Massage*. London: Penguin Books.

Merriman, B., 2017. The Editorial Meeting at a Little Magazine: An Ethnography of Group Judgement. In *Journal of Contemporary Ethnography*. Vol. 46. No. 4, pp. 440–463. Available at: doi:10.1177/0891241615615918.

Mittell, J., 2001. A Cultural Approach to Television Genre Theory. In *Cinema Journal*. Vol. 40, No. 3 (Spring).

Morrison, K., 2016. 53% of Women Made Purchases Due to Influencer Posts (Survey). In *Adweek*. Available at: https://www.adweek.com/performance-marketing/53-of-women-made-purchases-due-to-influencer-posts-survey//. [Accessed 12 December 2020].

Murphy, R., 2020. Local Consumer Review Survey. In *BrightLocal*. Available at: https://www.brightlocal.com/research/local-consumer-review-survey/. [Accessed on 12 December 2020].

Ng, E., 2020. No Grand Pronouncements Here…: Reflections on Cancel Culture and Digital Media Participation. In *Television and New Media*. Available at: https://doi.org/10.1177/1527476420918828.

Obeng-Odoom, F., 2014. Why Write Book Reviews. In *Australian Universities' Review*. Vol 56, No. 1. pp. 78–82.

Olszanowski, M., 2014. Feminist Self-Imaging and Instagram: Tactics of Circumventing Sensorship. In *Visual Communication Quarterly*. Available at: http://dx.doi.org/10.1080/15551393.2014.928154.

Pickert, K., 2008. Oprah's Book Club. In *Time*. Available at: http://content.time.com/time/arts/article/0,8599,1844724,00.html. [Accessed 14 December 2020].

Phatbasset, 2005. *Dangerous Curves*. [online] Available at: https://www.fanfiction.net/s/2353649/1/Dangerous-Curves. [Accessed on 23 April 2018].

Ramdarshan Bold, M., 2018. The Return of the Social Author: Negotiating Authority and Influence on Wattpad. In *Convergence: The International Journal of Research into New Media Technologies*. Vol. 24, No. 2, pp. 117–136. Available at: doi:10.1177/1354856516654459.

Roberts, A., 2007. *The History of Science Fiction*. New York: Palgrave MacMillan.

Rosenfield, K., 2017. The Toxic Drama on YA Twitter: Young Adult Books Are Being Targeted in Intense Social Media Callouts, Draggings, and Pile-ons – Sometimes Before Anybody's Even Read Them. In *Vulture*. Available here: https://www.vulture.com/2017/08/the-toxic-drama-of-ya-twitter.html. [Accessed on 20 December 2020].

Serendipity2909, 2017a. On Arrowheart, book one of The Love Curse. Wattpad [online]. Available at: https://www.wattpad.com/1497321-arrowheart-book-one-of-the-love-curse-series-one/page/5/comment/3874193188. [Accessed 28 April 2018].

Serendipity2909, 2017b. On Arrowheart, book one of The Love Curse. Wattpad [online]. Available at: https://www.wattpad.com/1497321-arrowheart-book-one-of-the-love-curse-series-one/page/5/comment/3874193188/replies/2383892068. [Accessed 28 April 2018].

Stewart, M., 2016. Interview on Publishing and Social Media. Interviewed by Miriam Johnson [phone].

Shriver, L., 2018. Writers Blocked: How the New Call-out Culture is Killing Fiction. In *Prospect*. Available at: https://www.prospectmagazine.co.uk/other/writers-blocked-how-the-new-call-out-culture-is-killing-fiction. [Accessed 20 December 2020].

Simpson, J. 2016. Interview on Publishing and Social Media. Interviewed by Miriam Johnson [email].

Singal, J., 2019. He Was Part of a Twitter Mob That Attacked Young Adult Novelists. Then It Turned on Him. Now His Book is Canceled: Kosoko Jackson, a Gay Black Author Writing about a Gay Black Protagonist, Gets Taken Down by the YA Twitterati. In *Reason*. Available at: https://reason.com/2019/02/28/he-was-part-of-a-twitter-mob-that-attack/. [Accessed 20 December 2020].

Singer, J.B., 2011. *Crowd Control: Collaborative Gatekeeping in a Shared Media Space*. The Association for Education in Journalism and Mass Communications Annual Conference, St. Louis. 10–13 August.

Sky, R. 2015. *Arrowheart, Book One of The Love Curse*. Wattpad [online]. Available at: https://www.wattpad.com/1497321-arrowheart-the-love-curse-one/page/3/comment/489392002/replies/497892796. [Accessed 25 April 2018].

Sky, R. 2017. *Arrowheart, Book One of The Love Curse*. Wattpad [online]. Available at: https://www.wattpad.com/1497321-arrowheart-the-love-curse-one/page/5/comment/3874193188/replies/4275791617. [Accessed 25 April 2018].

Smith, A., 2014. What People Like and Dislike About Facebook. Pew Research Center: Fact-Tank. Available at: https://www.pewresearch.org/fact-tank/2014/02/03/what-people-like-dislike-about-facebook/. [Accessed 14 December 2020].

Srinivasan, R., & Fish, A., 2017. *After the Internet*. Cambridge: Polity Press.

TheGeekyMe, 2016. On Arrowheart, Book One of The Love Curse. In Wattpad. Available at: https://www.wattpad.com/1497321-arrowheart-book-one-of-the-love-curse-series-one/page/5/comment/1092671996. [Accessed 28 April 2018].

Thelwall, M., 2017. Reader and Author Gender and Genre in Goodreads. In *Journal of Librarianship and Information Science*. Vol. 51, No. 2, pp. 403–430. Available at: doi:10.1177/0961000617709061.

Thelwall, M., & Kousha, K., 2017. Goodreads: A Social Network Site for Book Readers. In *Journal of the Association for Information Science and Technology*. Vol. 68, No. 4, pp. 972–983. Available at: doi:10.1002/asi.23733.

The Vida Count. 2019. The Vida Count. Available at: https://www.vidaweb.org/the-count/2019-vida-count/. [Accessed 8 December 2020].

Thomas, C., Jayagopi, D.B., & Gatica-Perez, D., 2019. *Booktubing Across Regions: Examining Differences Based on Nonverbal and Verbal Cues*. Proceedings of the 2019 ACM International Conferences on Interactive Experiences for TV and Online Video (TVX '19). Association for Computing Machinery, New York. pp. 145–156. Available at: https://doi.org10.1145/3317697.3323357.

Van Dijck, J., 2012. Facebook and the Engineering of Connectivity: A Multi-layered Approach to Social Media Platforms. In *Convergence: The International Journal of Research into New Media Technologies*. Vol. 19, No. 2, pp. 141–155.

Vu, H., 2014. The Online Audience as Gatekeeper: The Influence of Reader Metrics on News Editorial Selections. In *Journalism*. Vol. 15, No. 8, pp. 1094–1110. Available at: doi:10.1177/1464884913504259.

Waldfogel, J. & Reimers, I., 2015. Storming the Gatekeepers: Digital Disintermediation in the Market for Books. In *Information Economics and Policy*. Vol. 31, pp. 47–58.

Wattpad, 2017. Published Samples. Wattpad [online]. Available at: https://www.wattpad.com/44013622-wattpad-stories-published-as-books-pop-fiction. [Accessed 16 January 2017].

Wojcik, S., & Hughes, A., 2019. Sizing Up Twitter Users. Pew Research Center. Available at: https://www.pewresearch.org/internet/2019/04/24/sizing-up-twitter-users/. [Accessed 8 December 2020].

9

UNDERSTANDING AND INCORPORATING THE CONTRADICTIONS AROUND THE BOOK

This book has critically examined how the idea of what a book can be is changing in relation to the growth of digitally social communities and the writers and readers who congregate in these spaces, and it has identified how this connectivity is altering the balance of power between the traditional industry and those who choose to write and share their work in a global village. It can potentially help publishers determine if they need to alter the way they provide access to the industry in relation to the author-agent-publisher (bookseller, reader) hierarchical gatekeeping system in order to take advantage of new authors who are writing in digital communities and building a following there.

It has explored how social media platforms can be used by publishers to find content generators for traditionally published products and provides a new understanding of how the book is changing in reaction to the development and adoption of social technology, which in turn has led to a shift in power. Foucault's genealogy provides a means by which authority is explored as a force which changes hands and is not held by one entity over another but often moves from the bottom up. Within the bounds of the book, those at the bottom are citizen authors and readers sharing work in digitally social spaces.

The ubiquitous nature of the mobile and linked web, and the ease of access for a majority of users, makes it easier than ever for writers and readers to find, build, and join like-minded communities within the global village. It is important to consider the context of what a book can be and who has the power to say what it can be in the current technological environment of Web 2.0, with its focus on prosumerism; Web 3.0, which uses semantic data and metadata to better link parts of the internet and allow users to find their communities; and Web 4.0, which has drawn on the role of AI and complex algorithms to usher in the era of the Web of Thoughts, which works to interact with users on a more abstract and emotional level (Müller, 2008).

DOI: 10.4324/9781003186649-10

The main sites considered in this volume were Twitter, Instagram, Facebook, FanFiction.net, Wattpad, and Medium in what has been just a sampling of platforms and which should not negate the inclusion of others in future writing on this topic. The focus on Twitter as a place to scrape and mine hashtagged data grounds this study within a specific space that informs and highlights how citizen authors are using social platforms, in real time, to develop and share stories. Likewise, the use of in-line comments on Wattpad shows the growth of these communities and their interactions.

Key findings: TL;DR

Social media is altering the way a book is defined by making its content social

The role and definition of the book is changing in a way that specifically incorporates aspects of sharing and community into the process of writing and distribution of a work of fiction. It is this changing understanding of the book that has allowed for the rise of authors on social platforms. A book's content in the digital setting is reflowable across containers[1]; it is able to be shared in different locations, across different platforms, and at different times.

Interviews with authors highlight the role social media plays for them, where traditionally published authors use it as a marketing tool and citizen authors use it to share their works, gain new followers, and find readers. Traditionally published authors tend to have more narrow views of what a book can be, whereas citizen authors feel more thoroughly that a book can be a myriad of structures, formats, and types and delivered across a variety of platforms that allow for sharing stories.

Citizen authors and their role in online community spaces is a driving force behind the changing definition of the book. These authors go beyond what self-publishers do in writing works and publishing them via a press or directly to Amazon, Smashwords, or other service providers. Instead, a citizen author actively seeks out communities of interest where geographical barriers collapse and they can surround themselves with readers who are potentially willing to enter into a feedback loop based around the work.

By being moved into a digitally social space, the book no longer has to adhere to the properties that make it a book according to the industry. Through processes such as the mining of the hashtag #Twitterfiction and blogs and repositories such as Wattpad and FanFiction.net, it is made clearer how a book can be developed and shared within a digital setting and tell a coherent story even in the case of cross-platform fictions. Monetary motivations can be seen as secondary to the sense of freedom a citizen author has to try new writing formats within and across different platforms and connect with an audience. Choosing to write and share works in new settings is an act of breaking away from the constraints of the industry with its formal structures and processes. It is the idea expressed by Lopés that "a book need only be what the writer intends a book to be" (20 January, 2017) that highlights the changing definition of a book in relation to the global village and borderless connectivity.

Citizen authors have more freedom to develop works that do not need to conform to a gatekeeper's standards in order to reach an audience of readers. This enables authors to be more experimental in their content and format, as can be seen with Grant's 'cluster' stories on Twitter, which mix characters and contexts.

Publishers are gaining access to the spaces where the citizen authors are writing and sharing work

The possibilities of the book are limited only by what the gatekeepers allow the traditional industry to publish. Works that fall outside this are those by authors who choose to write, share, and develop communities around a publishing model that does not depend on the acceptance of a work by gatekeepers. Gatekeepers are inherently biased due to their position within the industry, their organisation, personal tastes, and institutional factors.

Publishers are beginning to look at the spaces and works of citizen authors. They are doing this by reaching out to authors directly on social media or via brokers from platforms. Publishers such as Unbound have unique business models that incorporate social media generated content, and some literary agents are having pitch days on social platforms to draw citizen authors back into the publishing model, such as the one in which Askew took part and eventually found representation for her novel.

Part of the freedom that a citizen author embraces, in the absence of access to the traditional industry, is the opportunity to test the limits of what a book is in relation to new technologies and formats; publishers would do well to consider a book in relation to the technology on which it is shared. As a citizen author is not tied down to an understanding of the book as a physical object, audiobook, or eBook, they can experiment with how they share their writing as new options become available to them (new technologies such as AR and VR overlays, connecting to the internet of things, AI writing, etc.), as has been shown by Kaur, Todd, and Stewart, etc. This allows them to test the limits of the fuzzy edges, where works are easier to consume in the non-traditional format, something that publishers in Asia have been tapping into for several years.

Publishers can also learn from citizen authors' interest in building relationships with readers. This focus on the connectivity of authors and readers frees the author to access new platforms and develop writing in different digital locations and formats. This ranges from using hashtags to link parts of their stories, interacting in the comments, mixing imagery and writing, and geo-locating works in a physical location, to developing algorithms and AI that can write new works based on what it has learned from reading previous ones. In addition, in recent months, we've seen the growth of virtual book clubs, digital author tours, and literary events held online on video platforms (zoom, google hangouts, etc.) and more specific literary event platforms that have popped up (VANE, MyVLF, etc.).

A citizen author chooses their own communities

Citizen authors have risen from the spaces where new technology and access to this technology has caused disruptions to the status quo of the publishing model and its outputs. These disruptions have given authors the opportunity to reach and develop a community of like-minded readers in digitally social spaces, sharing their work outwith the traditional publishing model. It is in these spaces that communal and professional ties allow authors to feel supported and willing to put their work out there with the understanding that it will be received in a way that is based less on rejection than it would be if sending work via the traditional publishing model.

Citizen authors can gain the authority to state what a book can be by participating in the digitally social communities. They take advantage of the ease of access to the platforms and the opportunity to be read sooner and often more widely than in traditional publishing. They value connectivity over sales, which is underlined by the growth of platforms such as Wattpad, Medium, and FanFiction.net, and value the prolific nature of blogs. The act of writing in these places is a move away from the hierarchy of the industry, and citizen authors often purposely choose instant readerships and relationships over the socio-economic gain of publishing with the traditional model. Citizen authors are freer in what they can write when they no longer need approval from agents and publishers.

Gender plays an important role in the reading and writing communities online

We can see gender playing a significant role in the way writers and readers develop relationships in online communities in three key ways:

- the gendering of 'free labour' as 'women's work' in digitally social spaces;
- the perceived authenticity of an author or reader as tied to the gender of those involved within the community;
- female-identifying authors and readers congregating in communities where there is limited censorship on the works shared.

The majority of social media users on the platforms considered in this book are female, with the notable exception of Twitter. Female-identifying citizen authors and readers react differently than their male-identifying counterparts in the communities where they are writing and sharing work, by either altering their tones, changing their writing, not sharing their work at all, or by remaining as lurkers in the space. This can limit both the writing that is shared and the feedback and commentary that comes from readers. As such, authors actively choose where they want to share their works based on the expectation of specific demographics of readership.

The idea of 'free labour' as 'women's work' comes to the fore in the consideration of the gender of citizen authors. Much like in traditional 'women's work', which relates to work done in the household and not for cultural or economic gain, a female-identifying author chooses to forgo the cultural and economic benefits the traditional publishing industry can provide in order to have the freedom to share their work directly with readers. This creates the potential for relationships to be built around that work – a work given freely to the community. Part of this relates to 'hope labour,' where the citizen author shares works in the community and develops relationships with the distant hope that this will result in opportunities related to the traditional industry, as many citizen authors would jump at the chance to be published in the traditional model – as seen with Rebecca Sky, who moved from Wattpad author to traditionally published author after she gained a large enough following on the platform.

Female-dominated social spaces are more supportive and interactive than those that are mixed gendered or predominately male. This fosters a feedback loop that is more inclined to be positive and encouraging and where the citizen authors are more likely to interact directly with the readers. As these female-identifying readers and writers interact with one another they develop a sense of community that grows beyond that of having communal ties based around a topic, genre, or style of writing. These ties can develop into relationships that enable two-way conversations between the citizen authors and readers, where the author gives personal responses to comments and questions from readers, further enhancing the connection between not just the reader in question but also with others who observe this connection and can see the potential to create an intimate though public connection of their own.

Female-identifying citizen authors often choose to inhabit spaces which censor them the least. This leads to a large number of subgenre works being written and shared by them in digital spaces that are less governed by the rules of the traditional industry regarding what can and should be published. Fan fiction archives and subgenres of erotica and non-mainstream writing thrive in a digitally social setting. The gender split of science fiction writers on platforms such as Twitter often echoes the traditional publishing model's gender split of being two-thirds male, evidenced by the hashtag #Twitterfiction.

Communities of readers and writers in online spaces both embrace and exploit the authors of subculture genres

Citizen authors are writing genre fiction in a larger percentage and across a wider range of genre and subgenre works than the traditional industry is willing to publish. Because of a lack of acceptance by the traditional publishing industry, they have turned to sharing their work in digitally social spaces, where the barriers of entry are lower and the form of the genre is reflected in the format of the writing itself. Here, in the digital communities, citizen authors are taking advantage of retrospective framing that gives their writing a place in the wider generic canon.

It is this framing that enables the repeatability of genre tropes within the discourse of the book. This allows for the platforms themselves to have a say in what acceptably falls under a particular genre. Much like the industry has guidelines for works of fiction, genres, and subgenres, the digital structures and algorithms of the platforms themselves are "fuzzy set[s]" (Rieder, 2010, p. 194) for what a citizen author can produce. Further to this, some citizen authors, such as Stewart, Grant, and Lopés are using the mediated structures of the platforms, such as the character limit on Twitter and the use of hashtags on Facebook, Wattpad, Twitter and Instagram, as integral parts of their works. This allows their fictions to cross platforms, timeframes, and accounts to develop a style of genre fiction that finds its home in their definition of what a book can be.

A key element of the growth of genre fiction in the digitally social communities is the refusal of the traditional industry to meet the needs, or the diversity of interests, of readers within genre fiction. Where the publishing industry does not focus on publishing a wide array of genre fiction, the number and variety of these works on platforms such as Wattpad and FanFiction.net are growing exponentially (Herman, 2014). On these platforms, the ghettoisation of a genre works in favour of citizen authors and readers seeking out these works in a singular location. It is the social setting, the potential for instant feedback, the ability to use previous works and worlds as a starting point, writing without deference to gatekeepers, and the agility of the format of digital media to echo the writing style and content that all serve to enhance the place of genre fiction in the digitally social setting.

The communities online are beginning to echo the hierarchy of the traditional publishing industry

These communities operate less in contradiction to traditional publishing models than might be expected. They can be seen to take on attributions of a traditional publishing house in that they offer edits, critiques, and plot suggestions on a work. Sometimes readers work as first reviewers, such as in the case of works like Sky's *Arrowheart* on Wattpad, where readers of the first chapter commented in-line about how excited they were. At other points in the chapter, the in-line comments say things about the characters and their likeability, or lack thereof. Comments like "Well hello bitch" (SecretlyHere, 2017, May 10) and "If she was in New York, this cab driver would have killed her…" (Lokokina, 2017, June 18)[2] are typical of how readers show their feelings about the characters the author creates. The author can then decide if this is the effect she desires and can alter the characters accordingly.

Likewise, the readers here can also play the role of marketer for the work, sharing it and promoting it in other digital spaces, enlarging the author's network. This isn't to say that the communities in digital spaces will take over from the wider industry, but there are ruptures in these communities that provide a new definition of what a book can be, shifting the power dynamic from the publisher to the author. This has developed space for citizen authors to write new works of fiction in their online communities and get direct feedback from their readers. These feedback loops echo the agent/author and author/editor relationships in the industry model. However, in the digital communities, the feedback is crowdsourced, and the citizen author does not necessarily risk alienating their readership or potential publication if they choose not to take feedback on board. In fact, a citizen author can choose to speak directly with the readers who have left the feedback, a process which bolsters the relationships, as is seen throughout the in-line comments in *Arrowheart*, where Sky consistently replies to readers and interacts with them.

This movement has shifted the idea of a reputational economy that meant that the publisher itself bestowed prestige to an author and their work by means of producing a traditional publication to a reputational economy where the prestige is measured in interactions with a wider, digitally receptive audience. It is the sense of community and the potential for direct interaction with, and feedback from, the readers that is a driving force behind citizen authors writing in digitally social spaces. It is "social presence," in a place that is mediated by technology (Vrasidas & Veletsianos, 2010, p. 9), that the author seeks out in joining in and sharing their work. Here, in their chosen communities, they can interact with readers who are interested in their work and willing to do their own 'free labour' in reading and commenting on the writing.

Likes and shares are valuable cultural capital and an incentive for a citizen author to share and continue engaging with online communities, especially when a critical mass of cultural capital can bring them to the attention of the traditional publishing industry. What this means for the wider publishing industry is that citizen authors are no longer reliant upon the industry for an audience and, in some instances, for economic capital.

These relationships provide outlets for new work and the potential for feedback from readers to reach the author immediately, often pinging through directly to their mobile devices, a process that the publishing industry has trouble replicating due to the time constraints on the individuals involved in the longer process of traditional publishing. As citizen authors and readers become more accustomed to the speed of interaction in the digital spaces, the publishing industry has a hurdle to overcome in replicating that speed.

There has been a change in the power dynamic between the publishing industry and the writers and readers who choose to forgo the traditional route of publication

The power relationships that arise between the citizen authors and the gatekeepers is a push-pull dynamic that, in many situations, positions cultural and financial capital against community-driven connectivity in online spaces, which, as shown in the previous section, deals in the format of reputational economy. This results in the hierarchy of the publishing industry being shaken, but not dismantled, and making a play to pull citizen authors back into a traditional model. This is most easily seen when platforms broker deals with publishers for a work to be moved back into the traditional publishing model. Authors such as Anna Todd and Rebecca Sky exhibit the crossover between traditional publishing and writing for a live and interactive audience on social media.

The hierarchisation of the gatekeepers of the industry is echoed within the social communities, who have their own rules about the acceptance of genres and subgenres into their canons. Readers can, and do, reject the acceptance of works where they do not feel the author has aligned themselves enough with the genre or subgenre in which they are placing their work. This is especially true of the niche subgenre of fan fiction but less so than that of erotica, where there is less gatekeeping.[3]

Furthermore, the distribution and wielding of power in the discourse of the book does not come from above and cannot be owned. It is not stable at all levels, and it alters depending on the position from which the new statements about the book are being pronounced. Those who traditionally have the power to say what a book can be are the gatekeepers of the industry, among them authors – who self-censor as they send out their work for consideration by the publishing hierarchy and take part in a publishing model that does not rely on the acceptance of an agent or publisher – and the readers at the end of the process.

The extension of knowledge and its relevance to the industry

This book set out to show that publishers can, and are, using social platforms as a place to locate content. The benefits of this are threefold:

- Citizen authors are themselves influencers in their genre and chosen communities and come with a ready-made audience, thus helping to make their work economically viable to produce in a more traditional fashion.
- Accepting the use of social media as a place to write and share fiction will likely make traditional publishers more accepting of future publishing models, where, perhaps, the writers of the book might work alongside AI and data-led content to create works and link social channels and written content to a users' social presence via mobile devices.
- If the industry model does not provide outlets for digital authors, it will be circumvented by other models. Not meeting the gender and genre needs of readers and writers will mean they will look outside the traditional publishing model to connect.

This book has brought to light how digital communities are affecting the publishing industry in terms of how a book is defined and who the new generation of citizen authors are. This has given new power to readers and writers who choose to read, write and make their audiences in online spaces.

Notes

1 This is as long as the underlying coding is flexible and accurate for various outputs.
2 Both SecretlyHere and Lokokina are female-identifying, based on their Facebook pages, and use of female name on Wattpad.
3 As long as the writing is tagged appropriately for the sex acts found in the work, most gatekeeping in the generic sense is relatively lax in erotica repositories.

Bibliography

Herman, B., 2014. What is Wattpad? The 'YouTube for Stories' is Transforming Book Publishing. In *International Business Times* [online]. Available at: http://www.ibtimes.com/what-wattpad-youtube-stories-transforming-book-publishing-1710151. [Accessed 9 September 2016].

Lokokina, 2017. Comment on Arrowheart, Book One of The Love Curse. Wattpad [online]. Available at: https://www.wattpad.com/1497321-arrowheart-the-love-curse-one/page/6/comment/2219533904. [Accessed 25 April 2018].

Lopés, M., 2017. Interview on Publishing and Social Media. Interviewed by Miriam Johnson [email].

Müller, N., 2008. The Web Expansion: From Web of Things to Web of Thoughts [diagram online]. Available at: https://flatworldbusiness.files.wordpress.com/2010/11/smartweb_web_5-0_evolution_confidential_-v004.jpg. [Accessed 15 June 2018].

Rieder, J., 2010. On Defining SF, Or Not: Genre, Theory, SF, and History. In *Science Fiction Studies* [online]. Vol. 37, No. 2. Available at: http://www.jstor.org/stable/25746406.

SecretlyHere, 2017. Comment on Arrowheart, Book One of The Love Curse. Wattpad [online]. Available at: https://www.wattpad.com/1497321-arrowheart-the-love-curse-one/page/6/comment/4241558253. [Accessed 25 April 2018].

Vrasidas, C. & Veletsianos, G., 2010. Theoretical Foundations of Social Computing and Virtual Communities. In Zaphiris, P. & Ang, C.S. (Eds), *Social Computing and Virtual Communities* (pp. 1–20). Boca Raton: CRC Press.

INDEX

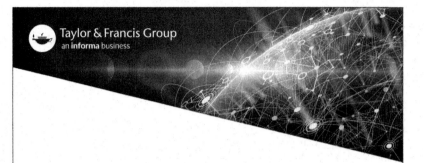

Taylor & Francis Group
an **informa** business

Taylor & Francis eBooks

www.taylorfrancis.com

A single destination for eBooks from Taylor & Francis
with increased functionality and an improved user
experience to meet the needs of our customers.

90,000+ eBooks of award-winning academic content in
Humanities, Social Science, Science, Technology, Engineering,
and Medical written by a global network of editors and authors.

TAYLOR & FRANCIS EBOOKS OFFERS:

A streamlined
experience for
our library
customers

A single point
of discovery
for all of our
eBook content

Improved
search and
discovery of
content at both
book and
chapter level

REQUEST A FREE TRIAL
support@taylorfrancis.com

 Routledge
Taylor & Francis Group

 CRC Press
Taylor & Francis Group